REA

Table of Contents

A Note On Definitions, References and Statistics

In the text that follows, the multidisciplinary nature of the subject rules out a set of precise definitions and interpretations. The field of conflict and violence belongs to a hybrid of philosophy, psychology, history, biochemistry, biology and much more. As regards statistics, numbers have nothing to tell us without interpretation and interpretation can be both biased and erroneous. For one thing, statistics from different sources or communities purporting to be about the same phenomenon often differ in definition widely enough to require circumspection before any conclusion is attempted. What counts as *youth* and what counts as *serious assault* are not the same in all cultures, for instance. Also, in presenting data on violence, there is always the certainty that not every instance has been reported, social and personal pressures enforcing understandably a silence that the statistician cannot pry open. Not every country gathers statistics as conscientiously or as thoroughly or as quickly as others, nor does every country wish to do so or wishes to do so honestly.

As for definitions, words are often used interchangeably in the way they appear in modern speech. I have not attempted to define exactly what are the differences between concepts such as aggression, assaults, violence and so on, which to most people are interchangeable. One person's idea of aggressivity could be another person's idea of violence. In brief, however, violence in this book is usually taken to mean extreme harm done to self or others. Murder and homicides are also used interchangeably and so are words such as adolescent, youth and teenager. A child is usually under eleven years of age, an infant less than 2 years and a fetus or embryo is of course an unborn child.

As for references, those from scientific books and journals appear in the text by name of authors and date of publication and are listed in full in the bibliography. All other sources such as personal quotations, newspaper articles, conference notes or television news sources are given a footnote number and are given in full at the end of each chapter. Brief recommendations for further reading are given at the end of the book. Finally, readers should be aware that much of what is presented in the text are ideas. There are, I think, few absolute truths.

Preface

In the course of my career in both peaceful and war-torn countries, I have become increasingly indignant over the ways children's welfare and survival are being compromised by the violence they are subject to and exposed to. Furthermore, children are not only passive victims, but they can become agents of destruction.

An investigation into what are the contributing factors for all this in different cultures becomes not only a question of scholarship but also one pitting fairness over personal biases. I let personal values impinge. Perhaps however, that is not so bad, for this book is also about indignation. Mine. About how children can be poisoned by environments that breed and let fester, hostility, frustration, humiliation. About how brains are poisoned by ideology, or irresponsible mass media or substances that modify moods.

I started the research for this book out of a curiosity about how some cultures could appear to behave rationally to themselves, but not to others. The transformation of children into violent beings has to be looked at from the possibility of its usefulness to any culture or, on the opposite, as a pathology that could undo a culture. If over-violent behavior was negative for a culture, then — following a biological or Darwinian logic — it should not continue to exist. However, it does. Its extreme consequence is warfare. War casualties continue to rise in absolute numbers (war casualties probably numbered 200 million in the 20th century), as well as in proportion to the world's population. Of even more concern, wars are increasingly killing and maiming civilians, rather than combatants (civilian casualties were 10% of war deaths in 1900, as compared to 90% in 1999). Similarly, murder can be the first cause of death for young men between the age of 15 and 25 in several countries at peace. Thus, extreme violence could be a biological way of thinning our ranks or else a form of disease, perhaps a pathology. In that case, one must see whether *agents* exist that could *infect* us in a typically

V

epidemiological pattern. We could behave violently as a result of biological events that affected us at the embryonic or post embryonic stage and not only as a result of our upbringing.

Within the appropriate cultural milieu, the combination of harmful chemistry and say, neglect or humiliation may be an explosive mixture. How much so? Could this affect whole groups of human beings not just individuals? These ideas brought me closer to my original training in Public Health and Biology and kept impinging on the *culture only* argument.

I divided chapters into broad themes of current concern. Into each a distillate of research material, ideas and philosophy were poured in. Academic texts, papers and lectures mainly from periods in Geneva and then Oxford were intermingled with material drawn from newspapers and current events.

My experience growing up in Egypt, where people are basically very kind, but where religious extremism and corruption increasingly contaminated the minds of very young people was also a factor in trying to determine why some populations could go from gentleness to fierceness in a relative short period of time. Years in field work and negotiations with all sorts of people and governments in several conflict areas was of course an added ingredient. References are made to poor, middle income and rich countries that I have worked in, as well as to others I have read about to see how patterns of indoctrination of children could differ.

These themes predominate in the chapter entitled "Cultures of Violence" and to a lesser extent in those about "Some Aspects of Religion and Violence" and "The Influence of Mass Media."

The Chapter on "Childhood" deals with children upbringing as it relates to violent behavior, notably the effect of single parenthood, abandonment, neglect, forms of disciplining and humiliation. A fair amount of space is taken up on the differences and age patterns for violent behavior in boys and girls.

This led into looking at violence by women and against women. While looking at the difference in the form and the incidence of violence between women and men, I realized how statistics are not very illustrative of what happens in some countries. The chapter hints at the sensitivity of a subject still very much hidden in many societies, where violence against women or committed by women is embroidered into cultural taboos. There are also references to the harm done to women by abuse or neglect and how this could then be "transmitted to a current and future child.

VI

The Chapter on Biology looks at some of the mechanisms of biological transmission as well as discussing both the way the brain and the body's reactions are dependant on substances we ingest or produce. Animal behavior studies are also looked at in this chapter. A friend asked me: "We are not birds or dogs, why are you referring to them?" The short answer is that I am a biologist among other things and I believe in the transmission of some basic processes. Other than that, it is fascinating and fun to speculate.

The Chapter on Environments refers to work done on the relationship we may have to our immediate physical surroundings, the effect of some substances we may breathe or eat, the effect of overcrowding, noise and perhaps even electro-magnetic radiation on our moods and our propensity to violence. Much of it rests on shaky evidence but again it is a subject that fascinates me.

Finally violence against self had to be mentioned even though this might approach mental illness, a dividing line I set for myself and did not want to go into. There is no way I could do justice to established clinical syndromes in a book of this kind but a few words on suicide had to be added if only to show how some cultures hide this phenomena more than others or else use it as an excuse for murder against women, for instance.

There is too much on the USA in the text. The main reason is that the USA publishes more than the rest of the world on the subject of violence. Perhaps because 3% of its population is behind bars or on probation — the highest rate in the world. One is 20 times more likely to be killed in a barroom brawl in Los Angeles than in a bar in Sydney, Australia, wrote someone. But it is not the most violent place on earth. Nevertheless, when asked what is the most dangerous place to live in, I cannot give a quick answer. There are too many forms of unacceptable violence. Certainly some countries today such as Algeria, Colombia, Pakistan or South Africa are very violent, much more than others, but then there are geographical areas, within the Caucasus, South Asia or the Near East where violence has been chronic for much longer. It is not my intention to write about *all* the forms and places of violence. Just a few of them.

It is my hope this account may serve to lessen the number of such places. Children are born seeking warmth, safety and comfort. It is my hope all children will one day be allowed to have that.

Samir S. Basta
February, 2000

VII

Acknowledgements

Many wise men set the stage for me to write this book. Nevin Scrimshaw of MIT, Adolfo Chavez of Mexico, Robert Mc Namara of the World Bank were the first to provide me with training and opportunities. Later, James Grant, the late Executive Director of UNICEF gave me a lot of inspiration and the conviction to find solutions to the most difficult problems. Richard Jolly provided more opportunities.

Dr. Pierre Dasen, Professor of Educational Psychology at the University of Geneva, was the first to offer me encouragement and to provide me with references in the realm of cross-cultural studies on aggression and violent behavior. He opened a window for me with a formidable and wonderful view.

Professor Peter Bryant, Head of the Dept. of Experimental Psychology at the University of Oxford enabled me to obtain a Visiting Scholarship at Wolfson College, where thanks to the unequalled atmosphere that University can provide, I read and read about so many things. Not always about violence, but things dealing with history, sexuality, neurology, ancient literature, medicine, anthropology, psychology, politics and everything else under the sun, that have contributed to many chapters. The lectures I attended at Oxford given by eminent professors, dons, scholastic visitors, were of such high standard that they will remain in my mind for ever.

I must also thank Professor Marshall Segall of Syracuse University for looking at parts of the first draft in 1996 and telling me it needed much more work.

There were also friends, secretarial assistance and librarians connected to my office in UNICEF Geneva without whose help much of this may not have taken off, especially Howard Dale and Mary Martin. Suzy O'Shea providing me with historical notes. Later, Mandy Dowd, poet and feminist, did a lot to help me improve on the ideas of violence done to and by women. Special mention goes to Robin Davies, who provided much needed criticism regarding many parts of the text. Jonathon Brown helped me with the editing.

Finally, the two most important people who pushed me to finish this book were my daughter Sarina and especially my wife, Marina.

Introduction

It is extremely difficult to separate out one risk factor for violent behavior from another. Similarly, it is difficult to separate out the meanings of some words. Thus, I have not made important distinction between words such as aggression or violence. I use them interchangeably because it became too difficult to decide where one starts and the other ends. I try to limit them in this book to mean "serious harm to a human being." Where possible when quoting statistics a distinction is made between physical assault figures and those involving homicide.

There is also a continuum between fear, frustration and humiliation. Again, it did not seem important for me in this book to define them or give them a sequential order. More interesting to me was to find out at which age they begin and whether we can always find a cause for them. I did not really find out but I advance some ideas and hypotheses.

As to the statistics and numbers quoted throughout the text, the well known caveats apply with even more force in this book, since much of the subject matter regarding violence is either embarrassing to some governments or too difficult to collect properly or is selectively used by authorities for all sorts of purposes. Statistics on violence can be collected and interpreted differently from one authority to another. Some represent actual crimes as reported by the police, others may be the result of surveys on a population.

Many readers may object to me connecting some monstrous behavior with another type of behavior that is in violence terms of a lesser magnitude. They may be right. It may be quite wrong to speak of a Hitler or Pol Pot in one paragraph and then jump to a tribal leader in Somalia and then to a Wall Street tycoon or an abusive husband in France. That is deliberately done so at times, because it is a form of both enquiry and provocation on my part. It is part of the question I ask: at what point must we take steps to avoid tiny, small and huge Hitlers from doing terrible things?

Chapter 1

Cultures of Violence

One in four children around the world (540 million children) lives in a war torn country or in a country where tensions are so high that violence can explode any minute, according to UNICEF's 1999 Report. While lip service is given to equality between different human beings in most national constitutions today, the reality is quite different. Intolerance and internal conflicts abound, sometimes state-sponsored, sometimes state-tolerated and sometimes contrary to state policy.

While the perception of what is threatening to oneself or to our communities will differ in various societies, there is nonetheless a majority of people in the world that would like to live with less violence around them.

Learning how cycles of violence are transmitted to children may help us to better control the process leading to a reduction of both individual and group violence.

The historical, psychological and cultural reasons for dragging children into combat, into hatred and into individual acts of violence are many. They are, in some ways, also victims of certain state's intolerance to some of their own inhabitants as well as those living outside their borders. Let us see how this process takes place in different cultures.

Modern Conflicts

Each day, countless children around the world are exposed to dangers that hamper their growth and development. They suffer immensely as casualties of war and violence; as victims of racial discrimination, apartheid, aggression, foreign occupation and annexation; as refugees and displaced children, forced to abandon their homes and their roots; as disabled; or as victims of neglect, cruelty and exploitation. (World Declaration on the Survival, Protection and Development of Children, UN 1990)

War Casualties

Most modern conflicts erupt within a country and 90% of today's victims are civilians, the majority children and women. Soldiers and para-military gangs kill indistinctly the old, the infirm, women and children. Children kill other children, women other women. There are fewer wars in which soldiers battle other soldiers.

For example, nine million European soldiers were killed in the four years of the First World War, of which 500,000 alone died during the 10 months of the Verdun battle.

Whereas 14 % of First World War casualties were civilians, the corresponding figure for the Second World War was 70 %. In the latest wars in Angola, Sierra Leone and Yugoslavia, an estimated 90 % of war casualties are civilians. Indiscriminate bombing in the Second World War is estimated to have killed at least 1 million civilians, but 30 years later the war in Vietnam is estimated to have cost some 2 million civilian lives. Most civilian casualties are children, who are being killed in quantities as never before. According to the UN, war-related deaths of children in Mozambique between 1981 and 1988 were 454,000. In the past decade 2 million children were killed in conflicts, 6 million disabled, more than 12 million are now homeless, one million orphaned. In 1992 alone, some 20,000 girls and women were raped in Bosnia, while the corresponding figure for Rwanda was 15,700 for 1994-95,. It is difficult to assess the much higher number of children, who by just witnessing many acts of barbarity are psychologically traumatized.

Length of conflicts may also be greater today than before. Angola's civil war has already continued for 30 years. In Afghanistan, the war is almost 20 years old, in Sudan 25 years, in Sri Lanka 11 years and in Somalia 10 years old. Whether this is a function of the type of weaponry used, the meddling of super-powers or because the extent of fears and hatreds is greater, is difficult to ascertain. A generation of children in these countries will never have known peace.

Arms Race for Peace?

International alliances and agreements make it suicidal for a country to attack another (cf. Iraq's aggression of Kuwait). Yet countries are still spending a huge share of their budgets on defense.

There are examples of national quirks that are so puzzling that it may be difficult to explain why and how that value-system has developed — for instance the continual and dangerous rise of the military-industrial complexes in both Russia and the United States, at unendingly spiraling costs and more and more weapons of mass destruction. Is it because American culture does not accept or want to think of itself as ever being threatened and a similar mind-set has existed in Russia for the past 200 years? Why this threat of annihilation and genocide at the hands of the other?

Like a plague of old, fear wafts and weaves its way into other countries, carried by word of mouth by the 9 or 10 million current refugees, by television and radio and newspaper accounts, by the arms merchants and politicians who reap benefit from arm sales, and even by the racists and misfits, who can either be rich or unemployed, unhappy and scared. The arms race between groups and countries can be defined therefore as a neurotic response to mostly unjustified fears of cultural annihilation, but it deflects millions of dollars from other constructive aims.

With the ready accessibility to sophisticated weapons, the risk of civilian massacres is greater today than ever before — and with that risk comes fear. And that fear is not only confined to these countries at war. Even in countries at peace, clever, manipulative leaders use much of this fear to increase spending for their armies and militias. Not only is official arms spending calculated today to be around some $700 billion a year, higher than ever before — 14 times as much as is dedicated to development, according to former Costa Rican President and Nobel Prize winner, Oscar Arias[1] — but approximately one third of that arms spending comes from developing countries, most of whom are not threatened by their neighbors.

Fear and ambition, prestige and corruption are all mixed here — countries have increased their defense budgets, such as Malaysia from $2 billion in 1994 to $2.4 billion in 1995; Thailand from $3.6 billion to $4 billion; Singapore from $3 billion to $4 billion.[2] They have no enemies, no boundary disputes of any significance, no wars that are on going or that seem to be sought. Could it be that they fear that if the other raises its defense budget, this may not necessarily just mean a potential threat. It may also mean someone in the next country is going to make more money?

There also seems to be no limit in the race to invent new weapons of death. For instance, currently there are no international safeguards as regards the possibilities of gene warfare using the new recombinant DNA technology. Thus, it is now not only possible to design biological warfare agents that would evade natural immunity and existing vaccines, but it is also possible to inject DNA directly into tissues to disrupt normal transcription processes. The invention of large-scale sprays or bombs that may have the same effect is not far off.[3]

The arm race is also exploited for economic gain. It is a huge industry in the USA, Russia, France, the UK and an ever-increasing number of developing countries. Many respectable individuals are employed in this type of legalized violence called arms dealing. Arm dealers, corrupt and not so corrupt government officials benefit from the constant competition to be safe from one's neighbor. In a personal communication with a Middle Eastern arm dealer in July 1989, I learned that commissions on arm sales could be as high as 25 %. If $700 billion is spent yearly and the commission was as low as 1%, this means that some $7 billion is circulating yearly as available commission money!

"Those with guns survive," said the Director of Liberia's Red Cross in 1990, speaking about what made children as young as seven years of age take up arms (UNICEF 1996, 17). Fear was the reason inner-city youths in the USA gave for bringing arms to school and the reason given by the 600 or so women and children who are in prison in Rwanda, when asked "why they attacked their neighbors?"

Fear can be a most lucrative business…

Landmines

For years, some of us have been concerned with the banning of the production of landmines, whose principal victims in this modern age have been civilians — about a thousand women and children are maimed and 800 killed *each month* from mines in actual or former uncleared war zones. Some 110 million landmines are said to be lying in the ground waiting to explode (UNICEF 1996, 17).

Yet few countries have so far put a halt to the production of landmines, although many have banned export of anti-personal mines as a result of the international campaigns. Is it greed that prevents a complete ban on landmines? Their production is justified as being essential to a national economy. Arms firms, from cottage industries to huge multinationals, say that the production of landmines creates employment and easy profits and that if they do not produce them, others will. Army officers will argue it is fear that the other side will use them. Poorer countries will say that they are the only cheap defense weapons that they can use to stop infantry and tank attacks.

At a UN-sponsored meeting to ban landmines in Ottawa in 1998, the USA delegate made the remark that the USA was willing to ban their deployment "except in conflict areas" (UN April 1996). Aren't landmines always deployed in conflict areas? Pakistan, China, Italy, Russia, former-Yugoslavia considered that their economies and security depended on landmines. Even the Czech republic, with its most humane President Havel, continues to justify exports of mines, guns and Semtex explosives as being essential to its economy. In 1996, Belgium (PRB industries) and Switzerland (Von Rolle) were still providing Iraq with the elements needed to make a super-cannon even after the UN imposed an arm sales embargo.[4] So did a British firm. What is to be done about individual violence if nation states continue this spiral of fear, profits and pointless aggressivity?

War-Like Nations

Are some nations chronically more war-like than others? I asked this question in 1991 when I got involved in the Yugoslav conflict. On the one hand, most of the Yugoslavs I had met had been well educated charming people, independent thinkers and civilized Europeans, on the other hand, many of them seemed to be possessed of a certain toughness and unmercifulness whenever the subject of their internal politics came up. Even before the war, many seemed to hate other ethnic groups in their Federal Republic. Why were they so? Why did they go to such extremes as killing each other in the 1990s? Was it the fact of their upbringing, their history? Is it because their culture is one of violence?

Most of us would agree that the headhunting Yanamanoto Indians in the Amazon, some New Guinea or Afghan tribesmen are *nation-tribes* of warlike violent people. But to themselves their violence is perfectly normal behavior. Is that violent Indian or that bloodthirsty proud tribesman a product of his nation, or does he, by his inherent violence, cause his nation to be classified as violent?

Both are true.

It is difficult to present an argument as to which comes first. Most of us would agree that it is individuals who make up nations. And individuals are born (fairly) innocent and their parents may also be quite peaceful people. Small children are extremely sensitive to the suffering of others. This concern evolves from the sensitivity of a one year old to the crying of another baby, to the concerns and hopes expressed in countless exercises carried out by kindergarten children on their wishes and hopes. I was struck by how these children, when asked what they hoped for in the new Millennium, almost invariably said they wanted to see an end to wars and violence, injustice and unhappiness, such as no more abandoned children, abused children and also more care about the environment. Every inquiry reported in the press from schools in the UK, the USA, France, China, Thailand, Russia and other countries quote, as priority, peace in the world and for all children.

Yet, at some point a group, a nation, a culture may influence a child into becoming a very violent young individual.

If we divide the world into the UN-accepted regional breakdowns, it seems that the South Asian region had the most wars or internal conflicts in the past 15 years with 6 of the 7 countries in the region having had some sort of war. This region is followed by the Middle East and North African countries, then some distance away, the Latin American countries, the Sub Saharan African countries, the countries of the former Soviet or Communist bloc, lastly, the East Asia and Pacific nations. The industrialized countries come last.

It seems that today the most war-like region is one extending in an arc from the Eastern Mediterranean to the Indian Ocean. This region, in which sizeable population moves, occurred over the past 100 years, was also the route of much migration in the past and much aggression.

Does the Propensity for Violence Change over Time?

Operating out of Mongolia in the early 1200s, Genghis Khan and his hordes went on to conquer territories which extended from what is now Eastern China to the Middle East and Southern Russia, killing hundreds of thousands of people on their way. Ala-ad-Din Juvaini[5] talking about Genghis Khan and his hordes claimed that: "in retribution for every hair on their heads it seemed that a hundred thousand heads rolled in the dust." So many different chroniclers have reported the range of killings and the sheer brutality of the Mongols that we can readily believe that they were unusually violent for their times. Yet how can such a once brutal people be relatively placid and peaceful today? Why the change and when and how did it occur?

I assume that it may be possible to conclude that after such an orgy of killing and pillaging, over a period of some 100 years, the Mongols were not only defeated but also psychologically exhausted or spent. Perhaps, after a paroxysm of violence occurs a refractory period takes place spanning one or even several centuries, whereupon the *mentality* of that tribe or nation or group changes, becoming fixed in a more peaceful mode. What happened in Germany and Japan this century, culminating in the *peaceful* nature of these countries today, may be a similar process. Lebanon after 10 years of civil wars is now largely peaceful, so are Cambodia and Nicaragua. Perhaps even today's very violent Afghanistan, Somalia or Sudan may soon become models of passivity and placidity — assuming, of course, that each has reached or is about to reach its *violence-peak*. Otherwise, nations or peoples would destroy themselves, which, in biological terms, would be counter-productive.

Can a Nation Effectively Commit Self-Destruction?

In the 1920s the sociologist Marcel Maus, a follower of the French philosopher Emile Durkheim, put forward the idea that certain cultures could suddenly or occasionally negate their instinct for self-preservation, by a series of violent, suicidal acts (Maus 1997, 19-20), Several animal species, notably whales, dolphins, wild horses and others also occasionally go through this suicidal type of behavior. But it is only a tiny part of these species that do that and only very few individuals and only very occasionally. Such behavior is usually preceded by a mass migration.

Humans throughout history, whether in ancient Palestine, Massada, Greece, or Carthage, have at times gone to war or acted out scenes of provocation knowing full well that they would lose, be massacred, or have to commit mass suicide; and almost all these episodes were preceded by a shift in population movements after or before invasion. Today, we have seen migratory colonies, such as various pseudo-religious sects, do the same — at Jonestown, Guyana, in the 1970s; in Valais, Switzerland, in 1994; the Dravidians in Texas, in1994; or even in Japan in 1995.

It could be argued that contemporary civil conflicts such as Bosnia, Cambodia, Chechnya, Kosovo, Lebanon, Rwanda or Sierra Leone represent acts of collective, almost hysterical, self-destruction by groups of men intent either on *purging* or *re-creating* something that would necessitate wholesale destruction of their own environment.

A biologist may argue that this is a kind of renewal of a *gene pool.* And yet...

Justifications for Violence

Rousseau in the 1700s and others have expressed the idea that Man is a kind of *noble savage*, basically good and non-aggressive, and that it was *civilization* that corrupted him and introduced hatred and envy. All very well, but what factor in civilization caused this? What is it that Man wants, or wanted, from other men that led him to become so war-like? Was there not enough food or sex or women or trinkets to go around? Hardly possible! Did one mother or father say to primitive children: go and get *more* of this or that and by any means possible, even the most violent ones? Why so?

Competition for resources obviously decides whether an organism will try to fight. But at what level does the absence of a resource reach the point that it is worth going to war for? People fight even when they have enough resources for survival. Iraq, with huge oil reserves of its own did not have to invade Kuwait in order to survive, or even to live better! Here we have an example of the folly of one man, Saddam Hussein, leading his people to disaster.

I shall list possibly universally *acceptable* justifications to take up arms:

- To have a minimum amount of food or other essential resources;

- To have a minimally acceptable living space;
- To protect one's family, children especially, against aggression;
- To defend one's nation or environment;
- For an ideal such as to be free.

Even though most of the above are *primal* urges, necessitating action, our beliefs in what is worth fighting for may lie in the way we are brought up rather than in some biologically determined origin. If our upbringing, traditions, beliefs or any of the factors linked to our overall culture demands it, we can be violent *and acceptably so for reasons that* are far removed from primal urges such getting food for one's starving family. Thus, North Americans may feel it is more justifiable to fight for freedom, than a Chinese person, who is used to others controlling him. A Sicilian or an Arab may feel more at ease killing someone because he insulted his wife or mother, than a Scandinavian.

De Toqueville predicted over 170 years ago that people who were more free would take up arms and defend whatever privileges they deemed necessary, more so than people who lived under centralized government, even a democratic one.

Whatever the reason, some groups or nations may be more vulnerable to violence and it can take just one individual or a group of individuals to plunge a whole society into physical violence against another.

Different Perceptions

Before embarking further on some of the political and cultural endeavors that lead to the maiming of thousands of children, it may be worthwhile to first examine how perceptions of what is aggressive or provocative differs in some modern cultures, as well as how these different groups will consider what is an acceptable response to aggression and provocation.

Aggressive Speech and Attitudes

Aggressiveness is sought for in business in the Anglo-Saxon World. In the USA, for example, job offers and ads openly call for *aggressive* candidates to apply. A few years ago such ads would be unthinkable in the UK, now they are quite common. A better word might seem to be *assertive* candidates but in the US context the qualification *aggressive* is actually preferred in business, law, and many other professions. In parts of South East Asia today, aggressiveness is equated not so much with fighting skills, but with the cunning and prowess of making money. In Hong Kong, Taiwan, Singapore and parts of China, this aggressiveness can be vicious enough to label it as a form of violence. It can also be a compliment to women doing business there, quite unthinkable in most so-called *traditional* societies.

Is there a connection between cultures, which encourage aggressivity in business, and increasing youth violence? Or do we see less youth violence in countries such as Afghanistan or Cambodia where adult men fight more?

Within other cultures there were also differences in what was considered fair competition and rewards. Indian Hindi students seemed more willing to make monetary allocations on the basis of need than were their American counterparts, who preferred merit over need when assigning rewards (Berman, Murphy-Berman & Singh 1985, 65-67). Obviously, concepts of distributive justice are influenced by norms rooted in the economic and social characteristics of societies (Segall, Dasen, Berry & Poortinga 1990, 220). Once more, we note that the less *collective-minded* societies are more conscious of individual needs, which may lead to more of a predisposition to act on the basis of lesser self-control and hence perhaps more towards an overly aggressive mode.

The competitive-cooperative dilemma in behavior of different groups has been looked at by several researchers (p. 221). However, there seems to be insufficient attention given to the links of this either to violence or to psychiatric tension — psychopathic behavior indeed? — Or, even more importantly, to the question of how children obtain the mannerisms that mimic their elders' behavior. In other words, does a Hindu or Chinese child transported to America remain *less competitive* than his native-born counterparts, less aggressive, calmer, and so on, because family influences matter; or is there a physiological, biological tendency to be that way?

There are however instances where men, who live in a generally peaceful environment, still use violence towards individuals in their immediate circle. An example is wife beating, which is considered normal or even desirable in some parts of the world, while it is generally severely condemned in most parts of the West.

On the other hand, in the Middle East any insult or derogatory remark about a female member of one's family can and does lead to a very violent riposte. Saddam Hussein's previous right-hand man, General Kamel Ali, who double-crossed him, was accused of having a dishonored mother. One of Lebanon's Druze leaders, Kamal Jumblatt, was also said to have been the son of a loose woman, accused as such by Christian fanatics in 1970s Beirut. Similarly, the worst insult that could be hurled at sadly departed King Hussein of Jordan, when the latter was embroiled in disputes with Egypt's Nasser in the late 1950s, was that his mother was also a loose woman. In Argentina, a Latin culture seeped in Mediterranean influences, calling Evita Peron a *loose woman* was liable to get one killed.

In France or the USA, it is worse to be called stupid or to make a racial slur than to say *motherfucker* or *nique-ta-mère*. As to China and the Far East, any shame or insult brought upon one's ancestors or grandparents is horrific. In the West, it is much less so. Accusation of corruption in the latter is very hurtful while in parts of the Far East it is accepted as equivalent to having *clever* or *sharp* business practices. In Scandinavia, an allusion to a violent character is worse than an allusion to being stupid, whereas in many other parts of the world, it is often the opposite. In fact, in some societies, such as in the Arab world, being called a bully or a violent man is a good thing in non-intellectual circles.

Each culture has set limits about insults, but these limits are a function of what the differing cultures consider to be important. The more the character of the personality being insulted is thought to be synonymous with wisdom, piety or affection; the worse is the insult. This may indicate that for most people, regardless of how violent they may seem, there is a secret or not so secret admiration for wisdom, piety or affection. This is indeed encouraging. Maybe man is not so bad after all!

Provocation — Cultural Threshold

"Venom", as one writer to a popular US publication reported "is on the rise in America." A couple of years ago, a judge in San Diego overturned a jury's murder conviction for a man accused of *killing* a neighbor on the grounds that the neighbor was a *despicable* character. He sentenced him instead to a lesser charge of manslaughter.[6]

The way cultures look at what is acceptable and what is not is a fascinating mystery. What is corrupt or violent behavior in one society

**Case Study 1.1.: Afghani & American
Contrasts in Speech and Attitudes**

As an example of many of these issues and parameters, let me contrast an individualistic society like the USA, and a lesser one such as the Afghani society. The two societies may appear to be too different to make any possible comparisons, although, in the realm of violence, I consider the two societies at the top of their class, though the form of violence, however, differs.

Social patterns of speech differ. The Afghani, however fierce he looks in his turban, wild beard and Kalashnikov, puts a high value on personal greetings and the rhetoric of courtesies when he is meeting with a friend or a stranger. The American keeps flowery language to a minimum and gets down to business. He doesn't have time to waste on too many greetings, doesn't see why he should prepare you a cup of tea before beginning talking and, anyway: time is money.

If the American is going to be seated, he may even lift up his feet and put them on the table. The view of the underside of his shoes may be profoundly shocking to people in other cultures, but to the American it is not. The Afghan may wonder with some bemusement how this man was brought up. If seated in front of someone of a higher religious, hierarchical or older generation, the Afghan will assume a position of deference, eyes and head slightly lowered and a strict attempt not to overwhelm the other with too many words and directness. To the American he may look shifty.

In some cultures aggressivity is considered to be a function of class. An *educated* person, especially in the East, is not supposed to be overtly aggressive in speech or manner. In other societies it could be the reverse: the sign of success may be verbal violence, ruthlessness and even the implied threat of physical violence. Speech patterns in the USA, for instance, are indicative of one's power over others and one of the many signs of success of heads of big corporations. But the difference here between that head of a corporation and the Afghani tribal chief is that the latter while usually more courteous and hospitable to friends and strangers alike will find it much easier to murder someone who insults his honor. He finds it easier because he has the tools to do it, the society expects that, and his culture brought him up to do so.

is perfectly normal in another. Thus a Finn may find it extraordinary to have to slip a piece of money into a document to have it officially stamped, while it may be quite normal to a Mexican, an Indonesian or even a Spaniard or an Italian, who, in turn, may find the Finnish seriousness about these matters admirable, strange or ridiculous...

In various political systems and in different cultures there are limits of tolerance to perceived provocation. Are these limits that dictators, politicians or populations set for themselves? How *inbred* are these limits, how old may they be and, what are their historical origins? Why is it that what is perceived as an insult in one society may not be perceived as such in another?

Incitation to violence or to a violent riposte will have cultural roots and, most remarkably, the *trigger* for this is not the same for humans living in different societies. Why is there this geographical variety? Is it because some societies have been more downtrodden, invaded or manipulated than others?

A popular TV program in Russia which uses marionettes to make fun of politicians (Kulki on NTV) did not incur any official wrath when the politicians and the Head of State, Yeltsin, were for some time portrayed as butchers or killers. This was of course as regards their heavy-handed approach to the aspirations for independence of various small republics and autonomous regions. Yet as soon as the program began to portray — that is, disguise — Yeltsin and his cronies as petty thieves, tramps and beggars, with all sorts of allusions to the corruption and theft of state property, the State Prosecutor began legal proceedings against NTV, accusing the program of insulting "the honor and dignity of the State."[7] Presumably, in Russian political circles, it is not bad to be portrayed as a bully, butcher, or vicious bear, or as the assassin of other (non-Russian) people, but it is a crime to be portrayed as a thieving beggar.

In Poland or the Czech republic (also Slavic) it seems that it is worse to be considered a bully or murderer than it is to be a thief. Is the tolerance level different because the latter countries, having few imperial pretensions and in fact having been victims throughout most of their history to outside *bullies*, would resent the latter portrayal more than being accused of dishonesty?

Punishment and Lightheartedness

It is important to consider how frustration and humiliation contribute to a rise in tension both within individuals and in whole cultures. This tension may lie dormant for generations, but it is a contributing cause to group violence in many societies. The release of such tension in societies where lightheartedness and emotions are encouraged to appear may act as cultural safety valves to hostile behavior.

It is said that today in some societies the urge for punishment, for uniformity, for political correctness and the surge in self-righteousness is a major impediment to spontaneous expression. Coupled with loneliness, people may be more frustrated, hence, more liable to sudden explosions of violence. Rates of depression are said to be doubling in these countries every ten years. Are they *too* serious? Is there too much unreleased tension in these populations, which transfers itself into violence against self?

For instance, an American resident in Germany mentioned that neighbors were extremely critical of each other, that they repeatedly complained if the autumn leaves of one neighbor drifted into the garden of another, that residents who did not scrub their outside staircases and pavements were criticized and that everyone was always *snooping* on the other in a way that would be unthinkable in the United States. This snooping on neighbors is common in other European countries such as Switzerland.

There is also the theory, that laughter, lightness of spirit and a certain *insouciance* without guilt or fear of punishment is vital for the release of all sorts of tensions, and the transfer of others, including violence, to less harmful modes. It is also possible that in cultures where laughing is common (e.g. sub-Saharan Africa), one may find less individual violent behavior — even if collective violence may be much worse. Can we correlate indicators such as laughter in societies with less violence, including self-violence?

Anxiousless societies have supposedly less cortisol levels. High cortisol is linked to nervousness and to violent behavior. Social isolation, a major problem in affluent societies may also increase anxiety levels. If people cannot *ventilate their feelings*, will there be more likelihood of sudden outbursts of violence? Today, for instance, 25 % of American households consist of a single person. In 1940 the figure was 8 %. Is there any link between that and the doubling of crime rates since the 1940s?

Information-overload, the lack of street life as we knew it before and the substitution of professional contacts for friendship may be further indicators of a dysfunctional society, which no amount of welfare programs can compensate for. But some people prefer to be free to make choices regarding their personal happiness. And many in the industrialized world consider that a family is either not that important or that it must not stand in the way of their personal happiness.

Part of the theological objections in conservative circles to a greater equality between men and women is in fact based on fear of loosening the ties that bind families together. Indeed, this is explicitly stated in a communiqué put out by Islamic leaders opposed to the participation of Arab countries, such as Saudi Arabia and even Egypt, to the 1995 Women's UN Conference in Beijing. It is not just fear of women being free or a strict interpretation of the Koran, it is a feeling articulated in various groups, both by men and women, that if the traditional nurturing and *pacific* world of women is disrupted, some sort of societal breakdown, including increased violence, will occur. They point out to the despair, loneliness and violence in Western societies — as if this was too rare to be taken seriously in their own societies... — attributing this to sexual liberty, single parenthood and the phenomenon of working women.

Parental violence against children is considered by UK authorities to be the major determinant of violence in adolescence (Gulbenkian 1995). In Germany, with around 15.6 million children, one million are said to be beaten regularly by their parents. It is estimated that 70% of these children have been beaten or made to suffer to such an extent that they exhibit psychological symptoms classified as "severe, permanent distress".[8]

Even worse are so-called *silent societies*, that is to say, ones in which punishment might not be so obvious, where a child is not allowed much expression, where non-physical means of discipline are practiced with such cruelty, that more harm to a child could occur. I am thinking here of cultures that force children to remain silent, that forbid them outings, expressions of sexuality and rebellion and that speak of divine retribution or a god-inspired vengeance. In sum, those societies where religious conservatism is rife and where Puritanism had taken hold.

In these cultures, the expression of certain types of emotion by children is so restricted, that a child who does show a tendency to be emotional is judged to be disrespectful, spoilt or brash. It may be that children brought up in a *straightjacket* atmosphere are a time bomb of inhibited feelings that could lead to hatred and violence. Evidence from England, Germany, Scotland, Scandinavian countries and the USA indicate that most mass murderers were from very inhibited, stern, punishment-orientated backgrounds.

Can Non-Violence Be Taken Too Far?

A quick look at a more surprising question that comes to mind: can even non-violence be taken too far?

In Norway for instance, corporal punishment of children is not only forbidden in schools, but also in the home. Recently, a father in Norway was fined the equivalent of $500 for smacking his daughter and in Sweden the sale of war toys — even a water pistol — is banned. Is this carrying things a little too far? More to the point, is there any evidence such action has reduced violence in Norwegian and Swedish society?

Indeed, in Sweden, there has been an increase in violent acts by youths in the past five years, much of it directed against immigrants and in Norway the child murder rate has actually gone up, although it is still very small compared to other countries.

Some may even argue that the determination to impose norms of pacific behavior and moral uprightness is counter-productive because, by inhibiting spontaneous exhibitions of passion and violence, society has fewer outlets left for spontaneous behavior — and that therefore suicide, depression and alcohol- or drug-taking may increase.

A non-violent society may not necessarily be an easier society to live in than a violent one. For a child, the inhibition of aggression may lead to more aggression later on, but since overt acts of physical assault are discouraged, aggressiveness may manifest itself in much higher levels of alcoholism and violence against self. Thus conversely, it may be that room for the expression of spontaneous or emotional behavior, including fighting, may protect an individual capacity to do harm to him or herself, although not necessarily to others.

Problems of Correctitude

The typecasting of groups according to race, religion, sex preference is to be tackled with utmost care. While the fear of antagonizing the other or reinforcing prejudices is legitimate enough, the problem associated with too much correctitude in discussing different points of view regarding people we consider *different, bad or inferior* is that these topics can then become the exclusive domain of hate groups and far-right movements. The failure to have open forums of discussion on this subject may indeed backfire and lead to a lot of misunderstanding. In the end, it may reinforce certain prejudices people have. For instance, when a specific group is perceived as having a higher crime rate than the national average, people may conclude that the particular group is suffering from a *genetic predisposition*. By showing it is not genetics that may lead to a particular minority having a higher concentration of crime, but rather the conditions they are living in and to unemployment, one may be in a better position to correct the problem. A sociologist or economist may show that contrary to widespread assumption, it is not a minority group in a given contrary that may have the highest rates of violent crime, but rather youths belonging to the majority (as in the UK and Germany for instance). In France, where discussions about race relation is limited to some acceptable platitudes, there has never been as much prejudice against immigrants from North Africa as today, because it is considered unacceptable or politically incorrect by the government to link crimes in some areas to certain ethnic groups. Thus just why certain immigrant groups resort to more crimes is not discussed and hence solutions are more difficult to find.

High Murder Rate and Origins

There are 25,000 murders a year in the USA for a population of around 254 million. In Colombia, in 1996, there were over 25000 crimes a year but for a population a little more than a tenth of the USA. Murder rates in Columbia are around *nine times* the rate for the USA, making Columbia as one of the most violent country on earth. In South Africa, the rates for rape, physical assault and murder are estimated to be even higher than in Columbia.

It is worth looking at the history of *invading* populations in these three violent countries, Colombia, South Africa and the USA. In each of the USA, Colombia and South Africa, there were different invading groups, who either for religious, linguistic or geographical reasons, did not only find it difficult to mix together, but actually tried to impose themselves over the other invading groups by force of arms. In the process they also used and divided the indigenous populations into warring groups. The hatred these divisions caused led to constant friction and to the arming to the population. Differences then as now were often solved by reaching for one's weapons.

There may be more pressure in new migrant groups to be aggressive. Since there is no prior ownership of land they covet (the indigenous do not count) it is acceptable tot fight ot hold on or get a pieced of territory. This obsession leads perhaps to a form of deep mistrust against others and feelings of rebellion and independence from a central government. There maybe more individualism and belief one must get what one wants. Children are led to believe that it is their right

---

Case Study 1.2
Columbia – A Culture of High Criminality

Data summarized by Paul Rutler[9] indicates that 26 % of Colombians believe the use of violence has helped them reach some of their goals. To those surveyed at random justice was closely allied with causing reciprocal harm to others.

The spirit of individualism is so strong in Columbia, that farmers periodically take up arms and kill government officials for provocations such as attempts to destroy coca plants or because of new taxes. Contrast that with the placidity of farmers in nearby Peru or Bolivia, nations more centralized and previously more under Spanish control.

According to the Columbian Institute of Legal Medicine (1996), assassinations account for one death every 20 minutes in the country and are the leading cause of mortality before any disease In 1995, there were 77.4 homicides per 100,000 population, a mortality rate higher surprisingly higher than the mortality from both heart attacks and cancers and about equal to the death rate from heart attacks in a developed country.

In 1995, the number of deaths due to murder was 25,273 in Columbia (population 36 million), as compared to 25000 for the USA, which is eight times more populated, or 16,682 murders for China, which is about thirty-three times more populated. India has 48,000-recorded homicides a year, but its population is 27 times higher than that of Colombia.

Did all this change the way Columbians think and make them more susceptible to justice, revenge and retribution? Judging by the size of anti-violence demonstrations in 1999, a shift in attitude may be taking place in Bogota.

to indulge, grab, or reach out, as they want. Societal disapproval or condemnation of such behavior is perhaps less than what it is in more collective-minded, traditional *societies*.

In each of the three *violent countries* mentioned above, the role models for children were men and women who in the face of much physical and personal adversity, traveled, fought and survived lonely and dangerous situations. Faith in oneself played an important role. Indigenous populations could be enslaved, beaten or massacred, because they were not considered to be civilized, but considered to be *heathens* and not to be friends with. There was little wife- or concubine-taking from the indigenous society, unlike the case of the French in Africa, the Portuguese and Dutch in Asia or the Spanish in Mexico and Cuba, for instance — and thus little assimilation.

The generality of such circumstances is all the more convincingly established by the rarity of the voices of dissent. Following the precedent already established by Dominican friar, Antonio de Montesino in the early 1500s, Bartolome de las Casas, a Spanish monk who was Bishop of Chiapas in the New Spain (Mexico), complained bitterly to the Spanish 'Council of the Indies' that policies of non-assimilation and violence directed to the Indians were non-Christian (Pike 1969; Collard 1971). He called for sanctions, including excommunication, against those who committed excesses and his text may thus constitute the first instance of threats issued to rulers in defiance of their violations of other people's rights. This led the Spanish crown to publish the "New Laws" in 1542 and, in 1573, the "Instructions for Discoveries", which gave some protection to the Indians. These efforts were also supported and became successful because a fellow Dominican became Pope Paul III in 1537 and granted the Amero-Indians spiritual equality with the Spaniards. One can say that this is a rare enough example of a Renaissance religious structure bringing about universal benefit, protection and kindness to a different race of humanity.

This also led to a much more tolerant attitude towards the inhabitants of the Philippines, conquered by the Spanish in 1560-1580 (Open University 1990, 324, 331). Note also that the Council of Constantinople in 1414 had condemned the idea and practice current then, of depriving people of their property rights because of their mortal state of sin (p. 335). For me, these are the first human rights advances.

Collective Mould

Let us now look at the opposite, that is a society where individualism is suppressed and collectivism worshipped. Ho (1985) exploring values in the East, notably in Hong Kong, as well as in the West, wrote that the Judeo-Christian tradition "affirms the uniqueness, autonomy, freedom and intrinsic worth of the individual, that the latter himself only can make the effort necessary for change, and that if he fails to achieve self-reliance he is viewed with contempt and rejection." Ho claims that by contrast in the East collectivism, group and extended family well-being is much more important. In a different study, Hui & Triandis (1984a) showed that Chinese students were more equality orientated and more conscious of helping others in their group, than American students. The argument is made that even when individuals there fall sick from mental stress, various kinds of support groups help that individual in difficulty, whereas in the West the clinical psychologist or psychiatrist feels that he alone should treat the individual.

However, obedience to group norms leads perhaps to a more malleable or loved individual, but not necessarily to a less violent one — as those who suffered at the hands of Korean, Vietnamese or Japanese soldiers during and after the Second World War may attest. Need I add here that aggressive behavior may not necessarily be connected to overt physical violence, but only to the threat of causing harm, pain or anguish to others. There is a universal hypocrisy in people who are supposedly *polite*, but still intend to harm others.

Japan is a society with little in or out migration where violent and racist rhetoric is at a high level but where actual violence is at first sight low. There is there a firm belief that "Japanese" collective norms are to be preserved from outside contamination. While courteous behavior must be practiced between Japanese, it need not be practiced in the same manner with foreigners whose feelings are less important or different. However, contempt for foreigners can explains the brutality with which Japan conducted itself in treating other population just before and after the Second World War. Japanese writers continue to mention in magazines and books that certain races like the Jews are plotting to take over the world, that Africans are primitive, that Koreans are not to be trusted and that Westerners are racially inferior – mainly their love-hate friends, the Americans and, especially, black Americans.

Shame versus Guilt: Japan

Stephen Wrage,[10] Professor of Advanced International Studies at John Hopkins School, wrote recently, "when the question of whether Japan ought to officially apologize for the suffering caused in the war was being debated in the Diet recently, 4.5 million people signed a petition against the resolution." He goes on to describe some possible reasons for this: Christians are taught about guilt, Confucians about shame. A guilty conscience is cleared by confession and contrition. Shame, on the other hand, is renewed, and not relieved by confession. "Hitler was seen at war's end to be as evil incarnate and conveniently killed himself, whereas, the Emperor of Japan survived, reigned, and continued to be a figure of affection, awe and worship" — despite the Allies wish to stop worship of the latter. He states that many open archives, memorial exhibitions, study centers of the horrors committed by the Nazis exist in Germany, whereas they are few in Japan. In fact, Japanese politicians go to pray every year at the Yasukuni shrine, which is dedicated to the glorification of kamikaze. We should note that Admiral Yamamoto is considered as a war hero (war criminal, some would say) and the hero of countless comic books. Moreover, there is little account of Japan's aggressive policies in the teaching of school history.

This is not to take a stance against Japan. It is simply to offer an example of a country, where guilt is not expressed as compared to the USA or Germany, where it is — and the mystery of why, despite all this, Japan today has a homicide rate a little more than half of Germany's and one tenth of the United States.

Is there also a double standard about which we decide to kill? Could it be that killing foreigners is more acceptable in most societies, Japan included, than killing your own people? We must also take into consideration the fact that the policies of the American occupation authorities, led by General McArthur in 1946-48, to rewrite a constitution and expunge all references to militarism — Japan has officially no army and renounces war — may have also been a powerful factor in reducing present day violence in that country.

It may also be that the horrific numbers of casualties that nations like Japan can suffer in a relatively short number of years (1940 to 1945) are enough to reduce violence later on. The horror may be just too great. In other words, it may take many casualties, a paroxysm of violence to reduce the aggressive instinct in man for a few generations at least. Maybe that is how a society becomes peaceful!

Japan is one of the least crime-ridden country of the world and its stress on civism is probably responsible for the low crime incidence since outlandish or emotional behavior is frowned upon and children are taught to conform from a very early age. Violence that was no longer allowed to be channeled towards military conquests after the Second World War seems to be channeled to violent pornography, high level of male alcoholism and work. However, this is changing. In the past few years there has been a rapid rise in school violence and youth delinquency. This will be looked at in subsequent chapters.

Cycles of Conflict

Asserting One's Uniqueness

We are talking increasingly about one world, even one global village. Mobility and communication technology enable people to get closer together. Distant lands become close neighbors within reach by airplane or the Internet. All sorts of media and consumer attractions, largely Western, especially North American, seem to point to a more global culture. True, but is it a global or is it a Western, especially a US generated culture?

The Victorians and the Spanish Conquistadors before them also spoke about one big new world of increased communication. The reality was of course quite different. There were first class subjects, who were Europeans and second-class subjects, their non-European lackeys. There was a lot of condescending, little empathy, a caricaturized identity and no real communication between these subject people.

The mid-20th century has, however, seen some radical changes in how formerly subject populations see themselves. The Afro-Asian Bandung Conferences of the 1950s, the waves of nationalization of oil, transport, utility, industries, the independence from colonialism and the creation of Marxist states in every continent awakened hopes as well as revenge and a determination not to accept controls imposed from or by others. The influence of non-European figures such as Gandhi, Mao, Nasser, Fidel Castro, who challenged and stood up to the White, Western and Wicked forces of tradition and privilege, consumerism and racism, influenced a whole host of future politicians, dictators and clerics. Power was now to be had and it rested on the *waking up of the dispossessed* and the marginalized, not only on a national basis, but also for the first time on an international basis.

The World was getting smaller. It was also getting more complicated. You were supposed to be united to others, but you were also supposed to scream out your uniqueness! Movements proclaiming equality for class, race, gender or freedom of religion mushroomed everywhere Paradoxically, people also felt the need to proclaim their uniqueness, as individuals but also as groups or nations. This need increased with independence of countries from colonialism. Indeed, the later half of the 20th century indicates that there has been a multiplication of ethnic, racial and religious influences, which have polarized different societies around the world.

These two opposing forces of globalization and assertiveness of differences were bound to cause confusing identities as well as a behavior of rejection, exemplified by revolutionary changes in the way young people would behave.

What was regrettable was the profusion of narcissism, selfishness, obscure nationalistic sentiments and eventually, after the 1960s, the creation of mini-states and minority movements everywhere.

Such polarization has been the principal cause for a new type of warfare, where yesterday's schoolmates are led to hate each other and eventually to kill each other. Whether this trend towards polarized societies is a reaction to globalization, that is to Westernized influences, or is due to a better awareness and pride in societies brought about by the liberalization of many societies from the mould pressed onto them by colonial forces is not important here. What is important is that too many groups today want to rediscover some identity and that this searching process leads to an increase in violent behavior both at the group and the individual level. Too many — as many as 15 million people in a decade — have died because they wanted to replace their identity by another or re-discover some past identity that would guarantee them absolution and happiness in the future.

That certain peoples have significant claims to express themselves as a people, such as the Kurds or the disfranchised Palestinians is not disputed. A more difficult concept to accept is that smaller population groups have to have their own independent entity, because linguistic, religious or other differences make it impossible for them to coexist with others in a geographical region or in a common state — there is simply no reason to suppose that the Christians in the Middle East, the

Maori in New Zealand, the Serbs in Bosnia, the Chechens of Russia or the Lombard of Italy or the Flemish of tiny Belgium would necessarily suffer less if they had their own nation states.

The ambitious and the insecure, those who suffered at the hands of a majority and those fearing such suffering tell us they would be better off alone. This is also of course how they gain sympathizers to their cause. But the effect on children is to increase pressure on them to take sides, to differentiate and to hate. Nationalistic conflicts probably represent the most common source of the brutalization of young people and potentially the most disruptive and dangerous source of human misery, far more than poverty, which is universally condemned, and for which remedies and political goodwill exists — in words and theory at least.

In many parts of the world, the media glorify or highlight nationalism and intolerance, thus stereotyping behavior that conflicts with homegrown racial, religious, ethnic or political objectives. Child-rearing practices in some communities are also very tolerant if not encouraging, of nationalistic, fanatical or extremist views, usually in conjunction with justifications linking these attitudes with economic advancement or with perceived injustices regarding upward mobility and more religious or racial hegemony.

> The rise of terminology such as *celebrating diversity* illustrates this deep change, and at the same time contributes to it. Celebrating diversity, however, utterly important as it is, should not be turned into idolisation of diversity. (Lindner 2000)

Humiliation and Revenge

Humiliation takes many forms and leads to many things. In this section, however, the end result discussed is violence. But before violence, one must pass through frustration. If one is humiliated often enough – and this includes groups and nations – a resulting anger builds up, which will manifests itself in an aggressive move or else remains in its frustrated mode. Sooner or later that frustration must also explode.

Frustration is also probably increased by today's tendency to believe that freedom or independence is possible for many more people than hitherto, that choices are greater, that rights are to be sought after and that prosperity and mobility are more possible. The frustration and anger level may become greater in today's society than it was when people were less individualistic, more traditional and more fatalistic than nowadays.

So, living in a changing environment may not be much better than a traditional, conservative one, unless there is the real opportunity to change, to liberate oneself from the things one wants to escape from.

Segall, Dasen, Berry & Poortinga (1990) in their classical text on human behavior seen from a global perspective show that socialization practices or social intelligence, differs in various cultures. Perhaps what we may at times consider to be *backward* societies are in fact more adept at engaging in social discourse, the airing of problems and issues and the creation of a sense of cohesion and shared values. We may be paying a price for not recognizing this. By not recognizing the contributions other poorer societies have to make, by making people feel ashamed of themselves, we may be increasing the likelihood of eliciting an estrangement, even violence from them. By our sneers and fears we may create a sense of shame in an already frustrated group because they are *different* from us. Scientists call this the "deficiency perspective," in lay terms, a tendency to look down on cultures which do not appear to be as rich or as *developed* as ours. Segall quotes from Howard & Scott: "Perhaps the ultimate conclusion ... is that the deficiency perspective, by labelling people as incompetent, tends to generate remedial structures that perpetuate powerlessness and dependence, thereby validating the initial judgements."

Violence can result from a history of repeated humiliations or from fear of an eventual return to a humiliating condition. History is replete with examples and psychiatrists have written much about this. In a wild part of Southern Sudan, I remember seeing primitive Taposa tribesmen going to war against a Kenya based tribe, the Turkana, in order to avenge a cattle raid that took place 10 years earlier. They had waited that time for their sons to get to fighting age, since many men had been killed in the previous raid. No amount of pleas on our part could dissuade them form this long awaited wish to avenge their humiliation. On a larger scale the humiliating conditions of the Versailles treaty at the end of the World War I lead to World War II. The Germans were requested to make complete reparation for all loss and damage caused. The allies' demands were ruinous and enforced in a high-handed way.

The hurt of humiliation created a hunger for retaliation. Hitler promised to do the job. He claimed that he could restore Germany's power and pride, putting it beyond the reach of enemies who wished to impose further humiliations upon it. He created a new *culture*, the *culture of the Aryan Übermensch* who, according to his advocators, had a right, even

an obligation to rule the world."
          Is it farfetched to perceive a correlation between the degree to which Hitler and his followers felt humiliated and the degree of alleged cultural superiority that they constructed? If this correlation exists, then humiliation is dangerous. It is dangerous because it does not just create cultural difference; it also helps to construct cultural arrogance and, - ultimately, - genocide and Holocaust. (Lindner 2000)

There may be a point at which humiliation leads directly to physical violence. What may be interesting to research further is whether this *point* differs among various populations and whether we can learn from that at what point humiliation must be reduced in order to avoid an explosion of violence.

Stereotype and Revenge

Stereotyping of other groups is evident in several modern cultures. It is in fact a surprisingly resilient human characteristic even in so-called open societies, such as France — where North Africans are perceived as dishonest or dirty — or Sweden, where other Europeans are not as honest or dependable as Swedes or Norwegians.

Were the Irish immigrants always more violent than the Chinese immigrants in the USA because the Irish were *expected* to behave in a violent fashion or because the Irish *are* a violent people? — Think of the intemperate prose of Jonathan Swift who advised the Irish to eat their children during famines in the 1700s (Glendenning 1999). He was probably tired at hearing that the Irish were akin to savage people. Did the English stereotype about the Irish and the humiliation they so endured influence them to become aggressive and confirm the views of others about them or did they become so because poverty, alcoholism and despair were so common in their impoverished serf-like existence? I doubt very much that they were born that way.

In France, a recent TV news program looking into violence in schools, interviewed a host of immigrant students in a difficult neighborhood around Paris. All those interviewed said that teachers and supervisors rarely smiled or greeted them, many were frankly contemptuous of the way they spoke French, and most screamed at them in class and recreation, calling them stupid, half-witted and worse. At the same time, the teachers — the three who had agreed to be interviewed, at any rate — said they feared the students. [11] The French penchant for segregating poor segments of the population into high-rise development at the outskirt of cities has led to several ghetto type environments with a concentration of poor first and second-generation immigrants. Violence is an everyday occurrence and a large proportion of immigrants are blamed for it. The humiliation unruly Arab-African youths suffer at the hands of police, municipal bureaucrats, teachers and potential employers tend to drive them even deeper into isolation, anti-social behavior and violence.

One further example of how prejudice could enforce stereotyping behavior. In the USA, in the aftermath of the Oklahoma City bombing in April 1995 several witnesses were said to have seen suspicious Arab looking characters, one even dressed in Arab robes running away from the scene of the crime. The newspapers, television and even some government officials repeated allegations involving an Arab suspect. One poor, hapless Jordanian was arrested on a flight to Rome and returned to the USA. Needless to say, he was innocent and the culprits were found to be white Anglo-Saxon types, with the first to be indicted a blond man with blue eyes and a typical American type crew cut! Pity the poor Arab-American child who will be looked upon with suspicion and who will therefore do as much as is possible to deny his origins — or, worse, fall prey to an adult who will convince him or her that there is little justice and that it is better to become as the society expects him to be by joining a terrorist group.

Origins and Intolerance

In 1547 Juan Gines de Sepulveda made the point that "natural law" justified the forced conversion, enslavement and war against the Indians of the New World, because they were "barbarians". Since anyone who was not a European Catholic was also accused of being a barbarian, a licentious person, a cannibal, or all three and more, it was easy to justify violence against such people by Europeans (Pike, Collard). Is our perception of others much different in this century?

Some cultures are led to think that it is justified for them to eliminate others who are not like them in order to protect themselves from losing power or to maintain a fiction about the purity of their uncertain origins.

In Spain, Jews and Moslems were allowed to convert to Catholicism before the 15th century, but not thereafter. This marked a turning point: one's Christian identity was no longer enough, one had to be of the right *race* to be a true Catholic. Doctrines of purity of blood and racist doctrines of original sin were thus introduced into Christianity.

According to the German historian Hagen Schulze[12] of the Free University of Berlin, the first mass ethnic purification was carried out by the Catholic Kings of Spain in the 15th century. At some point, therefore, the public or the king thought enough was enough and all those who were *different* (defined on the basis of race or religion) should depart Spain or be killed. Did their numbers become too large? Did they control too much income?

Schultze work is interesting in that it defines nations as a group of people wanting to live together, with a common *memory soul* and heritage. The creation of the first "modern" read nationalistic state was by Frederic II of Hohenstaufen (1194-1250) in the 12th century. Later, Nietzsche and Bismarck spoke of a certain *spirituality* of the German race. The Prussians, who became the dominant power, believed in the superiority of the German race over other non-Germans. This contributed to large segments of the German public prior to the Second World War believing that the Jews, Gypsies and Slaves had little of that heightened *spirituality*, hence little opposition. This made it easier for the nazis to exterminate them.

The attribution of *sinful* to people or races or religions is still heard today in places like Serbia as it is heard in parts of South Africa or in Iran and Saudi Arabia and in many fanatical groups in Europe or the United States. The French actress, Brigitte Bardot, once claimed that French Moslems were unusually cruel people because they slaughtered sheep during the Feast of *Eid el Kebir*. The belief that some people are more equal before God on account of their racial or religious background is still implied in many types of conversation and does much, I believe, to influence children to become intolerant of certain *others*.

The extent of prejudice within a *race* because of religion or place of birth is another anomaly. It can lead to more discrimination towards one another than towards outsiders. "Southern Slavs," one Pole declared to me, "were brutal people." Since all the Yugoslavs were essentially southern Slavs, he predicted mayhem and cruelty on a large scale. The West or the UN could do nothing to prevent these people tearing each other apart, because it was *in their nature* to do so. They were prisoners of a culture that admired *toughness* and lacked the *sophistication* of Northern Slavs, who were not a people that would kill each other.

My interlocutor failed to mention that a large part of Poles participated passively if not actively in sending millions of Jews and Gypsies to the gas chamber in World War II. The extent of delusion about one's group is amazing.

There is nothing inherently biologically different between races, and especially between Northern and Southern Slavs. What is different is history, the cultural setting — and the perceptive opinion of an interlocutor! Violence follows any systematic hostility against another group, be they from the same or different races. Are we not still influenced by such views, living in their shadow indeed, when we allowed the Nazis to destroy the Poles, Jews, Gypsies or Russians because they were *inferior*, or sanctified war or violence done by post-World War II big powers against smaller nations — or the continuing violence against minorities in other parts of today's world?

Some cultures seem to be uneasy about their origins. The more doubtful the identity in those who claim it, the more the need to assert it with emphasis. This was apparent from what I heard and saw in the Sudan, in the early 1980s, when the North-South war was being re-kindled by the dictator Numeiry; the ethnically insecure and fanatical Northern army officers, despite their dark complexions, were very voluble about their Arab backgrounds and Islamic piety. Many of them claimed that the Southern Sudanese, being Nilotic or of Negroid stock could not be *true Sudanese* — even though they occupied nearly half the area of Sudan and composed a third of the population! These Northern Sudanese are insecure about their *genetic* nature and their very geographical and cultural proximity to the despised *other* is clearly a factor as well as the more unspoken fact that many Northern Sudanese are descendants or part descendants of Southern Sudanese women brought into Northern Sudan through slavery.

In the case of a Bosnia, Bosnian Serbs, Moslems or Croats also have common ancestors. Is it this uncertainty about origins that makes a Bosnian Serb more hateful of Moslems than a Serb from Serbia?

This does not, however, explain sufficiently why some people are more comfortable than others as regards their identity. It may be that geographical and historical legitimacy are very important, in particular the idea that a place, a space or a country may or may not always have belonged to that group. A common memory may not be enough as Schulze said above. What is more interesting is that some people or groups may want to have perhaps a *mini-memory*, or a truncated memory that refers only to their immediate clan or group.

Also, in many countries, there is some ambiguity about the original ownership of the territory that the inhabitants are occupying. The vast majority of Jews in Israel came from elsewhere this century and it is mostly among them that we find the most hostility. By contrast, those Jews who remained in the Holy Land after the Diaspora seem to have descendants who are much more friendly to the Arabs. Similarly, Palestinian Arabs who remained in what was the original Palestine seem to be less militant than those who lived in other countries or in occupied territories, such as those of Gaza formerly under Egyptian rule. In former-Yugoslavia, the most violent people are those living in contested territory, whether in Bosnia, Croatia or Serbia, likewise in Kosovo. In Rwanda, the Tutsis are said to be originally migrants from far away Ethiopia and their presence in the country has been synonymous with the discrimination that began first against the Hutus.

Not belonging to the *right religious or ethnic group* encourages movement and displacement. Such groups of migrants, by the very fact of taking the risks of migration, are more adventurous, thus more open to being violent and having to prove themselves more as they carve out a piece of the space for themselves.

Mirror Images

The conflicts in Rwanda or in ex-Yugoslavia are tales of how one culture projects mirror image of its fear to another. It is a tenet of most countries prone to violence that a certain level of intolerance emanating from fear is more common than in countries where people are tolerant of the foibles and eccentricities of others. It does not always help even to know that some of this may be illogical. There is to the mind something akin to *conscious dysfunction*, that is, a certain reversal of certain behavior. People might not want to really change; we do not seem to know why. Thus, people can recognize that a behavior is negative, but they seem to want to pursue it anyhow.

Change in attitudes from an intolerant to a more tolerant viewpoint and vice-versa seems highly complex. Moreover, stereotyping seems as common in so-called advanced societies as it does in poorer societies (Segall, Dasen, Berry, Poortinga 1990, 332). The *mirror-image* problem, where each side in a conflict ascribes to the other exactly the same negative traits, was shown in surveys done in the USA and the Soviet Union at the height of the Cold War, and between Indian and Pakistani respondents — each side ascribed to itself positive and peace-loving traits, while accusing the other of the negative traits that the others gave of them (p. 334-5).

In an article entitled *Hitler's Willing Executioners: Ordinary Germans and the Holocaust,*[13] Daniel Goldhagen, Professor of

Government and Social Studies at Harvard University, argues that the collective anti-Semitism before the Second World War led to the Holocaust, not the Nazis alone. What should be added however is that the humiliating peace treaty after the First World War and an disastrous economic conditions may also have created the desire among many Germans to also humiliate their minorities. Thus a distorted image of the other fuelled by humiliation and centuries of prejudice exploded into irrationality and mayhem, a kind of collective madness kindled by a monstrous leader.

Prejudice and authoritarianism are correlated and assumed by some to be the outward manifestation of a "personality syndrome", that is to say, discomfort with what one is. Clearly Hitler and his henchmen suffered from this type of personality syndrome and he had a so-called charisma that seduced the masses. Did he alone transmit the fever to act to his humiliated masses? Is this power to transmit hatred a feature of megalomania?

There are also some societies where prejudice is not only sanctioned but explicitly encouraged by an entire regime, not just one individual, such as by the former apartheid government of South Africa, and to a lesser extent it is also present in Burundi, Iran, Rwanda, Saudi Arabia, Sudan, or in right-wing groups in many industrialized countries. The level of governmental sanctioning of such attitudes clearly differs between these countries, but the point to make is that some cultures and some governments actively promote discrimination and intolerance against other groups. While that is not surprising or new, it is regrettable that in this so-called modern or technological age they have not learnt from the past — namely that one effect of intolerance is eventually more violence for everyone.

As societies also differ markedly in economic development, it is clear that one way of reducing *differences* will be to close gaps between poor and rich. It is *not* equally clear how to do this. Marxism failed for example, for while abolishing class and income differences in some countries, it did not necessarily abolish the intolerance that has resurfaced in these countries with the demise of Marxism. In fact, the prejudices and stereotyping are now worse in these places than ever before!

A Clash of Identities : Rwanda

The elements of fear of cultural and economic domination by *others* are nowhere more obvious than in the mess of today's Rwanda and

Burundi. Some 40 years of inter-ethnic massacres of thousands, now millions, at regular intervals since independence in the 1960s are not only a testimony to the brutality, but also to the apathy and powerlessness of the international community to stop it. Since it is happening in remote Africa and there is little strategic value in the area, there has been no intervention until the latest 1994 massacres occurred in which over half a million died.

The fear that Tutsis and Hutus have of each other was transmitted to countless groups of children who in turn passed this to their children from the beginning of the Belgian occupation just after the First World War, when the Belgian colonial power chose the Tutsis as their *chosen people* and encouraged their social and economic domination over the Hutus. This is still is exploited by local thugs and politicians to amass power. From an early age children are forced to assume a tribal or cultural identity, which is differentiated from the other tribe. A constant and unremitting propaganda assumes that one side is out to annihilate the other. Fear of such pre-emptive strikes, as is related by several inhabitants, is what leads one part to attack the other before the *other* gets at them.

Their culture, despite a Catholic upbringing, accepts such behavior because it is reinforced constantly by a new series of killings, which reinforces negative attitudes. Even an idealist, or a pacifist faced with such repetitive killings would be bound to justify an attitude that calls for maximum alertness and some indoctrination of his children about the *other side*. Thus, what we have here is a Pavlovian feedback loop, which will trigger a counter-reaction, whenever the opportunity presents itself. Genocide seems almost as a cultural necessity.

In the case of Rwanda and Burundi, we seem to have a more extreme case of cultural paranoia leading to periodic murder of a large mass of people. The signal has rung so much that an attenuated response must now give rise to an exaggerated response. Identity itself is so threatened that every possible mean of survival is allowed, including the massacre of your enemy before he snuffs out your identity altogether.

Could it be that there is a need for a certain level of identification in order to minimize violence, but if there is too much, or where there is a perceived threat to identity already established, violence must occur?

> Social groups who find themselves in changing, contested identities are far more open to the ethnic and political definitions being suggested or imposed from the outside and more vulnerable to becoming

incorporated in the power play of others, [...] as in the case of the Zulu Inkatha movement in South Africa (Wilson & Frederiksen 1994).

Spiral of Group Violence: Yugoslavia

In 1991, during the Serbo-Croat war, radio and TV were immediately used by the authorities in Belgrade and Zagreb to whip up support for the fighting — and for the atrocities. In the first place this meant inventing stories about how the other side had massacred inhabitants of a certain village or town. Most of these first accounts were total fabrications, but they were widely broadcast, and each side was convinced this was indeed happening. Then a second stage took place with actual killings and atrocities to avenge what had been inflicted by the other side. The distortion of accounts of even how some casualties came about made this a *media war of the first category*.

The virulence of the propaganda, true and false, helped to open old wounds that Tito's Yugoslavia had not managed to *cleanse* from the collective paranoia. Every Croat, Serb or Bosnian would relate how a member of his or her family lost, fought, or joined one side or another during the Second World War, and — this is a deeply emotional culture — describe at times in great detail just what atrocity had been inflicted. Calls for revenge killings for atrocities committed four or five decades ago, or even before, increased the paranoia. Grmek, Gjidara & Simac (1992), three French-Croatian university professors, date back the ethnic hatred and brutality in Yugoslavia to hundreds of years. [14] At a private meeting in the fall of 1991, attended by France's then Minister for Humanitarian Affairs, Bernard Kouchner, and myself, I was assured by President Milosevic of Serbia that Serbs suffered so much first from the Turks, then later from the Germans and the Croats that, in his words, they were "never going to forget. Thus, we should *understand their desire to avenge themselves for all that had been done to them*. A chilling reminder that there was to be no forgiveness and that political capital was to be made from all this.

In Belgrade, I attended a meeting of some hundred people screaming (in some historical confusion) about revenge for killings by the infamous Croat-Nazi regime of Zagreb, who committed horrific atrocities on Serbs. What they wanted now was to exterminate as many presumably innocent Croats, for what happened 50 years ago. Children took part in these rallies.

Each side began to attribute to the other *contamination* by other races or religions. Bosnians became Moslem fanatics, Croats were Austrian or German contaminated, to the Croats Serbs were Turks despite their staunch Orthodox Christian roots and so on. Croatians became convinced of the purity of their people as compared to the Serbs who had mixed with invaders. "They are really Turks, not European "like you or me," an official said to me — he did not realize that I am Egyptian! Even church leaders began to warn against Catholic or Orthodox domination by the other side (as seen in Lebanon two decades before). In other words, people were different if they were Catholics, like the Croatian, Moslem, like in parts of Bosnia, or Orthodox, like the Slavs of Serbia or Montenegro – devil is the other despite a common language, a largely common recent history and thousands of intermarriages between the various groups!

The process of transformation and transmission of hatred continued. Criminal elements from the underworld became *religious*. They were to be seen wearing huge crosses, dressed in camouflage or in black, carrying terrifying knives and guns, claiming they would save the religion, their mothers, their sweethearts from all sorts of dishonor. Needless to say, the worst rapes, the worst beatings and sexual torture of men and women took place by these irregular elements, for example the criminal Arkan in Serbia or the Hos in Croatia (cf. Bassiouni & McCormick 1996). The presence of German-speaking young fascists from Austria and Germany in Croatia was, in turn, extremely important in reinforcing the fears and paranoia of the Serbs about a re-enactment of what happened during the Second World War. In Zagreb or Belgrade, youngsters as young as nine or ten years old were seen with these fanatics. The involvement of such young children in a European war seems to be without recent precedent.

In 1992, in Croatia, I witnessed the beginning of what was to become state sponsored ethnic purification, expulsion of Serb teachers, people with Serb names began to fear their neighbors. Croatian kids in Zagreb were beating Serbian schoolchildren. Serbo-Croat couples were having problems and their children were asked to choose between one and the other parent. In one incident I witnessed in Zagreb, at the end of 1991, very young schoolchildren were jeering a small boy in front of a teacher in a popular square in the city center, because he was a Serb. In another, a mock Serbian tank was set up near a school for children to stone. In Serbia, in 1991, I met people who were dismissed from their jobs because they were born in Croatia, or because one of their parents was a Croat or a Moslem.

In Zagreb, in 1992, a friend related to me how a mother, unable to stand the fact her husband was from the other side and defended Serb actions, knifed him to death in front of their child.

Professor Cherif Bassiouni, with whom I briefly collaborated when he was the UN Secretary General's Expert on Violation of International Humanitarian Law for the former-Yugoslavia, notes in a formal UN Security Council report how young children were forced to watch while their loved ones were being raped or executed — or both. It does not take much to imagine in what spirit of vengeance these children are growing up...

These stories and others relating cases of inter-ethnic murder, beatings or abandonment, were also spread by the media and intentionally or not revealed how impossible it was for Bosnians, Serbs and Croats to exist together. Hence, justifying, at the behest of respective governments, the complete separation, if necessary by force, of all sides and the taking of territory they felt was theirs.

Children were therefore easily duped into forgetting that essentially all the people of former-Yugoslavia were one Slavic race, that the language for Serbia, Croatia and Bosnia *is one and the same*. Violence became *normal* and children had been unscrupulously manipulated to hate, to revel in killings of the *other* — and to hand down all this to their eventual offspring.

The veneer of modernity that post-1930s Yugoslavia adopted was a veneer that failed adequately to cover a great struggle between rural and urban Slavs who had developed their slightly different ways thanks to foreign occupiers. Like many other societies, the veneer was not allowed to bind the people of that region into a whole because unequal socio-economic development, a North-South fissure, was allowed to grow. The poorer elements were assigned the status of a Third-World people and the more developed, more urbanized parts adopted the architecture and assumed the mannerisms of what they considered to be modern and European.

However, since the transmission of past horrors remains such an integral part of the culture, the veneer of modern "Europeanism" in Yugoslavia is indeed but a thin veneer.

Indoctrination of Children

As in any template, the early human being is ready to absorb or have grafted upon him or her a series of images, beliefs and sensitivities. But the template also exists in its own right and its little niches and secretions are not always overwhelmed by what will eventually come from *without*; the *within* also exists. This is the crux of the argument about whether people can control their behavior, or whether they will always be dependant on genetic or early environmental influences.

Behavior is of course not simple. Conformity with cultural norms is high up in the value system we have to bow under. Painful sanctions are applied to those who do not. Motives are singularly difficult to explain. Compatibility with role expectations are almost always in conflict with internalized motives.

While some cultures may behave in overall more violent patterns than our own, we may find more cases of individual barbarity in our own culture. Do different forces shape what I would call *group violence* as distinct form *individual violence*?

Coping with Violence

In societies where self-control is considered to be all-important, *violence* is going to be less *acceptable* than in societies where emotional behavior plays a more important role or where self-control is less of a premium. One is referring to self-control only in the context of *manifesting outwardly to others one's feelings of hostility*, a relative concept. For example, not answering somebody, who is talking to you or staring fixedly at him or her are outwards signs of hostility, but this is a far cry from picking up a cudgel and hitting him over the head. It is thus manifestly obvious that in some groups within some cultures there is proportionally more people who will favor the silent stare form of physical aggression while in others the physical aggression may be the most common form of riposte.

The *release factor* in openly expressing one's hostility or taking part in a fight may be an attempt to offset the negative aspects of self-control. While casualties or injuries may be higher in societies where there is less self-control, there may be less harm done to the self, than to keep one's feelings bottled up. Studies show that a child that is a helpless bystander to his parents fights may suffer more than one that openly takes part in street battles or wars where the risk of injury or death is omnipresent (cf. Berry, Dasen, & Saraswathi 1997, 388; McWhirter, Young & Majury 1983, 81-92).

Living in openly hostile situations may paradoxically also help children to *cope* with stress. However for the coping to be effective the child needs a feeling of belonging to a family, a gang, a group,. If not, the child is so bereft of support that he or she becomes almost mentally catatonic, oblivious to norms of behavior and to limits of violence. Maybe, that is what causes some to murder. As Aptekar & Stocklin state: "in the release of severe mental trauma, it could be that action, however horrendous, is preferable to non-action." Their chapter entitled "Children in Especially Difficult Circumstances" gives two interesting tables to enumerate the symptoms found in children suffering from possible war- or violence-related trauma. One table shows various effects such as increased delinquency, while the other shows improved coping skills or even improved mental health! Note also that almost as many authors find no symptoms as do find symptoms. This may indeed be a result of methodological difficulties, but also, as the authors themselves hint, because multiple trauma or several events are needed before a child's resiliency begins to crumble in both the visible and invisible sense (Aptekar & Stocklin, in Berry et al. 1997, 386-7).

Could that be a reason for the violence seen in some groups or cultures? That is a coping mechanism in these groups is created or results from past humiliations, oppression and violence (including massacres) such that peaceful behavior becomes more difficult. It may explain forms of Jewish extremism and hatred, as well as Arab or Moslem fanaticism. We see it also in Tamil, Kurdish and other minorities' forms of violence that include assassination and suicide bombers. Youths may feel so helpless and traumatized by their seemingly hopeless, negative, social and political surroundings, that they must react, just as what happens in traumatized street children who continue to steal and fight, knowing that there may be little psychological alternative.

But it is not just street children or extremists who can feel this way. At a UNICEF-sponsored seminar on "Violence and Children in the Arab World," held in Cairo on 26 August 1995, educated Middle-Eastern students said that they felt justified in being as violent as they could against others after witnessing brutal incidents in each of South Yemen, Sudan, and the West Bank, which they felt helpless to change. More importantly, they saw little change for the good in the future. One should also note in passing that this seminar calculated that the number of children displaced in the region due to wars in the past ten years were as follows: Iraq, 350,000 children; Sudan, 2.3 million children; Lebanon, 379,000 children.

Belonging to a Group

Two instincts govern the individual during their earliest years: the sentiment of *belonging* to a group, unit or parent; and *survival* — of the individual or/and the group.

If the group in question expects a certain behavior, the growing child will provide it in order to belong, since survival will depend on belonging to a unit or group that will protect, feed and shelter that child. Notions of common group benefits — the common good — may not necessarily enter into this, neither would *morality*, as the survival benefits of these are not primordial unless, as the individual grows older, they are also incorporated into the *belonging need*.

An important point is that as the culture becomes more complex and sophisticated, there is less of a permanent mode of behavior, less of a fixed pattern because the individual is either immediately susceptible to his group's changing priority or he may change or transfer to another group and have to adapt to its priorities — as adolescents do, for example. This freedom of action to *change* may paradoxically contain more risks, more tensions and perhaps is one of the principal reasons for the youth rebellion and violence that we see more in industrial societies. In some groups, survival is as dependent on sticking to such group norms as having the right food to eat.

However, belonging to a group is not synonymous nor does it necessarily result in conflict or intolerance. Groups are necessary, even desirable for purposes of self-identification, just as sexual or gender boundaries and the resulting games are. But once usurpation of another group's presence and land results, this constitutes another step towards possibly uncontrolled behavior. Just as street gangs, who eventually take over another group's *turf*, may find essential to dominate even destroy the conquered group's personality as did some colonial masters and slave owners (cf. Rutter & Smith 1995).

Group Identity and Cohesion

Some groups may adopt the mannerisms, sometimes exaggerated of a *superior* or *older* race or group who appeared stronger than they. The nostalgic costumes, crosses, ballads and such like, so often seen in conflict-ridden Slavic groups in Yugoslavia and parts of Russia, not to speak of the spears, feathers and dancing of male Zulu warriors, or even the costumes, hats, beards of orthodox Jews are cases in point.

In former-Yugoslavia, Rambo-like headscarves and T-shirts were very much in evidence among fascist groups known for their brutality, as they were among the young hoods of various Lebanese factions during their long and brutal civil war in the 1970s and 1980s. In Liberia's and Sierra Leone's on-going civil wars, child and adult soldiers wear women's wigs and dresses in a perverse twist of role playing, as if to accentuate the contrasts of male portraiture; adult soldiers make sure that initiation ceremonies for child warriors are mixtures of fantasy, dressing-up, role-model adulation and arms-training — a strong brew calculated to please, impress, attract, frighten and motivate youth into obedience to a new, previously risqué mode of behavior. Perhaps this is also related to a wish to identify or belong to a new race of super-humans, a race that in the minds of these ignorant and drug-crazed youths resemble the omnipotent northern cultures... The fancy-dress costumes are a symbol of a new identity. Conversely, new recruits can be inducted into violence by accentuating some ancient culture noted for its bravery and adopting its former way of dress: the new Cossack warriors in Russia, the Zulu Inkatha toughs in South Africa, the turbaned Islamic Talaban warriors in Afghanistan, the right-wing camouflaged fringe groups in the USA, the robed Japanese right-wing groups, and so on.

Such mannerisms are important for group identity, as well as cohesion, recognition and appreciation. Accordingly, there is a reward system — the individual can win recognition by acceding or accessing to the group when he or she is allowed to wear the *costume*. Once more, it will be the marginalized, the traumatized, those going through major life changes or economical or political upheavals that will be primarily drawn to such modes of initiation. And so will children! Children are drawn to costumes and make believe. Is this a way to recruit them into violence?

In the West today, and increasingly in parts of the East, there are more modern equivalents of these *culture spin-doctors*, clever manipulators who have managed to learn how to attract young people, how to be instantly aware of changing priorities, and also how to tune in to changing fads and fashions. The young everywhere thus want to belong to this *right* group. A whole industry, ranging from pop stars to impresarios to former or current addicts, feeds, influences, copies and inspires them. Hence the present penchant of wearing shoes with untied shoelaces, baggy pants, cap twisted around the head and the omnipresent T-shirt all formerly the garb of prisoners, whose belts and shoelaces were confiscated. This was first adopted by street gang youths from violent US city ghettoes pretending they were tough enough to have known prison life.

In developing countries, at least those in which child soldiers and child exploitation is common, a similar phenomenon operates, whereby a charismatic individual, religious or non-religious, adopts a style that others much younger find appealing. It is an approach that feeds upon their profound wish to avenge whatever social, familial or ethnic injustice has been inflicted upon them and to join or re-join a *master* race or group known for its power to create havoc.

The wish to belong to another *master-group* is not without risks for the young even in peaceful societies. In Japan, bullying of schoolchildren who dare to be different, by teachers and other students, has led to suicides of several young girls and boys during these past years. Yet, the group cohesion demanded of Japanese by other Japanese prohibits too much airing of such culturally sensitive topics. The result is that children continue to commit suicide as a result of this bullying and academic pressure. In Japan, it was teachers responding to what they perceived as modern — American — fashion and dress codes, who initiated pressure tactics on *undisciplined* students. They isolated groups of such students from others, encouraged discriminatory behavior against them and ridiculed them in front of others.[15]

At no time in history have the *young* been so targeted, have been the object of so many manipulators promising an identity. We are dealing here with the search for identity, which for many in North, South, East and West needs to pass through revolt — and hence violence — its most expressive offspring.

Child Soldiers

According to *Médecins Sans Frontières*,[16] as of 1995 there were 38 conflicts going on in the world. The number of children below 16 carrying arms was calculated to be between 100,000 and 300,000 in 1996 (Cambodia, Eritrea, Ethiopia, Guatemala, Honduras, Liberia, Sri Lanka, Somalia, Sudan, Zaire). Another gruesome aspect is the forced recruitment of young girls for sex with combatants.

Religious or ethnic groups sanction and even some governments actively recruit children as warriors and killers. This was deliberate policy in the Iranian response to Iraqi aggression in their 1980s war, just as it was deliberate policy in Cambodia in the 1970s, where children as young as eight were taught to kill adults and other children. It happened or is happening in Algeria, the Congo, El Salvador, Lebanon, Mozambique, Peru, Sierra Leone, Sri Lanka and other countries, just as it happened in Uganda in the 80s and 70s, where children as young as 11 became regular soldiers or *Kadogos*. Afghan, Somali or Liberian factions recruited children as young as 8, who, exposed to atrocities, encouraged in the use of firearms and taught that it was their religious or social duty to kill, could become very cruel. Child warriors' cruelty is of course the result of other individuals' influence, but it also stems from a society or culture, which allows these influences to occur.

A UNICEF study (Brett & McCallin 1996) shows that children are enrolled as soldiers in some 24 countries. The study estimates that about 45 % of the combatants operating in Afghanistan were male youths between the ages of 13 and 18. In Burma, the corresponding figure is about 40 %; in Liberia, 30 %; in some groups in Ethiopia, 38 %; and in some recent South and Central American groups, 20 %. Furthermore, children as early as 7 years of age have been observed with weapons in Burma, Bosnia, Colombia, Kurdish areas of conflict, Liberia, Mozambique and Sri Lanka.

While the authors of that study believe children are used primarily because they make up for adult losses on the battlefield, a growing body of field specialists assume that children admire or belong to armed groups in Africa and parts of Asia because the power of soldiers there instills so much fear and that the only way youngsters feel able to gain some measure of respect, while at the same time controlling their own fear, is to join the swaggering, brutal entity that goes for the name of army in most of the sub-Saharan African countries and a couple of South East Asian States.

Similarly, the police and armed forces of some of the African, Asian or Latin American countries are often made up of youths who not only as youngsters observed, but also suffered directly from atrocities at the hands of some armed group or other. While it could be that revenge may be a motivating element in their joining up, it is more likely fear of suffering again from some sort of atrocity or negation, that motivates them to join police or army units (cf. Azur 1994). This police or armed forces recruitment of youths, who are prone to violence or who have been abused, is a practice that leads to the brutalisation of so-called security forces and should be condemned and monitored worldwide.

Even in affluent countries, such as Iran, Northern Ireland, Saudi Arabia, Russia, South Africa, Spain, the USA, hate-groups, using religion, race or survival reasons, continue to indoctrinate young people, who otherwise may have become normal, peace-loving, unprejudiced young people.

Paul Fussel (1996) has explained in some detail how relatively peaceful, innocent US farm boys were trained to become vicious killers by the US Army. Likewise, young Egyptians, Pakistanis, Gulf Arabs and other Muslim nationalities were armed, trained and given money by British and US advisors or by Iranian and Pakistani trainers in Northern Pakistan in the 1970-80s, all in order to expel Russian troops and their sympathizers from Afghanistan. How many of these youths later went on to kill civilians in their own countries? Has a study been done to establish the link between army training and future killers? Note that military law in most countries clearly specifies that crimes by army personnel can only be tried by military courts, somewhat limiting any civilian judge or prosecutor from trying military criminals, even if they murdered thousands of civilians!

In addition, Aptekar & Stocklin rightfully ask whether abuses of children's rights — such as using children to pick mines on the frontlines of the Iraq-Iran warfront in the 1970s and 1980s — may not be a universally condemnable crime (Berry, Dasen. & Saraswathi. 1997, 381). The UN International Court of Justice needs to act on the crime of recruiting children in armed conflicts. It is a form of genocide for it condemns young generations to mental and physical destruction.

War Games and Initiation Ceremonies

This brings us to the question of war-like play and initiation ceremonies in traditional versus non-traditional or modern societies, a topic many anthropologists have written about. While we can reasonably assume that children are taught about warfare in all societies, the extent to which this determines their acceptance of warfare, as adults must vary.

In most traditional societies, if the male child is not ready to take war games and war talk seriously at an early age, he may be so stigmatized that he would probably not be able physically to survive. In the West, on the other hand, as well as most modern societies, a male child can still be appreciated even if he becomes the equivalent of *a sissy* or *a nerd* and refuse to partake in violent male initiation games.

Does this ability to choose in the West allow the child to become more of a pacifist, later on?

The whole question of participation in games is also related to obedience and ability to withstand or to succumb to group pressure. Thus, as we discuss aggression, we should attempt to associate this to value systems connected with concepts of benefit to self or/and to group.

While creating child soldiers is an extreme form of a child's recruitment into an adult's warfare, other forms of instilling war-like behavior and intolerance in children is widely practiced today. One doesn't need to refer to initiation rites of Masai or Zulu children in Africa to find the most stereotypic examples. Closer to us we find the Palestinians and the Israelis. All Palestinian children are made conscious from the earliest ages of their expulsion from ancestral lands and are brought up to believe that they are in a struggle to get their land back. Hardly a day in their lives will go by without this reminder, be it as a cause of their lives in so-called temporary settlements or because each adult or older sibling will refer to it. Boys as early as five or six are taught war-like songs and poems, learn to mouth curses about the Jews and in many cases are allowed to handle or admire weapons.

Professor Moshe Zimmerman[17] of the University of Jerusalem accused his fellow countrymen, particularly those in Hebron, of bringing up their children in a climate of paranoia and hatred as regards Arabs. Such state-sponsored intolerance, he stated, resembled the education given to young Nazis. He was referring in general about the absence of positive images regarding the Arabs in classrooms and in particular to the attitude of Jewish settlers in Hebron, who were not only celebrating the anniversary of the murder by a Jewish settler, Baruch Goldstein, of some 30 Arabs during prayers at the Mosque of the Cave of the Patriarchs, but who had composed *children's* poems and songs to that effect.

There is a philosophical problem about classification of such attitudes as delusional. Since history shapes behavior by handing down philosophies or stories to succeeding generations, one could argue that Israeli mistrust of the Arabs is justifiable in the circumstances. It is a type of Pavlovian reaction to terrible deeds carried out on a group of people since many years. A possible analogy may reside in the fear that lack of militancy may denote weakness; that after hundreds of years of accommodation in Europe, the Jews were unable to stop the massacres and genocides they themselves had been victims of throughout history. Therefore, indoctrination of the *power to exterminate* must be one of the tools the new Jew must have. There is some fundamental tenant of certain survival instinct: to kill before *they*, the others kill again.

On the other hand, blind and unpitying vengeance, like Baruch Goldstein's, taken as a proof of the *new* power vested onto a group that will never allow themselves to be victims of anyone again is taking things too far. We can say that children are being subjected to the irrationalities and phobias of their traumatized parents and grandparents and, since such fear and hatred is fed to children at an early age, we can therefore assume that further intolerance and hatred will be transmitted to further generations.

Cultural Stereotype for Masculine Behavior

Boys are easy to induct in war-like behavior because cultures relate their masculinity to it.

A fundamental characteristic of male behavior results from an insecurity about masculinity. Machismo, the boasting of physical or sexual prowess is a very real male behavior trait but the extent and the form it takes is very culturally specific.

In some societies — such as in the Middle East, parts of the Mediterranean, Latin America or the Pakistan/Afghan/Caucasian regions — females expect males to behave in a *hyper-masculine* way, to the extent of considering this not just normal but even highly desirable behavior. Such attitudes are rarer in other cultures. However, the geographical limits are not very well defined and clear cut here. For example, in some Pacific Islands, such as Tahiti, male machismo is less a cultural trait than in others, such as Fiji. In Northern Europe, it is more predominant in Germans than in Norwegians. In Asia it is more visible in Korea and Japan than in China. Thus, the proximity of a cultural group to another in geographical terms is no guarantee that male children will be brought up to the same level of militancy and machismo. It is the ancient experience that culture has lived through that will determine how aggressive boys should appear to be. Both conquest and uncertain group identity play a part as well.

It is symptomatic of certain cultures, that the names given to males are associated with warfare, bravery, honor, strength, and so on. In Middle Eastern Arab cultures we very often find the names Assad (Lion), Sharif (Honorable), Nasser (Victorious), Nimr (Tiger), Kebir (Great). Does this somehow lead to males having more of a penchant for fighting behavior, than in cultures where names are given more for religious, trade or poetic backgrounds? Is it a result of historical reasons, because these were cultures where bravery was at a premium, because there was so much insecurity? Cultural conditions differ and with them the way even the unprejudiced perceive violence. In the geographical belt stretching from Afghanistan to Algeria (East-West) and from Syria to Sudan (North-South) an aggressive young man is admired. It is the same for some Latin American and Caribbean cultures or, say, ghetto culture in the West. Men must fight and fighting in earnest begins when they are very young boys. Aggressive behavior is not a bad characteristic in these societies, which are very conscious of matters of *honor*. In fact, a young man would suffer from ridicule if he did not exhibit aggressive behavior. But whereas this aggressiveness takes too often the form of physical violence, other cultures encourage it to be channeled to competition in business or the arts.

Fears of Feminization and the Relation to Violence

Single children, especially males, living with an abandoned mother, may show more aggression than single children living in a nuclear family environment. This tendency is reinforced in the case of the absence of a father or where contact between child and father is minimal. These male children's aggressive attitude may be a reaction against the fear of feminine identification (Bacon, Child & Barry 1963). Several other authors support this hypothesis of a link between criminal behavior and fear of feminization (Whiting 1965). Boys react against their situation if abandoned by a father much more severely than girls. This seems to be true of most societies regardless of the culture, so that one may assume that the psychic damage of a father's absence leeds to what Segall, Dasen, and Poortinga (1999,267) call "compensatory machoism" (cf. p. 64 for additional discussions on this).

An equally interesting factor is whether the surge of testosterone during adolescence is responsible for aggression. If that was a sure factor then one should be able to say or predict that in all cultures there would be higher adolescent crime rates or even aggressive behavior than in other age groups because testosterone levels are highest in young males. This is not so — contrary to popular belief.

Mazur differentiates between dominance behavior and aggressive behavior due to this testosterone surge (in Segall et al. 1990, 277). He keeps a very open mind as to whether there might not be a reciprocal relationship, so that success in status competition may itself produce an increase in testosterone. It may also be that *culture* acts on the already *testosterone-primed organism* in such a way that no final conclusion can be reached without taking into account the *power* or *amount of influence* of that particular culture on either group or individual concerned. Therefore, in quantitative terms, culture may be more important than hormonal levels in influencing the propensity to violence. And the fear of not belonging fully to one's sex or one's group is a powerful tool that some groups and cultures use to keep the fires of male aggressiveness burning brightly. These reflections on how factors related to feminization and masculinity are transmitted sometimes into real and apparent justifications for different forms of violence are gone into more detail in subsequent chapters.

Work, Play and Risk Taking

It seems that culture influences the child primarily by the amount of social interaction provided to the child early on. Thus, in some cultures the child is left alone in a crib or playpen much of the time, whereas in others the child is never left alone, as in most African, Latin American or Asian societies.

What effect does this have on subsequent feelings of hostility or ability to socialize?

Play and inclusion in adult activities such as work are important factors that determine future behavior. Discouragement of the child from the latter and insufficient appreciation of the former — or at least lack of sufficient stimuli from the mother or substitute — may predispose the child to an internalization of conflict and hence to some risk of explosion later. In some cases, it may even be the reverse: children who are spoilt with play and socialization too early on may be predisposed to demand everything and to become violent when they cannot get it. This behavior may become a pattern in adulthood. It will perhaps seem a rare case but serves to underline the simple, obvious but so often overlooked truism, that a balance needs to be found; a child *can* work as well as play and *can* be disciplined as well as having its own emotional life, all without being spoilt, if such balance is present.

Several researchers also found that risk-taking in girls was much less common than in boys, although it is not clear whether this is due to the biological differences or to environmental conditioning, the pressure of correctitude. One would expect to find a higher level of crimes, killings, and abuses undertaken by women where females are rewarded more for risk-taking, than in societies where they are prohibited from risk-taking behavior. It is evident that in places such as Paris or New

York there are proportionally more female prisoners than in seemingly violent places such as Gaza or Karachi.

Girls receive more training in nurturance, socialization and obedience in the poorer cities of the world, but it is difficult to explain why Norwegian or Swedish women, say, who in most ways are brought up to be *independent*, are not much more violent than Italian or South American women. Perhaps, once again, the Scandinavian society's abhorrence of violent behavior over-rides the individual's propensity. It should also be noted that Barry, Josephson, Lauer & Marshall (1976) looked at nearly 150 societies to see whether anywhere, there were female crime rates that were higher or even similar to males. They did not find any.

Can we explain the lack of discipline and aggressivity of some children in Middle Eastern and Western cultures on the fact that they do not spend enough of their time learning how to work and how to interact with working peers? Studies in Kenya and the USA showed that whereas American children on average spent around five percent of their non-school time on some chore ordered by their parents, the equivalent in Kikuyu children in rural Kenya was around fifty percent. Furthermore, a clear gender difference seems to operate, with girls in several traditional societies spending much less time on play than boys, as they get older (Segall, Dasen, Berry & Poortinga 1990, 117-120).

Whiting & Whiting (1975) studied children in six cultures and noted that children who did more work were closer to being "nurturant-responsible", more often offered affection or assistance, than those who did less, those they called "dependant-dominant" and who sought attention or assistance and made selfish suggestions Other experts such as Munroe & Munroe (1977, 145-6) and Shimmin & Shimmin (1984, 369-379) confirmed these observations in other cultures.

Could we then say that is one of the reasons that girls are less violent than boys in these societies, because they are made *more responsible* early on?

If we compared playtime and socialization in different cultures to homicide rates or war-like episodes would we find a correlation? Perhaps what we might find is that when children whose social skills — an ability to play and communicate well with others, including the ability to partake in household and other social tasks — is very deficient, they will logically have more trouble in accepting social norms, requirements and traditions, and be less accepted by their peers, than those more sociable. A number of studies show how delinquent and violent children become when they were unable to develop socialization and cooperative play patterns (Gulbenkian 1995, 50-62, 127-147, 218, 262).

Inhibition, Games and Violence

Prescott (1968) considers that the absence of violence among adults in 48 out of 49 primitive societies he studied over 30 years ago was in part due to sexual freedom among the adults and youth. It may be that there is a good correlation between sexual inhibition and violence. The more free we feel to express desires, the more happiness and the less violence there is in us.

A healthier sexual outlook and upbringing may help to protect against the internalization of conflict within one's self and against others. This is not only about a lack of freedom to be what one wants to be, but also as a result of an *educational milieu* that is frustrating and inhibits many other emotions.

It could be that sexual freedom reduces the need or demand for violence by reducing or channeling certain frustrations and disappointments in the young. It may also be that the greater the amount of *hypocrisy* in a society, the more the disillusionment with that society. This could also be a biologically programmed reaction, a compensatory response to inhibition of one reaction by an exaggerated response, or substitution of another. Thus, violence may not just be influenced by a culture that encourages violence, by mimicry or visualization of violence, but also by inhibition of certain other feelings such as sexual hunger that is not allowed to express itself sufficiently.

The inability of some parents or their refusal to condone early sexuality leads them perhaps to substitute violent behavior as a kind of psychological replacement. In September 1996, a six-year-old boy in North Carolina was suspended from school for kissing a classmate on the cheek. The school authorities decided that was sexual harassment. A month later, in New York, a seven year old who kissed a girl, also on the cheek, was sent home as well.[18] If American parents, who complain about the accessibility of sexually stimulating movies, software or videos, spent a little more time studying how their undisciplined child was being manipulated by the cruel, avid, clever peddlers and makers of violent films, messages and weaponry, they would be more concerned than they seem to be — no doubt? However, their culture considers sexual exposure to be as bad as exposure to violence, if not worse. Much more is spent on purchasing computer programs or appliances that block access to sexually explicit programs than the equivalent to block violent programs.[19]

The reverse also happens. Despite Japan's professed peaceful nature today, we find the most graphic, brutal, violently pornographic films coming out of Japan, such as rapes of schoolgirls with all sorts of objects, sadistic sex scenes with men torturing young women and so on. In fact, a special name has been given to this post-Second World War Japanese film industry: *Eroduction*. Could it be that the Japanese have successfully substituted *virtual violence* for more taboo violent behavior or militarism?

Simpler and healthier are attempts to channel the potential for violence to contact sports. The tradition of holding competitive sports events, even very rough sports such as rugby, ice hockey, boxing or the traditional form of polo (in the Pamirs), was a way of channeling violence away from lethal ends. While this shows that society recognized the need to channel male aggressivity, the puzzle is that men continue to behave violently even if they have had a sports career involving a great deal of aggressivity. Thus the number of soccer, rugby and basketball stars, who also beat their wives and girlfriends, is disproportionably high. Do they go into these sports because they were violent to begin with or did the sport made them violent? Do they influence more youths to become violent? Probably. Society accepts this with almost a wink of complicity. "It is OK to be brutal in sports; that's part of the action." Another example of hypocrisy, albeit a more healthy one. Maybe, after all, we have not done away with the need for male initiation rites involving violence. The cultural excuse is a tenet of arguments against the applying of universal child rights.

International Protection of Children

Cultural Difficulties in Applying a Truly Universal and International Protection of Children

The 1989 UN Convention on the Rights of the Child now ratified by some 196 countries (all the countries of the UN minus the USA and Somalia) has around 40 legally binding articles pertaining to the welfare of children. A number of these articles specifically prohibits discrimination on the basis of race, gender or religion, prohibits the recruitment of children under 18 in armed forces, prohibits the exploitation of children for sexual and commercial purposes and protects children from violence, harmful traditional practices, early marriage, degrading treatment, adult prisons and so on.

In the deliberations carried out in Geneva between the ten member Committee of Experts on Child Rights and member governments, who ratified the Convention, the members of the Committee are supposed to point out to governments who claim exceptions from implementing various articles, that "culture and tradition are not acceptable reasons for violation of a Convention,"[20] neither can a state invoke national security to deprive people of human rights, unless that state is being attacked by outside forces.

In true diplomatic fashion, however, these reminders are rarely put so bluntly. In countries, where for instance girls are married off at 14, the reminder is usually that a lower marriageable age for girls than for boys is discriminatory. It is left at that. One rarely hears stronger condemnation such as the words: "violation of the article such-and-such of the Convention." Note that girls can be married as young as 9 in Ethiopia or 10 in Niger with the blessing of religious authorities, Christian or Moslem alike, and the connivance of official authorities, who recognize such marriages later at the official age. In Ethiopia Government policy to distribute land to married couples has led to reinforce the practice of early marriage. Impatient husbands often transgress the tradition of waiting until the bride reaches puberty to have intercourse. This has dramatic physiological and psychological consequences for the girl and can even put her life in danger.

About one third of the 196 countries that ratified the Convention as of April 1999 have lodged reservations, thereby stating their intention not to be bound by certain of its provisions. Countries that invoke culture as a reason not to implement any of the 45 articles of the Convention are many in Asia (such as Indonesia, China), nearly all in the Moslem group of countries and many in Africa. A real dilemma looms here. Once again, one can recognize the importance of cultural traditions and one is wary of applying ethnocentric views to other cultures, yet this is after all a universal treaty that was drafted by a group of widely different states and accepted by the majority of countries in the world. So, either we accept this is a *universal law* for all or we start chipping away at it, using the *culture argument* to placate all sorts of politicians and anthropologists — or apologists!

Conflict and aggression at the individual child level is facilitated by such attitudes of defiance to international norms of decency. In other words, refusal to abide by international conventions by use of religious, cultural or legalistic arguments also reflects and encourages the mind-set *leave us alone, we are fine as we are*. "No, you are not," we should cry out. "You cannot excuse universally condemnable behavior to protect your culture."

Djibouti, Iran, Saudi Arabia, which consider themselves as guardians of Islam say they have "reserved the right not to apply articles incompatible with Islamic Sharia." Others such as Syria or Pakistan join them, while they allow other rules *incompatible with Sharia* to persist, such as drinking alcohol or, worse, torture. According to the 1997 Amnesty International Report, 134 countries are engaged in coercive practices termed torture; that is more than half the current members of the United Nations, most of whom have signed the Convention on Elimination of Torture.

Economic problems are also cited by many Far Eastern and African states and, until recently, by some Latin American states, as an excuse not to implement or ratify human rights treaties, arguing that their current stage of development is too unique, backward or in need of jobs or social cohesion to allow them to carry out the reforms that richer nations can afford to carry out — an argument that loses some of its weight when one notices that some very poor countries have not only ratified these treaties, but also implement them democratically and equitably; Eritrea, Belize, Botswana, Burkina Faso, Swaziland all come to mind. How can any country invoke excuses such as the above to justify doing nothing to ban forms of children violence such as child prostitution, such as in Thailand, Philippines, India and Nepal, with over 5 million child prostitutes? (in the USA there are some 300,000 prostitutes under 18) (UNICEF 1996, 34).

The USA, like others, is reluctant to have a world organization that could meddle in internal affairs, an argument that many others use to put local needs above the common human good and thus justify violating international covenants dealing with peaceful relations, human rights and equity.

Most child malnutrition and the highest mortality rates are usually found not just in the poorest countries of the world, but also in those where ethnic or religious hatred is tolerated, even encouraged, in order to maintain or revert to some traditional culture. They are also those where female-male literacy rates are the most unequal (UNICEF 1996, 32-5).

International Intervention for Peace

Whether in post-colonial times as in Rwanda, or in post-communism as in the case of ex-Yugoslavia (and Chechnya, Armenia, Azerbaijan, Tajikistan, and so on), it is primarily in changing conditions that groups will be vulnerable to insecurities, to demagoguery — to conditions which will lead to mass hysteria of one form or another.

World bodies dealing with security should be able to better predict where such changes will develop into open conflict. Many early measures to curb the propagation of hate groups are possible without sacrificing democracy (and freedom of expression). Many steps could be taken to better monitor arm flows and purchases, occult financing of groups, the use of mass media to incite others to violence (as in Rwanda) and to provide more creative ways of educating children in cross-cultural exchange, cooperation and coexistence. One might have thought that this gives a major role for some UN agencies professing to care about peace, children and human rights, but it is one in which they have been too hampered by political considerations to take rapid action. This is a pity for an excellently trained and motivated network of UN and Volunteer agencies is already in place round the world; their staff can see when the need arises and they are ready for such interventions. However, thanks to the domination within of diplomats and politicians, the UN's hamstrung approach to anything that might constitute an interference with a status quo in a country is a serious blow to the hopes of millions of human beings who, while wanting to maintain their *identity,* also want to break out from the cultural straight-jackets that will eventually kill their children.

While there is an understandable reluctance to interfere in what is called a "country's internal affairs," there is room for a great deal of flexibility thanks to a growing world opinion about the need for peace in both North and South. In some cases, the application of economic incentives by the world powerful nations can also achieve much improvement.

Thankfully, the NATO intervention in Kosovo and the UN's late effort in East Timor may undo this reluctance to intervene for humanitarian reasons. In addition, one should mention the UN type intervention led by Ghana and Nigeria in Sierra Leone and Liberia. But the point here is that it is only after thousands of people have been killed or displaced that an intervention is considered. But why allow the arms, the hatred and the indoctrination of children to proceed for so long before action is even considered?

Conclusion

A brief foray into how different cultural factors lead to the perpetuation of violence in modern societies has been outlined. But if the tone has been more indignant than objective at times, it is because nearly 2 million children have died in the last ten years from man-made conflicts. Some 540 million children, or one in four of all the world children, live in violent environments (UNICEF 1999). There can be no objectivity with figures like these.

Throughout the rest of this book many examples will be given as to how child rights are routinely violated, lied about, or simply forgotten. It has been the objective of this first chapter to reveal some historical fears and some national responsibilities for these conflicts. Such conflicts are not always a single national responsibility. There are also global responsibilities. For example, Western powers provide financing to a developing country, which in turn buys excess arms dumped on the market from former Soviet bloc countries. These arms facilitate both internal repression and acts of invasion towards other countries. Then, these same rich countries find it difficult to provide sufficient funding for peace making and peacekeeping. It is thus common to find richer countries, so-called donor countries, provide one form of assistance that is counter –productive to a second form of assistance. There are other forms of danger that come from richer countries such as Iran and Saudi Arabia, which have directly or indirectly subsidized fanatical groups that affect children's tolerance towards others in several countries where these groups are active in the name of a purer religious or cultural identity. Finally, we may also ask where and how liberation movements in places such as Sri Lanka, Sierra Leone, Northern Ireland, Chechnya and Kosovo get their arms from, which entities finance their violent groups?

Newspaper Sources and Other Quotations

1 *International Herald Tribune*, 17 May 1996.

2 *International Herald Tribune*, 9 Dec. 1995.

3 *The Lancet* 348-9036, Nov. 1996.

4 *Tribune de Genève*, 18 January 1996.

5 History of the World Conquest, *The National Geographic*, vol. 190, N. 6, December 1996, 9-37

6 *International Herald Tribune*, March 1997.

7 *Le Monde*, 25 August 1995.

8 UNICEF and Save the Children, Germany, as reported by Agence France Press, 19 September 1995.

9 Paul Rutler for Agence France Press, *Cambio* 16, 15 September 1995.

10 *International Herald Tribune*, 17 August 1995.

11 French TV TF2, 29 January 1996.

12 *Le Nouveau Quotidien*, Lausanne, 9 May 1996. An interesting justification for this reversal was that too many Spanish noblemen were cohabiting or marrying native women in the Americas with a resulting loss of income inheritance and status for Spanish born women, who convinced the King and the church to limit such cohabitation with "Christian natives."

13 *International Herald Tribune*, 19 March 1996.

14 They also reveal much about their own biased nationalism in their portrayal of Serbs as brutal expansionists and their playing down of Croatian atrocities, especially those of the Ustachi movement during World War II

15 *International Herald Tribune*, 17 January 1996.

16 *MSF-Switzerland Magazine* No.3, 1995, 3.

17 *Tribune de Genève*; 1 May 1995

18 *The Economist*, 12 October 1996.

19 "Policing For Porn" *Newsweek*, 22 May 1995.

20 Statement by H. Badran, Chairperson, in UNICEF 1999, 29.

Chapter 2

Childhood

In this chapter on Childhood, I will cover a wide range of factors that I consider relevant to understanding how violence is transmitted to the young. Though much is contentious, first the quality of parenting and later peer group influences seem to be the most important transmission mechanisms for learning both antisocial and violent behavior in the young. Parenting factors are more important in the first five years of life. Peer group factors increases as the child grows reaching a peek in the teenage years. Older generation also transmit their trauma's and fears to children of succeeding generations. Unfortunately, most of the data cited in the following pages is from industrialized countries, as there is a dearth of data from poorer countries.

Young Child Criminality

Let us begin with homicide. The number of recent murders involving children as killers may or may not be on the rise since it is impossible to find statistics that go back more than a decade or two. The publicity and frequency with which this is reported today seems to indicate it is a relatively recent phenomenon. According to a report prepared for the US Department of Justice by Prof. James Fox of Northeastern University in Boston, homicides by youngsters aged 14 to 17 increased 22 % between 1990-1994. At the same time homicides by those aged 25 and above decreased significantly.[21]

The wave of very young child-to-child homicide is today big news. Would we have been informed of such killings three or four decades ago? Was there, firearm access apart, a kind of taboo in reporting such acts as crimes? Nevertheless, the incidences of such killing today and their frequency are alarming. In just the past three or four years, we have heard of 11 year olds in placid Norway killing 7 year olds; two children under 11 killing a five year old in Liverpool. From Oakland, California, came news of a 6 year old beating to death a neighbor's newborn baby.[22] Also in the USA, two 6 year olds, a brother and sister, were being trained by their now convicted parents how to beat each other until the blood flowed.[23] From Florida, we read that there are presently 37 children under 17 years of age in prison for murder.[24] In 1999, two 11 and 14 years old massacred more than a dozen schoolchildren and a teacher in Littleton, Colorado. In early 2000, a six year old shot another 6 year old in Michigan. There is even something fashionable about all this since there is now a video game targeted to the young called *Massacre in School*; it is produced in the UK and part of the action consists of aiming a firearm at the head of school children in the schoolyards.[25]

The wave of teenage night curfews in the USA has become a desperate response to increased vandalism and violence in general committed by young people. Some seventy-three percent of America's 200 largest cities now have laws requiring teenagers — up to 16 years old in some jurisdictions and 18 in others — to be off the streets after a certain hour each night, usually 10 o'clock.[26] For nearly 150 cities to have such draconian laws is indicative of something going very wrong. Never mind how many innocent children and parents are punished by this, we may well ask what improvement, if any, this will bring in the long term?

While the effects of mass media on violent behavior in children will be discussed in more detail in Chapter 8, suffice to mention for now that the phenomenon of very young (under 13) child violence in industrialized countries may be the result of two primary factors; one is the profusion of acts of violence on the TV screen and the internet that could awaken the *imagination* of youngsters and two is the isolation that modern lifestyles impose on these children.

From only a cursory review of pre-twentieth century literature, we have every reason to conclude that the lot of abandoned, depressed mothers, married or not, was much worse in the past than it is today; single parents or unmarried mothers were far more ostracized and maltreated, children were exposed to far more prejudice, and suppressed rage was presumably worse. At least in what was called the lower classes, males seemed to drink more, fight more, have less chance of upward mobility and resort to family abuse with much less ostracism or supervision than today. All other factors involving societal or parental abuse or mimicry thereof may have been just as bad before as now, if not worse. Yet, against that it must also be observed that the loss today of the notion of *extended family* as a cultural backdrop offering theoretically some support — even if it has been partly replaced by myriad social services — may make the anguish of loneliness that much more piercing now.

In some cases, criminal and terrorist movements become the peer groups for children replacing parents and friends as the main influence in teaching children how to behave violent. Their use of children to be killers, drug dealers or prostitutes is seemingly on the rise. Fanatical movements exploit children's credibility and vulnerability. Even worse is the use of young children as suicide killers and terrorists. Yet it is the fear of the individual school child that goes berserk with a gun in hand that captures the imagination and fear of adults in industrialized countries.

However, since it appears true that child-to-child murders and serious assaults are on the rise in industrialized countries, we must look at what has changed in children's environment to lead some of them to commit atrocious crimes at very young ages.

Behavior that we either learn or inherit from our parents is less important in some cultures than the desire to conform or bend to the rules of an age group. This is especially so in the more individualistic cultures of North America and Europe. Thus, any program that wishes to decrease the incidence of violence in youths should aim or target the age group as a whole and not just individuals.

Parenting And Violence

One has listed some of the factors that make children violent. There are, however, also protective factors that may help prevent children from leading a life of violence:

- At least one parent or caregiver with a stable relationship with the child;
- Positive, well-orientated and emotionally satisfying educational environment – this is a state or county responsibility. Too many teachers are allowed to continue teaching even when they have lost their motivation;
- Constructive coping mechanisms encouraged by others; a sense of balance in social responsibilities and achievement demands – this is about using volunteers or government workers who must work with youth groups; good, normal impulse control;
- And last but not least a positive image of oneself with a feeling of sense and structure (ICCB 1994, 9, 17, 19).

The absence, weakening or destabilization of any or all of these is a recipe for trouble.

But having said this, there is too much of a tendency to believe that parents are *always* the cause of extreme forms of anger in young children. But are they? The evidence is mixed.

The work of Professor David Farrington, Institute of Criminology, University of Cambridge (in Gulbenkian 1995) and others presupposes that most child criminality stems from either dysfunctional or criminal parents. Yet, neither the Norwegian case cited previously, nor the Liverpool case found evidence that the parents were such. Neglect may be cited, especially in the form of *not keeping an eye on* the child and not knowing where he/she is at a given time, but that can hardly be regarded as criminal behavior by the parents or evidence of dysfunction. True, separated or depressed mothers may be found to be an associated factor in most of the cases, but again, given the millions of depressed or separated parents, one would then expect many more child killers to exist than is the case. Where parents keep guns in full view and reach of children, as was the case for the perpetrators of the Littleton massacre, then we can attribute a more direct responsibility to them as well as in cases where child abuse by the parents or older siblings lead directly to violent behavior by their victims.

However, more scientifically fashionable today is the belief that it is peer group pressure that is the biggest or most significant influence on children. Thus older children at school or in the street can more readily influence a child in his or her manner of dress, speech and *acting out* than the parental dynamics at home. While this may be so in most cases it would be foolhardy to suppose that dysfunctional and violent parents, parents who withdraw or never give affection, as well as sexual or other types of abuse in the home will not have a more primary influence on a child propensity to violent behavior that the friends he or she has later in life.

Parental Abuse and Lack of Nurturing

The anthropologist Phillip Walker[27] looked at the bones of 5,000 children from pre-industrial societies and found no marks of battered-child syndrome; whereas he calculates that were they bones from today's societies, he would have found signs of abuse at a rate of one in twenty in children who died between the ages one to four.

Evidently, the death of a child from child abuse or neglect is only the tip of the iceberg. For centuries and today still in too many countries of the world, child abuse goes unreported. This is mainly because it usually happens in the intimacy of the home and there is a reluctance to interfere. This situation is changing at least in industrialized countries: there has been more reported cases of child abuse during the past decade than in previous ones. This may indicate that the overall increase in non-fatal cases represents better reporting to the authorities, that people are less reluctant to report such cases or that children feel more free to discuss what happens to them or others.

A universal definition of child abuse is difficult. Part of the reason is that it is culture dependant, and also may or may not include many types of violence done to the child. The European Conference on Child Abuse and Neglect (ECCAN) in Oslo, Norway, in 1995 decided to adopt the American definition of child violence, which states:

> Punishment exceeds the boundary of violence when one is beaten with an object, when a sensitive part of the body is beaten, or when there are marks left on the body.

A 1993 study, reported by the US Department of Health and Human Resources,[28] broke down the data about child abuse as follows:

Physical abuse	22 %
Sexual abuse	11 %
Emotional abuse	19 %
Neglect	70 %.

These segments total more than 100 % because children were included in every category that applied to them. A child, who suffers from sexual abuse, is also suffering from emotional abuse for example.

To give a brief indication of the scale and growth of the problem, note that in France, the United Kingdom and the Unites States for example, all indices for child abuse are progressively higher for every subsequent year since 1980. In the United States, rates of child abuse doubled from 22.6 cases per 1,000 children in 1986 to 41.9 cases per 1,000 children in 1993. The proportion of fatal cases remained the same. [28]

Of course a large part of the increase is better reporting since both children and parents, who were abused as children, are talking about a subject that used to be taboo. The problem is how much of the increase is due to better reporting and how much to a real increase in child abuse.

Country reports on child abuse incidence vary widely in the same year, because the sources cited are different. Thus agencies dealing with child abuse, especially those with hotlines will report much higher rates than police or government agencies. In addition, within a group of neighboring countries, such as some Western European ones, one country may report child abuses rates that are double another country's rate, because more attention is given to diagnosing child abuse in the former than in the later. It is moreover difficult to ascertain whether the beating of a child by a parent is less important than say, neglecting to show affection and support to a child.

For example, 90% of prisoner in Swiss jails said they were beaten as children as were 74% of army recruits, according to the Swiss Foundation Enfants et violence. [29]

The Gulbenkian Foundation Report on Child Violence (1995) offers much testimony indicating that violence in childhood led to violent adults; hundreds of scientific papers as well as anecdotal accounts also show this relationship. Much pertains to violence done by fathers but the literature also shows how some violent mothers affect their children. Indeed, many girls and quite a few boys have been adversely affected by the cruelty and violence shown to them by their mothers – not only by their fathers.

Moreover, Selma Fraiberg (1982) goes into detail as regards the "avoidance, freezing, violent" reactions of babies born to depressive, hostile or drug-addicted mothers (p. 612-635). Another important aspect of this study relates the age at which the early reactions to these syndromes occur; defensive reactions occur as early as three months of age. That these extreme reactions can usually be reversed by more affectionate behavior of the mother's — after treatment — points to non-permanent effects on brain structures. However, since there was treatment, there is no way of knowing whether the child would have shown more permanent effects. Fraiberg speculates that the avoidance, freezing, fighting reactions of the baby represents a "biological mode of defense" that is also present in other animals. The first 18 months of life represent a "sensorimotor period, the occurrence of defensive behavior in a pre-verbal period." The mothers in her sample were defined as "psychologically absent" and 12 of the 13 babies avoided their mother through every system of contact, in complete reversal of the social patterns that normally are exhibited at such development stages. Fraiberg claims: "It is possible that certain systems have not been activated by a nurturing person and as a result a pathological stage is reached" (p. 618).

She notes that this is maternal-specific selective behavior, for in some cases the baby only avoided the abusive mother, not the father or strangers. The author further suggests that there is a cut-off mechanism in young children which functions to obliterate the experience of intolerable pain. That is, a reaction which leads the child to respond to further punishment, by ignoring it. Does this explain the origin of *guiltless* or *unfeeling* criminals, those that are the most extremely violent individuals?

In other cases cited, children deprived of affection at as early as 16 months do not *ignore* the psychic pain but develop a well-established fighting mechanism and strike out at any available target, not just the abusive mother. Fighting may be a reaction against the "dissolution of the self" feelings, which accompanies extreme danger (p. 612-635). The threshold for pain in such cases may also be higher (p. 612-635).

There are in addition some interesting observations as regards *pain-pleasure* reactions resulting among other things in a type of smile that accompanies a hostile intention and the way in which this becomes a personality trait. Is this what writers and poets have referred to as *the cruel, or the sadistic, smile*? — Or what policemen look out for when rounding up *the usual suspects*? And so indeed, the sadist may begin as a child who was terrified and trained to hide that terror.

Adopted or Substitute Parents

Of a number of studies linking parental abuse of children to future adolescent and adult violence, let us look at data from the USA (Bloom 1995, 103), especially that offered by Daly & Wilson (1988), who have looked into parental violence in a variety of settings. Some of their conclusions regarding adopted or substitute parents are interesting. For instance: in the late 1970s, a child living with one or more substitute parents was about one hundred times more likely to be *fatally* abused than a child living with natural parents. Children who are adopted by one or both parents are at much greater risk of being maltreated. In turn, there seems to be a resulting tendency for adopted children to inflict more harm on their spouses and children when becoming adults. In a further study quoted by Bloom this time from a Canadian city in the 1980s, a child two years of age or younger living with a step-parent and a natural parent was seventy times more likely to be killed by one of them than if living with two natural parents. Insofar as non-fatal abuse was concerned, children under ten were up to 40 times more likely to suffer parental abuse, if living with a stepparent, than with two natural parents.

Let it be said right away of course, that these figures are not necessarily reflective of the situation in other countries. For one thing, the level of violence, regardless of the age of the victim, is higher in North America than in most other parts of the world. Secondly, in some societies — notably in parts of the Middle East or Africa — a widow usually remarries the brother of the deceased husband and her children are usually treated as if they were the natural children of the new husband. Thirdly, in most parts of the non-industrialized world, the *extended family*, particularly the presence of grandparents in the communal home, ensures that there is more love and attention to go around and the child is not so dependent on one parent or the other. Also, where there is polygamy, children are usually treated equally, since failure to do so would create so much havoc that one mother or the other risks being expelled from the home. Finally, in these same societies, the philosophy of ownership, of possession, is different. Unlike the custom in the West, children are more of a communal asset than an individual possession. Toys and other play objects are also shared more and children of either sex are taught responsibility and work tasks at an earlier age.

This may be a healthier concept, since it may better integrate a child into the values of a community or group — and do so earlier. It also lessens the chance for selfish behavior and the "I want, I get" aggressive syndrome. In the West, gratification is so much more permissible, that adults as well as children, are more prone to get into temper tantrums and learn to be violent earlier, if their self-gratification is not met or is hampered by another. Parental attitudes and uncertainties, hostility and competition are also more likely to be openly visible or demonstrable in small living spaces and apartments than in larger compounds or open settlements. Single children are bereft of the conditioning applied by older siblings. Their world is smaller and they are more dependent on their immediate parents.

Single-Parent Upbringing

Data show that between 1978 and 1986, the number of single-parent families in the USA has doubled — in less than ten years. The effect of single-parent family on school performance is shown in a 1986 study by Guidubaldi & Perry (cited by Sagan 1987, 104-5). While 30 % of children from two-parent families were high achievers, the corresponding figure was only *one* percent for children from single-parent families. The figures are reversed when looking at low achievers: two percent of children from two-parent families are low-achievers as opposed to 40 % for single-parent families. In addition, single-family children were shown to pay more visits to the school clinics, were more often late to class, were absent more often from class, had more cases of truancy, were punished more often by authorities, and were twice as likely to drop out of school before getting a diploma.

However, let us not overlook the fact that since marital instability is also a function of poverty levels and social class, the socio-economic milieu and the physical environment these children find themselves in may be to blame rather than (or at any rate in addition to) the fact of having one parent (Gelles 1985).

USA	21 %
Norway	15.4 %
Sweden	14.6 %
Denmark	14.3 %
Canada	13.4 %
Australia	12.4 %
Finland	9.5 %
Netherlands	8.4 %
Belgium	8.1 %
Italy	4.4 %

Table 2.1: Children growing up without a father in the home.
Statistics available only for these ten industrialized nations
Source: "Progress of Nations Report" 1996, UNICEF

As for statistics on the number of children growing up without a father in the home, the USA tops the list of industrialized countries with 21.2 % children living in solo-mother families. The lowest percentage is Italy, at 4.4 % (Table 2.1).

Separation or divorce is also likely to be correlated with poorer school performance, teen pregnancy, higher delinquency, and poorer mental health in both children and mothers. Divorced or separated fathers seem to fare better than mothers in treating their children, as far as reported cases of abuse and hardship are concerned. Mogens Nygaard Christoffersen[30] found for instance that children who stayed with their father reported being hit much less often than those living with their mothers, had less nightmares and were much less stressed or anxious. The sample size was 1,200 parent-child units, half of which lived with the father and half with the mother; but *caveat emptor* — firstly, there are over 100,000 single mothers in Denmark, as opposed to only 15,000 fathers; secondly, 73 % of these fathers were employed as opposed to only 54 % of the mothers; and thirdly, fathers had in general higher education and social status, better jobs and hence better *security* than the mothers.

Divorced and separated parents, those who are unhappy and those who admitted to being violent with their children give conflicting answers as to the reason for their comportment. But if you divide these into male and female, there seems to be one difference: males will tend to report that they want *loyalty*, *obedience*, and so on, from those they *love*; whereas females will report they seek *support*. Does the male penchant for obedience create more disciplined children? Does the female desire for support allow for more emotional behavior? Probably it does.

Poverty and Divorce

One of the main determinants of poverty is often the absence of a father, especially in the traditional role of principal breadwinner. In turn, in several investigations, it has been seen that the father's absence is one of the main determinants of violence in male children (Bacon, Child &, Barry 1963; Segall, Dasen, Berry & Poortinga 1990). This absence may be a physical separation or a refusal to take any part in childcare. One theory is that the resulting violence in male children is a compensatory attempt to separate from the female influence — "protest masculinity" as Whiting calls it (Whiting 1965). The interaction of low self-esteem connected to absence of the father may also be a primary cause of male violence (Kaplan 1980).

Divorce studies in the USA have shown that unemployment and low pay increase hostility between husbands and wives (UNICEF 1996, 44). Analyzing divorce during three recessions between 1970 and 1982, Donald J. Hernandez, Chief of Marriage and Family Statistics at the US Bureau of the Census, estimates that recession accounted for about 50 % of the increase in divorced or separated mother-only families between 1968 and 1988. Of white children born since 1980 in the US, about 50 % will spend some part of their childhood in a single-parent family. For black children the proportion is 80 %! According to the above studies, this difference is mostly accounted for by the rise in black children born outside marriage. Furthermore, according to Hernandez, "the size of the racial gap in joblessness, about 15 to 25 % in 1989, is at least two-thirds the size of the 23 percentage point increase between 1960 and 1988 in the comparative proportions of black and white children living in mother-only families with never married mothers" (UNICEF 1996, 44).

According to the 1996 UNICEF Progress of Nations Report citing the Luxembourg Income Study, a child living in a solo-mother family in the USA is five times more likely to live below the national poverty line than one where a father is present (Table 2.2).

Country	Children in 2-parent families	Children in solo-mother families
Sweden	2.2	5.2
Denmark	2.5	7.3
Finland	1.9	7.5
Italy	9.5	13.9
Norway	1.9	18.4
Netherlands	3.1	39.5
Canada	7.4	50.2
Australia	7.7	56.2
United States	11.1	59.5

Table 2.2: Percentage of children living below the poverty line in 2-parent families and solo-mother families, 1990-1992.
Source: Progress of Nations Report, UNICEF 1996, 44
(citing Luxembourg Income Study, Working Paper no. 127, August 1995).

Note that the poverty line is defined as 50% of national median income after taxes and transfers. Government policies mitigate the effects. Thus, Denmark, Finland and Sweden have high percentages of children in solo-mother families, yet less than 10% live below the poverty line. Without taxes and transfers for example, France and the USA would both have 25% of their children in poverty. In France, government action has slashed that figure to 6.5%. In the USA, government policy reduces the figure only marginally to 21.5%.

The percentage of children living below the poverty line is higher in solo-mother families than in two-parent families. In low-income groups, absence of a father is more common than in other income groups. Thus, there may be a double effect of poverty as regards to violent behavior: one, the absence of the father, and two, the hopelessness associated with poverty itself. Of course, more important still is the case of a father or male figure who espouses violence and/or who is a criminal.

Prejudice and Shame

There is a new technique given to the subject of predicting criminal and violent behavior in young children which relies on background checks on their family environment, their records at school, the area they grew up in, their father's absence or presence of a criminal background and so forth, all in order to build a so-called "profile" of the child as regards his or her chances of becoming a criminal. In 1995 the then British Home Secretary, Michael Howard, endorsed this technique to be applied to children as young as six years of age.[31] A committee using a computer would have done these assessments, whereby the probability of violent behavior would have been predicted from a history of violence in the home or criminality of the father and so on. The methodology is based on Farrington's research on 411 boys since 1961, which found that those who were labeled "troublesome" by their teachers, or who had criminal fathers, were most likely to become criminals. Four British computer companies are also said to have produced software for this methodology. We should be wary. Other than the obvious risk of typecasting people for the rest of their lives, of making someone even more prone to violent or criminal behavior by making them feel they are expected to behave in that manner, or by creating an even bigger cleavage between social classes in Britain, the technique would no doubt penalize the poorer segments of society simply because more rowdy behavior does take place in inner city schools, because that is where inner city kids meet and play most of the time unlike their richer cousins who tend to have other places to spend their leisure time. One can assume that criminal behavior will then become mainly linked to lower social classes and income, because rowdy behavior or a propensity to violence will be focused in ghettoes. This is not perfect, because it may overlook the increasing criminality seen in children born of more affluent parents and unfairly put the spotlight on poorer families who already feel they are singled out (which contributes to their distrust of the police, the teaching profession and the courts).

Lindner's work on humiliation, although it was done on cultural groups and not on individuals, also shows how humiliation can predict future violent behavior (Lindner 2000).

Unwanted Children

One of the most important studies to date on the effects on a child of being born unwanted — where the mother had wished but had been unable to have an abortion — is to be found in a little known book entitled *Born Unwanted* (David, Dytrych, Matejcek, & Schuller 1988).

The study looked at the effects over time of "unwantedness" on several age groups, children, adolescents, adults, from the 1930s to the 1980s, in the Czech republic, Sweden and Finland. Poor school performance, disruptive behavior, unsatisfactory relationships, depression, violence, divorce, alcoholism, and so on, was always higher in children born "unwanted" than in families where they were "wanted" and where no attempt at abortion had taken place (the data took account of socio-economic and other factors.) Boys showed a higher disposition than girls to disruptive behavior and depressive states. One of the authors/editors also hypothesizes that a permanence in psychological disorders occurs not only due to insufficient maternal stimulation at an early age, but may also be due to a passing of adverse factors from that child as he/she grows up to succeeding generations (p. 64). Thus there is a possibility, as yet not proved, that when a mother has been herself an unwanted child, she will pass to her yet unborn child some negative influence, even if she welcomes her pregnancy and the child to be born.

Transmission of Stress to the Fetus

A propensity to aggressive behavior can be transmitted to the child at the fetal stage. Animal studies show that maternal influences may be so important at the fetal stage, that a whole range of stimuli are transmitted, including the cultural and environmental milieu that affect the pregnant mother in a significant way such as happiness, sorrow, stress and fear.

Work with primates indicates that if pregnant rhesus monkeys were stressed by bursts of high decibel noise, their offspring had higher levels of aggressive behavior and were less conducive to social harmony.[32]

There is the possibility that more violent offspring come from families where the mother has been stressed a great deal during her pregnancy and it may be a function of socio-economic status, that stress is higher in poor families or those surrounded by a climate of loneliness or violence. The point here is that the change in response begins at the fetal level, not perhaps later as some would suppose. It would be interesting to see whether this makes for a permanent state of aggressive behavior, that is to say, one that would be difficult to change even if the environmental conditions later improved.

One can assume that brain structure and formation of the embryo is not complete until some degree of *cognition* is beginning to become operational. In other words, while the fetus is still in the womb, signals from the environment are being received and these signals may stimulate the timing of the closing of the neural tube and the creation of more sophisticated nerve connections leading to a proper brain. Cognition must precede behavior, the next stage in brain development. At this stage it may be better to call this mental development, since, presumably, mentality is being formed. It may be that stress translated or carried by different chemicals in the blood (cortico-steroids) is transferred from mother to fetus at this *cognition* juncture. Perhaps even before, during the first neural blastocytes — that is around the fifth or sixth week of gestation.

A further important example of how a brain can be programmed comes from animal studies during the period of development just before birth (or hatching in birds), when a surge of hormones leads to say, sexual identity, which as discussed is a factor in predicting violent behavior. For instance, in the zebra finch, a small bird studied in Australia and the USA, only the males sing a complicated song; however, if a cocktail of sex hormones is injected into the eggs just before hatching, female finches also begin to sing these songs.[33] It may well be at that stage that male-female differences in aggression behavior begin to be formed — male and female brains *are* structurally different. Spatial orientation and language abilities between male and female humans are not the same, and in most mammals, fighting skills are also different, since all males are endowed with brains that put a premium on turf protection and fighting for females.

Sexual identity, formed at a later stage (not sexual organs only) is crucial to the formation of aggressive sexual behavior. What we may take to be all sorts of male *cultural* cues, may therefore be behavior which is formed at the embryonic stage and quite independent of culture — although of course, it is further refined by influences affecting the child as he/she grows up.

Child Abuse and their Origins in Childhood

No society condones *cruelty* to children, although beating or physical punishment is considered normal in most societies. Yet cruelty may be most common at both ends of the income scale, since the neglect by rich parents may seem as cruel to the child's self-esteem as anything.

In most cultures, boys are said to be more at risk of being beaten than girls and this obviously perpetuates the whole cycle. Whether this is culture-specific or not is not certain —the definition of a simple beating as child *abuse* will of course differ in different cultures — but Buchanan (1994, 3) minimizes the culture specific pattern of this, so do Finkelhor and his colleagues (1988). I am however of the opinion that child abuse as definition is culture specific with the possible exception of course of forced sexual intercourse and very violent beatings.

Thus, it may be that a child will feel *abused* in some cultures because he is expected to perceive what another child or an adult has done to him as a socially condemnable form of *abuse,* whereas in a different culture the child would not feel the stigma of abuse for that same type of behavior. Nevertheless, the subject of what is and what is not child abuse cannot be dealt with either simply or swiftly. Let us assume that regardless of definitions, the psychological damage done to children, who feel abused or even those who do not consider it was abuse, but who were maltreated, will linger on all their lives. The consequence on society is the transmission to subsequent generations of this type of violence. In the USA and the UK, it is estimated that around 30 % of parents, who have been victims of abuse as children, will go on to abuse their own children. In other terms, abused children are six times more likely to later abuse their own children than parents in general – the national average is estimated to be 5% (Kaufman & Zigler (1989); Gelles & Loseke (1993), both cited in Buchanan 1994, p.5).

One of the best account of risk factors in parenting is found in a UK study (Gulbenkian 1995, 32-55). For instance, a study on a large sample of violent children shows that 72 % had been abused in some way mostly by their natural mothers and fathers. In another report, the American Psychological Association states that children who had "weak bonding" to their parents were much more at risk of becoming violent individuals. Poor parental discipline is also a factor.

However, as Buchanan (1994, 12) also shows there is not a uniform view among experts that all or even most abused and beaten children will go on to beat their offspring. A supportive, loving relationship with one's spouse, economic security and so on are protective factors, even if they are say, beaten, whereas, low self-esteem, low IQ, low EQ (cf. Goleman 1995), marital discord, single parenthood and living in a violent culture are much greater risk factors, as expected. Parents with troubled relationships are more of a risk factor than single or divorced parents, a fact that most children will attest to (Gulbenkian 1995, 162). Children may also copy the behavior of parents with troubled relationships, which in turn may affect their relationships with others.

Levinson (1989) studied 90 societies and found 16 in which there was no physical punishment of children and, interestingly, little or no family violence of any sort. Even more important, he found that where a society believed in and carried out a great deal of sharing, cooperation and *equality*, there was little family violence. As ever, we see that competition leads to more aggression.

Certainly, there seems to be at least anecdotal evidence that warm, physically demonstrative, loving parents (or grandparents) give rise to kinder children and adults than do cold, authoritarian or aggressive parents. Thus, we would expect to see less violence and psychological illness in cultures, which are affectionate to children, than in cultures which are aloof to children. Unfortunately, the scientific evidence for this is not very definitive. Nevertheless, parents who are not affectionate are shown to have more dysfunctional children (Gulbenkian 1995, Part 2; Kaufman & Zigler 1989, cited in Buchanan 1994). And I have already proposed the hypothesis that not only are some parents more biologically prone to be abusive (through inheritance, such as having been unwanted or having been the subject of a stressful pregnancy, alcohol or drugs as well as mental disease), but some children as well seem to be biologically more vulnerable to the effects of abuse and violence than others. More and more evidence seems to link stress during pregnancy to fetuses that are more vulnerable both clinically as well as psychologically once they are born (Buchanan 1994, 14-16).

The above account concentrated more on physical abuse such as beatings. Sexual abuse is another form of physical abuse that can lead not only to depressive states, sexual abuse of other children and suicides, it can also lead to violent forms of behavior that include the killing of other children. An interesting, but depressive account of how cycles of neglect, sexual abuse and maternal abuse can lead to a child becoming a killer of other children is in Gitta Sereny's recent book entitled "Cities Unheard. Why Children Kill: the Story of Mary Bell."

Child prostitution is both a form of child exploitation and abuse. It occurs not just because of parental brutality but also because there are economic advantages to those who sell children's bodies to eager customers. It also is on the increase because of drug dependency and what is even more recent in industrialized or consumer-driven societies, a desire by some young girls and boys to sell their bodies so that they can appear to be rich to their friends and peers. On a mission to the Baltic States in 1992, I saw prostitutes as young as twelve or thirteen. This led to a study on child prostitution in Riga, which revealed many disturbing patterns (Shilvena et al. 1996). From a sample of children who were interviewed and who had become prostitutes at an early age (one as young as eight years old), nearly half (48 %) gave parental discord, alcoholism or brutality as the main reason for running away from home and earning money by selling their bodies. Another 36 % gave as a reason the fact that both parents worked and had little time or interest in them. A number of girls also stated that they wanted to prostitute themselves because they wanted to draw their parents' attention, usually their mother's. A fair number also listed the appearance of an abusive or alcoholic father-in-law on the family scene as a precipitating factor. Even more disturbing were the answers of children in school. About 22 % of boys and 31 % of girls at school said they would consider selling their bodies if the cash was right and nobody could find out.

In Riga, from 26 % to 41 % of *prostitutes* are considered to be minors with a bunching around 15 years of age. We should not overlook the fact that the younger the age of prostitution the greater the physical and psychological toll on the child, therefore a greater risk of illness, violence and even suicide. In 1995 for instance, 9 % of all syphilis cases in the Baltic States were children between 15-17 years of age (Shilneva et al. 1996).

Discipline and Authority

Farrington's fascinating series of studies seems to point out that violent offenders had harsher and more discipline-orientated parents (Gulbenkian 1995, 35). Once again, it is a question not only of degree, but also, as Farrington's work suggests, age; for if discipline is applied too early and too harshly it may have different effects than in much earlier or later ages — age 8 seems to be a predictive age in his studies. It is also quite normal to have a more exuberant personality at a younger age rather than in later (teenage) years and so, the effect of disciplinary pressure is bound to vary. Moreover, impulsive and overactive children may be punished more harshly, putting them perhaps at risk of aggressive behavior later on. Different children's temperaments will also elicit different responses in parents (Gulbenkian 1995, 40).

Farrington's studies also show that children who have parents accused of criminal offences are more liable to violence (this is a predictive factor by age 10 already.) But there is some uncertainty about the explanation. It could be being *brought up* in a criminal atmosphere influences one markedly at an early age; or it may also be that the same conditions that influenced the parent to be violent will also influence everyone else in that milieu — racial discrimination for example. It could even be an illness of a hereditary origin. But separating out these cause and effect factors is very complex.

We should point out that peer or parental rejection of a child who does not do well in school, may also worsen anti-social attitudes in the child and lead to violent behavior. This is well shown by the studies undertaken in the USA in 1987 by Patterson & Snyder (in Quay 1987). The clumsy, socially inept child may also suffer from so much rejection that unless parental concern, love and attention is particularly strong, there is probably a higher risk of violent outbreaks later on in life (Gulbenkian 1995, 49).

If violence is shown in the home, the child will obviously feel that he or she can only behave in a defensive or aggressive way; to do otherwise would be to *allow* the child to suffer more abuse. Eron's work (in Bjorkvist & Niemela 1992) showed such a relationship in the six countries that were studied. They were all industrialized countries, but others have shown the same from studies in Nigeria, Solomon Islands, Palestine and one or two Latin American countries. There is nevertheless a dearth of well-designed studies in most non-Western parts of the world, so that much of the foregoing conclusions are very Western biased.

As the UK study amply shows, the concept of a "good hiding" or a smack is common in the UK, as it is in many parts of Europe. (Note that in the UK the mother does most of the smacking (Gulbenkian 1995, 52, 58). But is it so in all of the world? I have rarely seen a young child in sub-Saharan Africa being beaten as often as I have seen it in North Africa. Could it be that in say, sub-Saharan Africa, it is more culturally unacceptable to beat a small child? Is that why these countries have fewer problems with violent youth? Or does that have nothing to do with it? On the other hand, parental behavior, which is too lax, may also lead to problems of discipline and possibly violence in the child. Anecdotal accounts claim that discipline is more lax in the USA than in Germany or India, but that would not explain why there is more violence in the USA — unless there is a *necessary* level below which child indiscipline increases. American parents may on average be so lax that the child does not adequately learn submission behavior. Perhaps it then follows that where fathers are absent — as in many inner city neighborhoods and several suburban ones too, be it said, where fathers are working and traveling excessively — submission behavior is difficult to learn; the potential for violence is thus higher than where a father is much more present. Dog breeders know, for instance, that a puppy that has not learnt the submission-domination cycle from its mother and siblings, because it was taken away from its litter at too early an age, has a likelihood of being a more violent dog than one taken away at 3 months or more.

Interesting information from Canada indicates that children may not necessarily be adverse to physical punishment. In a telephone-&-questionnaire survey on 56 girls and 66 boys, aged 15 to 18, in Nova Scotia, in 1994, 55 % of the boys and 41 % of the girls believed: "it was all right and even sometimes desirable for *parents* to physically punish their children." However, only 8 % believed that *teachers* had a right to use physical punishment (Covell & Howe 1996, 255). On the other hand, in Japan, the sometimes very brutal beating of schoolchildren by teachers is not only sanctioned by Japanese society as a whole but by some students themselves [34]

Submission to parental authority has traditionally been a prerequisite for submissive behavior to other adults who come to occupy a position of hierarchy in the individual's life. If there were no submissive behavior learnt early on in life, the chances of violent rejection of any sort of authority would presumably be greatly increased. This would lead to a society of chaos. People would not only be doing whatever they wanted, but fights, arguments and killings would increase, because there would not be an authority or respected figure to respond to. Thus, one of the values of parenting is the *learned response*, that is the acceptance of something called dominance or authority by offspring — or in more colloquial terms, *the pecking order*.

However, finding the appropriate limit to parental disciplinary action not only will depend on individual family factors, but also on cultural ones. In addition, too much parental dominance may lead to abuse; *too much* is of course culture-dependent, but I would call too much of anything that the child feels is repeated, cruel behavior. It could be that unordinary violent youth have either rejected parental authority because of too much abuse, or, having had to accept it and suffer, react violently to any new, outside form of authority. Indeed, various studies have shown that where parental discipline has been excessive, the offspring have become anti-social, violent — and even suicidal (cf. Gulbenkian 1995, 46-53, 129-136, 162 & 177).

Paradoxically, an obedient and respectful society, where the young are forced to *listen* to their peers, may be more polite, civic-minded and non-violent at face value but may have a greater degree of hidden anger, suicides and explosive episodes of mayhem, as we have already noted in Chapter 1, p. 21 and 49, when discussing Japan.

Authority does not necessarily stem from within the family, of course, and dominance is achieved within the *pecking order*. Dominant male animals have more power to elicit behavior, which creates submission and esteem in others, than do non-dominant males. The same biological process occurs in humans. Youths learn what cues are necessary in order to dominate others. Thus, powerful drug pushers, pimps and gangsters, who are dominant figures in some poorer neighborhoods, will replace (or rather, displace) the weaker biological father, and cues the young pick up from that dominant figure will be reflected in speech, dress, and behavior. Hence, the gutter language, shoelace-less footwear, outsized trousers of inner-city youth in America that resemble those of prison inmates — most of whom become their role models.

Power or dominant behavior also seems to lead to a rise in blood serotonin levels, which in turn, causes a real or relative drop in the level of the same chemical in submissive animals and humans. The response to dominant behavior may thus also act itself out via the body's hormonal system. Since serotonin production has a beneficial effect on mood (cf. Chapter 5), the person who lacks opportunities for its production in sufficient quantities will be depressed and presumably more likely to submit to authority. Unhappy youth may therefore fight to increase the level of that hormone. A recent study has indeed found that people with lower serotonin levels are more likely to commit impulsive crime (Wright, quoting Linnoila et al. in Masters & McGuire, 1994, 243-4).

Anti-Social Behavior, Mistrust and Crises in Self-Esteem

Moffit (1996) informs us with some humor that anti-social behavior is one of the most stable human attributes — with a continuity or uniformity that matches that of human intelligence. Does this mean that as intelligence progresses, so will anti-social behavior in youth? This is not just a philosophical question. It may be that as we learn to exercise more fully our brain, say in playing with computers, we also increase in as yet some unknown way our mental capacities to indulge in real or virtual scenes of violence or anti-social behavior. Machines become more important than friends and duty.

Societies that profess and indeed do worship individual freedoms may also, wittingly or not, encourage poor discipline in children; or at least a healthy tendency to question parental authority. Thus, if such freedom-loving, anti-social behavior is encouraged by the culture or by the parents, it may be difficult to expect anything but a violent adult to ensue (cf. Robins 1978, 611-622; Olweus 1979, 852-875).

Freedom — especially excessive liberalism — may have other effects on parenting or the responsibilities of spouses towards children. In the more *free* societies, not only may spouse abandonment and infidelity be more common but also both parents may find it easier to make difficult demands on each other. When these demands are frustrated, disappointment arises. When this happens, it is easier for anger and violence to break out and the weakest — most likely the child — will suffer the most.

The concept of protecting the most vulnerable members of a society, the old, the weak and the child, has also less place in a competitive, individualistic, atavistic society, than in one where custom, tradition and respect for the old or the young is ingrained. In more traditional parts of the world, men are also less protective or gentle with women that have had prior sexual experience, other consorts and others' children. Perhaps this is due to a primitive biological inclination, to mistrust females who are more readily available to other males. But if that mistrust of women occurs in a systematic way, then it is easy to see that male violence towards women will increase.

Mistrust between the sexes may have also changed for the worst — and in *both* directions – at least in some countries. And a new cynicism reigns. In a survey undertaken in the USA in 1970, most women interviewed were most likely to call men "basically kind, gentle and thoughtful." But in a 1990 survey, conducted by the same pollster, most of the women interviewed described men as "valuing only their own opinions, trying to keep women down, preoccupied with getting women into bed, and not paying attention to household affairs." With that kind of attitude, justifiable or not, a child is bound to become even more confused because his respect for the traditional male authority figure may become more uncertain.

Young men who kill earn respect in some cultures. Others who flirt with any form of danger are worshipped. Politicians stoke their people's intolerance and bigotry to become more important. How much of all that is due to poor self-esteem? How much does a bigoted dictator's thirst for power belong to his humiliation or depreciation during childhood? Would Hitler have become what he was if he had been a highly respected and loved pre-teenager?

In some cultures, children's self esteem is deliberately destroyed in order to encourage anti-social behavior. Children's low self esteem has close links to adult violent behavior and is even predictive of later criminality (Moffit 1993, 674-701). In such cultures, parents, usually the father humiliates the child; if female, the child is informed of the contempt men have about her sex, and if male, any show of weakness, emotion or overt warmth is discouraged.

Crime as Profession, the Answer to Poverty

In France, street violence has risen sharply as compared to violence in general. It is responsible for 50 % of all violent crimes, and about 25 % of all such crimes are now committed by minors (below 18 years of age) compared to 14 % fifteen years ago. It seems that in *cités* (low-income housing development, usually at the edge of towns), youths are increasingly turning to crime of all sorts as a popular and professional pastime. Crimes in *cités* has risen by 400 % from 1992 to 1998. The proportion of crime committed by minors as compared to the general population has tripled in twenty years, from 5 % of all crimes in the late 1980s, to 10 % in 1993, to 15 % in 1998.[35]

Scattered interviews with these youths serve to debunk theories that only poverty and overcrowding led directly to crime. In France, generous social and unemployment benefits and the provision of sometimes rather well-designed low-income housing, with relatively little overcrowding, as in parts of the Riviera, should in theory protect youths from the traditional desperation associated with poverty-stricken families. Youth crime is high there too and an increasing number state that to rob and attack is *cool*.[36] Many youth also refuse jobs that their parents were willing to do, justifying their refusal by stating that the jobs are too demeaning or that the pay is not worth it, being scarcely better or actually lower than available unemployment benefits. Thus do more fashionable alternatives thrive: crime, drugs, bag snatching, even prostitution.

According to the French authorities, an increasing proportion of these violent young people are girls. More interestingly, the same authorities feel that girls are no longer a positive factor of stabilization or protection against violence in teenage groups, but rather a factor of *incitation to violence*. Furthermore, the largest increase in violent school crime has come from young immigrants from North Africa, girls included. This is not to discredit the idea that poverty is a major cause, only to emphasize that it is *relative* poverty, not absolute poverty that matters; and that when such relative poverty is combined with racial or ethnic discrimination, group pressure to destroy and behave illegally, increases.

A parallel phenomenon is highlighted in recent findings in the UK.[37] The point is made that it is not absolute poverty that causes the most health problems in the young, but rather their concept of where they stand and how they stand relative to others. The article also argues that when poorer people have less access to possessions and services that are available to the better off, they suffer and fall sick more often. Compared with youths living in the wealthiest groups, the study shows that those living in poverty are 5 times more likely to die from accidents, 5 times more likely to be diagnosed as having schizophrenia and 2.7 more likely to commit suicide. One in four two-parent families and six in ten single-family in the UK now live in relative poverty, which adds up to 4.2 million children, a three-fold increase since 1979. Between 1979-1994, the incomes of the poorest 10% fell by 13% and those of the richest 10% rose by 65%.

The phenomenon is not confined to the UK. It seems to be happening not only in other European countries such as France and Germany, but also, more ominously, in many urban areas of the so-called Third World as well. In parts of the Middle East, such as Egypt, which now has a population approaching 65 million, the gulf between the haves and have-nots is so great that any tourist visiting Cairo or Alexandria is struck by the contrast between the opulence flaunted by some increasingly rich kids and by their parents, and the misery that exists in the popular districts of these cities; a contrast so great indeed that the government has created *tourist Mecca's*, far from the maddening crowds, where entertainment is provided and where visitors are protected from the risk of both terrorist attacks — as well as the risks of seeing such contrasts that may be difficult to accept. China has the same problem today in some of its cities and so did Indonesia, which, until it deposed the dictator Suharto, sought to give the illusion of just one big happy family. Only when the riots began in Jakarta and elsewhere did correspondents and foreign observers suddenly notice that there were unusually high numbers of poor angry youths, desperate, violent and articulate about the massing of wealth that Suharto's friends, cronies and officers had done.

Heredity, Class, Intelligence and Race In Early Years

Controversies and comparisons involving aptitude experiments using either racial or social class or both — they are sometimes difficult to separate — may be very confusing. In France for example, the school failure rate for working class children is four times that of children from the professional class (Rose, Lowentin, & Kamin 1990, 83). While proponents of racist and elitist theories will try to claim this reflects breeding, the more liberal scientists will claim that differences in status, wealth and power explain why poorer children fail more often in school than richer ones. The same can be said to apply to differences in the propensity to violent behavior between poor and rich children and adults. It may be that all the differences cited here between nationalities and groups as regards violence, are also explainable on the basis of status, wealth and power.

The same holds for tests trying to establish the inheritance of *intelligence*. The testing for IQ (Binet's tests) at the beginning of this century led to much misinterpretation as well as to abuse, including, for instance, in the USA the passage of compulsory sterilization laws in 1907 aimed at *genetically inferior degenerates* most of whom were supposed to have a violent disposition. This measure did not reduce the incidence of violence in the USA; in fact, even though thousands were sterilized between 1907 and the 1940s, it went up! Rose, Lowentin, &

Kamin (1990) discuss the methodological problems that have plagued tests of IQ heredity on twins (p. 80-129). Notwithstanding their exhaustive account, the evidence still seems to favor the theory that in identical twins at least IQ are closely related. If IQ are related, then why not other parameters as well, such as predispositions to aggressive behavior? However, children reared by the same mother, whether adopted or not, black or white, seem to have a closer link to the adoptive mothers' IQ (but not the father's), than those of others whose genes they share (p. 113).

The inheritability of a trait only gives information about how much genetic and environmental variation exists in the population in the current set of environments. Change the environment and perhaps you will change the trait — but maybe not its ability to be transmitted to other generations. Some inherited diseases, such as Wilson's disease, are cured by an antibiotic or other drug. Similarly, IQ variation could be 100 % heritable in some populations, yet a cultural shift could change everyone's performance on the IQ test (p. 116). Heritable does not mean *unchangeable*.

Another misconception is that it may be possible to find a gene completely changed in one race or population of humans and completely different in another. This does not seem possible, although the proportion and position of alleles on a gene may presumably differ in different populations. Thus, there is no *pure* race of humans in the strict genetic meaning of the term. A Spaniard and a Masai warrior share about 85 % of the same genes. In that regard, no group seems more hybrid in its origins than the Europeans, who have been so preoccupied with racial purity for most of the 19th and 20th century? Europeans are the product of the mixing of older Europeans and invading tribes from the East and the South, Celtic, Germans, Franks, Vikings, Ostrogoths, Visigoths, Arabs, Jews and others.

Racism can be disguised in subtle forms. In 1967, well known scientists such as Mark, Sweet & Ervin (1967) in the USA, put forward the theory that those who carried out the urban riots were perhaps suffering from abnormal brain wave patterns. Poor impulse control and psychosis, presumably inherited, were the result. I should like to ask these scientists whether all those that took part in the Boston tea riots in 1775, the French revolution in 1789, and all other great urban riots, such as the St. Petersburg and Moscow riots in the early 1900s, were brain-diseased? In a later book, Mark & Ervin (1970) also put forward their view that psychological treatment or education of such people would not succeed, since brain structures were irreversibly damaged.

Only brain surgery might succeed, namely, destruction of the part of the brain (amygdala) (p. 7). Indeed, they even calculated that 5 % (11 million) Americans were affected! In Africa also, the belief exits that darker people are more inclined to criminality (Sudan, Morocco, Mauritania).[38]

In England, a more novel theory was put forward in the 1980s to explain urban rioting. This is the theory that lead from urban pollution, namely gasoline fumes, may result in hyperactivity (David, and also Needham, in Rose, Lowentin & Kamin 1990, 171 ref. 12). Such a theory still needs to explain why some people riot and others do not, since everyone in London is exposed to such pollution! That a chemical pollutant may indeed affect an individual's behavior is widely accepted, as is the brain damage so caused. However, nobody has yet shown that this occurs at group level — nor of course is there any conclusive proof so far that a gene exists for violence, paranoia, or even schizophrenia.

Some may even argue that heightened aggression is not an abnormal trait — after all, if it is true that in the USA alone, some millions of children suffer from a form of violent personality known as obsessive-compulsive disorder, then such huge numbers may call into question what is *normal* and what is not, if we assume normality is a function of the number of people who possess a human trait, particularly since we now read that the number of preschool children taking psychotropic drugs increased several hundred folds between 1991 and 1995.[38b]

The Legal Aftermath

Violent crime committed by ever younger people is increasing in many countries — in the USA alone, murders by minors tripled between 1984 and 1994; and so, more and more jurisdictions begin to judge and sentence minors as adults. Provisions in the Convention on the Rights of the Child to protect minors from imprisonment with adults and execution for capital crimes are not always being respected, even in advanced Western societies. There is an increasing tendency for some States in the USA to punish youngsters harshly as young as 14 years of age, with Texas and others allowing capital punishment by age 17. In Florida, in 1996, there were 37 children under 17 in prison for murder.[39] Since 1992, at least 44 states in the USA have adopted new juvenile justice laws that allow more children to be tried as adults. In other countries the custom of putting children with adults in prison is common. Very few people seem to think this is inappropriate. Of all the principles in the Convention of the Rights of the Child this one seems to be one of the least respected. Few members of the public seem to think that releasing them in the care of their parents or in halfway homes is justifiable. Yet Sereny's book has shown, prison will not rehabilitate them. Understanding, friendship and love will.

In some industrialized countries, where children below 18 are now responsible for 20 % to 25 % of serious crimes, both parents as well as the youngster are increasingly liable for criminal damages, imprisonment and public condemnation.[40] In France for example, a mother has been jailed in Mulhouse because she did not do enough to discipline her violent delinquent sons.[41] Her defense rejected by the court was that she was too afraid of them.

In 1997, President Clinton signed a new law from Congress, mandating imprisonment for children as young as 13 in response to growing teen and pre-teen violent crimes and murders. We are thus witnessing a massive increase in not only youths who are becoming more violent, but also societies that are becoming more intolerant as a result. Yet because they are becoming more intolerant, they are buying more guns to defend their homes and more of their children are finding these guns to maim and kill others including their own parents. While, four times as many juveniles are using guns to kill their victims as 10 years ago, the National Rifle Association (some 10 or 20 million members with huge electoral influence) refuses to allow significant limitations on sales of guns.[42]

According to statistics in a UNICEF Report (1996), which quotes information published by The Children's Defense Fund of the USA, run by a remarkably courageous woman, Marion Wright Edelmann, every two hours an American child is killed by a firearm. Every four hours, a child commits suicide. Every eight hours a child dies from an act of violence or one of neglect, every fourteen seconds a child is arrested; and every 15 minutes a newborn child dies. The majority of these horrific statistics occur in poorer families.

Now my question: are the parents of these children to blame in the majority of cases? It is difficult to answer that question. In some cases, parents leave guns lying around or even teach their children how to shoot as part of character building or sport. In other cases, the poverty, drug abuse and hopelessness of the mother or the father enable undesirable characters to come into the home and the child is exposed to them.

Finally, we have another, more recently researched phenomena, which implies that children become first fearful and then hyper aggressive because they inherit a trauma that has been transmitted through generations, such as the Holocaust or Black Slavery. Figley (1985, 295-313) well explains a traumatized parent's influence on a child's feelings of guilt, anger and victimization, and how this trauma is transmitted through succeeding generations. The effect of trauma transmission to other family members and their descendants may lead, given the right milieu, to a greater propensity for risk-taking, violent or suicidal behavior.

In the Biology Chapter I go into some of the consequences that maternal stress may have on an offspring's later propensity to violence. Walker (1995), for example, supposes that overproduction of stress hormones by the mother can affect the sensitivity of fetal brain tissue, which in turn would lead to perhaps a more exaggerated response to stressful or annoying events.

During my work in Africa and Asia, as well as in Mexico, I noticed that children who were ill or apathetic were isolated by their mothers and left alone. This would have serious consequences later on.

As early as 1951 Widdowson had shown that children put under the care of angry foster home adults in Holland grew at a much slower rate than children put under the care of loving caretakers. Other studies quoted in Dasen & Super (1988) for example also show how a parent may involuntarily through disease, malnutrition or stress transmit poor psychosocial development to a child.

Mothers traumatized by some earlier occurrence may also transmit, a feeling, especially during pregnancy — and not only a virus, a disease or a nutrient imbalance. This could be through a hormone or other chemical that affects brain development in their offspring. More recent studies imply that the fetus is so sensitive to the mother's moods that anger felt by the mother during pregnancy can be linked to character traits that remain with the offspring not only during the early childhood phase, but also into adolescence (Goleman 1995, Ch. 5; cf. also Sagan, 1987, 38-40). By the same token, Hagerty (1980) reports how a large study to determine the reasons for streptococcal infections in schoolchildren, found that chronic family stress was the major explanation why some children frequently displayed the infection and others did not.

Can we really call that poor parenting?

Yet all in all the cues and the messages one gets from one's family and one's culture are not to be minimized. Time after time, well-meaning but overly ambitious parents have also indirectly or directly caused such anxiety and stress in children that these children have become either dysfunctional or overly aggressive adults. For instance, in an article "And what about America's Stunted Gymnasts?" Bowring[43] argues that the administration to young athletes by some parents, gymnasts or trainers, of hormones or other drugs (such as in the attempt to delay menstruation or menarche in young girl athletes) or by transmitting to them feelings of over-competitiveness, results in a form of physical or mental damage. This is often overlooked in a culture or family intent on *winning*, where young sports hero's or heroines their parents are paid millions and where the means apparently justify the ends. Bowring also writes that this is not much different from the child labor or exploitation, which occurs in countries such as Pakistan or Bangladesh: "Parental responsibility, East or West, is about protecting children from exploitation and self-destruction."

The most vulnerable children

This report on childhood would not be complete without citing what would be the biggest injustice of all as regards children. This injustice is the shockingly high mortality rate of children that fail to reach their fifth birthday because of the violence done to them by a combination of war and poverty.

Thus quoting from the 2000 UNICEF State of the World's Children Report, we note from Table 8 (p. 114-117) that those countries in a chronic state of internal warfare have the highest under 5 mortality rates. These countries are: Sierra Leone, Angola, Niger, Afghanistan and Somalia

No amount of indignation or philosophizing about the violence done to children in other countries, including rich ones, can come close to the indignation we should feel about the violence being done in these areas of the world where cruel and ambitious warlords, sometimes assisted by greedy diamond, drug and arms merchants, allow the killing of so many children in this year 2000. This is both murder and suicide.

Newspaper Sources and Other Quotations

21 *Tribune de Genève*, 21 Aug. 1996.
22 *International Herald Tribune*, 27 April 1996.
23 ABC News, 2 July 1996.
24 CBS News, 29 June 1996.

25 *Tribune de Genève*, 17 Oct. 1996.
26 *The Washington Post*, June 1996.
27 *Time Magazine*, 28 August 1997.
28 *The Lancet*, vol.348, August 1996, 606.
29 Ostermunigen 1995
30 "Un mythe s'effondre." *Tribune de Genève*, 16 Aug. 1996.
31 *The Sunday Times*, London: 15 Oct. 1995.
32 From a lecture by Susan Clarke at the Harlow Primate Lab., Wisconsin University, Madison; 1994.
33 "Sexual differentiation and cognitive function." Lecture given by Prof. Lucia Jacobs of Berkeley, California at the Department of Psychology, Oxford University, 10 November 1995.
34 *International Herald Tribune*, 9 Dec. 1996.
35 "Violence des jeunes: les vrais chiffres." *Le Figaro Magazine*, 17 Oct. 1998.
36 From interviews I conducted with youths in 1998, in and around Nice.
37 "UK Young People's Health Affected by Relative Poverty" *The Lancet* 349, 19 April 1997, 1152
38 Based on personal observation.
38b *International Herald Tribune*, 21 March 2000, quoting a recent Journal of the American Medical Association Report.
39 CBS Evening News broadcast, 29 June 1996.
40 *Le Nouveau Quotidien*, Lausanne, 24 May 1996.
41 TF 1 News, 8 March 2000.
42 according to US Attorney General Janet Reno, *International Herald Tribune*, 9 March 1996
43 *International Herald Tribune*, 7 Aug. 1996.

Chapter 3

Suicide

Suicide, the ultimate form of violence towards self is said to affect more and more children. Yet many are unsure of whether this represents a real trend connected to cultural factors or whether it is a form of mental illness that is on the increase.

A study on teenage risk factors in suicide in Boston in 1987-1988 is worth examining for it reveals interesting results that may be applicable to other societies (Rubenstein, Heeren, Houseman, Rubin, & Stechler 1989).

Based on the answers to a questionnaire put to 300 ninth- to twelfth-graders from public schools, 20 % of the sample was categorized as suicidal based on their self-reports of having tried to hurt or kill themselves in the past year. This is a startlingly high figure. Furthermore, it should be noted that 43 of those 60 cases were girls and only 17 were boys, a huge difference, well illustrating the greatly increased risk as regards attempted suicide in girls.

The parental factor, that is unhappiness with one's family does not always seem to be a principal cause of these teen suicide attempts, even if divorce rates are increasing. The reason for these suicides seems to lie more in the poor image these children have of themselves and a lack of cohesion with family and friends.

Stress, depression, *acting out* — presumably, highly aggressive behavior — poor peer relationships, problems with sexuality, low school achievement, death, departure or suicide attempts in the family... these were all considered to be associated factors, even predictive at times. As might be expected, problems related to sexuality, pressure at school, family suicide and personal loss were the most serious risk (92 % of the students who scored very high on these four risk factors were judged suicidal.) The highest *protective* factors against attempted suicide were family cohesion, family adaptability, positive friendships and parental support in that order. The highest protective mix was a high-cohesion family combined with low stress in the child; the most risky factors, low cohesion in the family combined with a high stress student. Whether this is a cause-&-effect continuum is not certain.

We should note that all these results came from students who volunteered for the study; it is impossible to state with any certainty whether these results are representative of even the Boston area much less the USA, or indeed of the people who then do commit suicide. We should also note that *total stress* (the above four factors) was a more potent predictor on its own of suicide, than depression alone. It should also be noted that these students were from middle-class families, so that economic hardships, poverty, violence and so on, chronic stress factors in low-income families, were not factors of great importance in this sample. Since suicide is beginning to be linked with low serotonin levels,[44] we may hypothesize that when both stress and depression reach a certain level, the risk of suicide becomes much higher. Note that generally more girls than boys attempt suicide, but more boys than girls actually kill themselves in industrialized nations. However, is there a difference, a threshold for different cultures?

Pattern of Suicides

What pattern of suicide rates is there between countries?

The lowest overall rates by far are in the countries bordering the Mediterranean — Israel excepted. Does this strengthen the hypothesis that where the extended and nuclear family is strong, there is less solitude, more outlet for discussion and argument, less hidden depression and more affective behavior? Does the high rate of suicide in Eastern European and Nordic countries also result because there are high alcohol and alcohol addiction rates there, more violent behavior among the young, and more wintry gray weather? Does this affect males more than females in terms of actually killing themselves (and not just attempted suicides), because males are more prone to take risks and ingest more alcohol and drugs? About four times as many young males as females commit suicide in the industrialized nations (World Health Annual Statistics 1993-1995 in UNICEF 1996,4).

Places where indifference and aloofness are more of a cultural trait may be a greater risk factor for suicides, than places where a great deal of conversation and interaction between neighbors take place. Moreover, cultures, where forgiveness and flexibility may not be as forthcoming, may carry more of a risk. Experts have described to me how institutionalized Danish children in the 1950s committed suicide after being forced to eat their own vomit, having been forcibly isolated for long periods from other children. These children had often been severely beaten by alcoholic parents, before they were placed in institutions.[45] The causes of death of these children should be labeled *homicide*, not *suicide*.

The 1990-95 suicide rates for Europe show that the *sunshine states* of southern Europe have suicide rates that can go as low as one-tenth that of the Northern European states.[46] Greece's rate is 3.5 per 100,000, whereas Finland's is 30. Italy and Spain have rates of around 7.6, whereas Switzerland and Belgium have 22.7. Malta is at the same level as Bahamas and Barbados, who are at the lowest end of the global scale; in the former USSR, Tajikistan has a rate of 5.4 compared to Lithuania at 70. Even in France, where the rate is 20.1, sunny Corsica has a suicide rate three times lower than Brittany, although youth unemployment is higher in Corsica.

Might the differences be more easily explained on the basis of alcoholism rates? Alcoholism can be both inherited and a result of certain lifestyles. Mexico has a very high alcoholism rate, yet suicides there are more rare than in more northerly countries and states where alcoholism rates are lower. It may be the outgoing, so-called Latin warmth provided by neighbors and others, rather than the sun, that protects best: from these lists we find that the *friendliest* countries, admittedly a very non-scientific measure, are those with the least suicides.[47] In the absence of firm statistics I would however hazard a guess that these countries may be more friendly to boys than to girls. Hence, in developing countries these may be actually more females than males that kill themselves.

Developing Countries

Data on suicides from developing countries is even more difficult to obtain than all other social statistic in these countries. Indeed, it is simply impossible to find data for suicides for most of these countries. Families and authorities all combine to hide the origins of certain mysterious and sudden adult deaths.

The stigma of suicide is enormous, even in educated families. The poorer the country, the worse the stigma seems to be. Looking at the little information that occasionally surfaces, we find that female suicides represent probably a much higher proportion of suicides in people from developing countries than in non-developing countries. The rate of suicide is also higher among women than among men in UK immigrant populations (Gulbenkian 1995, 189). This is the opposite of the trend seen in non-immigrant, native white populations. One suspects this gender difference for suicide to be true in the immigrants' country of origin as well, for the reasons mentioned previously regarding the difficulties of being born female in some of these countries. The data obtained by the Murray & Lopez for WHO confirms this. The second highest global rates for female suicides come from the Indian subcontinent, the origin of the majority of UK immigrants.

We must also take into account that the murder of females is often passed on as suicide — murders such as the immolation and poisoning of wives in India in order to re-obtain dowries and, in the Middle East, North Africa, Sudan, Somalia and Ethiopia, the murder of girls who lose their virginity before marriage. These murders are often passed on as suicide. So do the shockingly high rates of the murder of unfaithful wives in some countries such as those of the Near and Middle East. In tiny peaceful Jordan (population 6 million), for example, around 40 to 50 very young married women are murdered each year by their husbands who suspect them of being unfaithful.[48] Suicide is often listed as the cause of death even though gunshot and other wounds make it clear that it is a murder.

In China, where recent WHO statistics show the highest rate of female suicides anywhere (as high as 56 % of all reported female suicides in the world), the maltreatment, neglect, hard work, isolation and pressures inflicted by in-laws on brides, may not be the only causes for such high rates of female "suicide" (cf. Murray & Lopez 1997a, 4-19). Murder of young and not so young wives because they are *undisciplined* also occurs frequently in some rural areas and is passed off as suicide. I learned this from a Chinese female doctor some years ago.

"Why are women in India 2.3 times more likely to die from a burn, whereas in all other regions combined, men are more likely to die from burns?" (cf. Murray & Lopez 1997b). In the same report, we note that both the rate for unintentional injuries as well as intentional injuries is much higher, by a factor of 4 for the first and a factor of 7 for the second in the developing world as compared to the so-called developed world (p.1274). The highest rates other than in China found were India, other Asian states and sub-Saharan Africa (the Middle East had the highest rate for intentional injuries, after China and Africa south of the Sahara).

The developing world still has a long way to go before admitting and publishing the true cause of certain deaths and injuries.

Suicide and Politics

We know that during warfare suicides increase. As we would expect, that may be partly due to deprivations and loss of close family members. However, even in peacetime, urban violence and political assassinations can reach such proportions that they lead to a significant increase in suicide rates. In both Spain and Italy, where suicide rates shot up in the 1980s, terrorist and urban bomb attacks also increased just prior to these rapid rises in suicides in the early 1980s. The same is true for Northern Ireland, where rates rose significantly after terror increased in cities and towns there in the early 80s.

The suicide rate for adolescent and young men (15 to 24 years) in the United Kingdom rose from 7 per 100,000 in 1982 to 12 per 100,000 in 1992, that is it almost doubled in ten years. In England and Wales, for this age-group of men suicides are second to traffic accidents as a cause of death, but in Northern Ireland, where young people are one-and-a-half times more likely to kill themselves as in the rest of the UK, suicides claim more lives than traffic deaths, as in France. For young women (15 to 19 years) one in every 100 suicide attempts succeeds. This UK figure is said to be close to all the other EU countries. While 80 % of all deaths from suicides in all age groups are male, 80% to 90 % of *failed* suicide attempts are by women (Gulbenkian 1995, 189-192).

The UK figures have been skewed much higher by the Northern Ireland data. The reason for the high Ulster data may be the terrible economic, social and religious problem in that Province, but it could also be due to the ongoing violence there, which may facilitate violence against self.

Another interesting observation is that in the France, the UK and the USA at least, more young men were being sent to jail in the 80s and 90s than ever before. The rise in incarcerated youth offenders parallels that of suicides in jails and the rise in young male suicides overall. Thus, there may be a more direct connection between youth violence, punishment (real or feared), and suicide.

It is the most depressed that kill themselves. But could it be that the rise in depression that we see in all affluent countries is not only related to but is even preceded by an awareness that the world as these victims see it is not a pleasant place to be in, and that on seeing so much violence around them, people will increasingly try to cause violence to themselves? In times of affluence and optimism, as the period between 1947-1970 in Europe was, suicides rates were much lower than in the period preceding the Second World War, when economic hardship and political terror was rife, and much less than in the mid-1970s to 1990s when unemployment, urban terrorist violence and crime also increased.

Statistics from France

A country not previously known for its high suicide rate — unlike Scandinavia, Hungary, Austria, Russia and former communist states — France in the past 30 years has so drastically upset some previously *suicide stabilizing* factors that suicide rates have soared. Indeed, they keep increasing, even overtaking Sweden in 1980-81.

The trend was:

- 6,402 suicides in 1950;
- 7,223 suicides in 1960;
- 7,774 suicides in 1970;
- 10,405 suicides in 1980, as peaks were being reached;
- 11,644 suicides in 1992;
- 12,200 people for 1993, an increase of 5 % in one year

Since the population has remained stable at around 55 million from the 1960s to today, this represents a very real increase. About 2 % of all deaths in 1991 were suicide, a huge proportion: this is about one third *more* than deaths due to traffic accidents in a country that already has one of the highest rates in the world.

In terms of age and gender, suicides rose most rapidly since the 1960s for 15-24 year olds, particularly females, but this acceleration decreased between 1976 and 1980, only to accelerate again after that (as traffic and other causes of death in the young decreased); currently the suicide rate of the young is the one increasing major cause of death.

We should also note that reported attempts at suicide stand at around 150,000 cases per year, mostly by teenage girls. Men and adolescent boys attempt fewer suicides than females, but their successful suicides number much higher than for females. It is however the elderly who commit the highest number of suicides. Thus, even if young and middle-aged men have experienced a rapid rise in suicides since the 1960s, this is still some 7 to 9 times less than the number of suicides in the over-75 age group. As the population in France is also essentially aged or aging, birth rates being less than replacement, this is to be expected.

The high suicide rate in France for young people today may be connected to the ever-increasing rates of juvenile crime. Thus, whereas in 1994, 92,000 minors were accused of crimes, the figure for 1997 rose to 154,000. Urban violence went up from 3,466 serious incidents in 1993, to 15,791 in 1997, a five-fold increase in just three-and-a-half years.[49]

Newspaper Sources and Other Quotations

44 See Chapter 5.

45 G. Neilsen gave me these details in a personal communication; Mougins, 1998.

46 World Health Organisation figures quoted in *The Economist*, 5 October 1996.

47 ibid.

48 TF2 Report, 7 March 2000.

49 "La Violence des Jeunes," *Nice-Matin*, 12 May 1998.

Chapter 4

Women

The reason for looking at violence committed by women in a book that is concerned mainly about children is threefold:

- Women are the primary caregivers and care takers of children. Their role in shaping much of the personality of the growing infant is more important than that of adult males;
- The role and pattern of behavior of women is changing rapidly. Will these changes adversely or positively affect behavior in children?
- Abuse of women is widespread. What effect does this have on children?

The Statistical Phenomenon

Women are much less inclined to resort to physical assault or homicides than men, but how less so?

Interpol International Crime Statistics reports are the best way we have of looking globally at the difference in the numbers and nature of crimes undertaken by men and women.

Country	Murder Cases per 100 000 pop.	% of Murders attempted or committed by		% of Serious Assaults committed by	
		Women	Juveniles	Women	Juveniles
Industrialized Countries					
Austria	2,47	19,50%	6,70%	13,00%	9,70%
Canada	2,43	12,03%	8,48%	9,50%	12,74%
Finland	0,57	11,40%	5,70%	9,70%	16,60%
France	4,70	13,78%	5,87%	10,28%	10,26%
Germany	4,12	12,00%	5,20%	10,90%	14,10%
Israel	1,77	5,00%	2,00%	18,10%	6,10%
Japan	0,99	21,70%	7,00%	7,10%	36,90%
New Zealand	4,01	8,70%	6,10%	6,00%	6,70%
Norway	2,61	8,00%	16,00%	4,00%	31,00%
Spain	2,29	12,57%	2,85%	6,79%	7,41%
Sweden	8,90	7,70%	1,90%	8,60%	12,00%
Switzerland	0,26	15,10%	5,60%	10,90%	9,50%
USA	9,31	9,70%	14,50%	14,80%	14,70%
Eastern Europe					
Azerbaijan	9,55	2,80%	5,30%	2,60%	8,20%
Poland	3,01	18,70%	2,40%	6,80%	10,30%
Rumania	3.62	7,14%	5,50%	4,89%	6,20%
Russia	15.47	11,40%	4,00%	8,80%	3,80%
Hungary	4,15	15,70%	5,90%	9,10%	8,50%
Latin America					
Chili	5,04	12,90%	4,21%	6,58%	3,63%
Ecuador	6,19	2,10%	2,80%	4,10%	4,50%
Peru	9,28	17,80%	9,20%	19,30%	8,10%
Asia					
Bangladesh	2,21	4,76%	2,65%	0,96%	7,31%
Hong Kong	1,81	8,20%	N/A	9,00%	10,10%
Malaysia	2,36	9,50%	4,01%	6,65%	7,02%
Nepal	2,55	5,52%	0,14%	1,46%	0,19%
Sri Lanka	8.13	7,69%	0,76%	4,10%	1,57%

Table 4.1 a): Percentage of Murders and Violent Assaults
Committed by Women and Juveniles in some countries
(Adapted from Interpol — International Crime Statistics 1991-1992.

Country	Murder Cases per 100 000 pop.	% of Murders attempted or committed by		% of Serious Assaults committed by	
		Women	Juveniles	Women	Juveniles
Africa					
Benin	1,42	6,00%	2,00%	8,25%	26,00%
Cote d'Ivoire	2,53	2,83%	2,02%	13,30%	2,89%
Kenya	6,40	8,50%	4,00%	3,50%	2,90%
Malawi	2,60	2,08%	2,08%	7,65%	1,58%
Senegal	1.78	1,58%	6,20%	29,05%	8,85%
Middle East and North Africa					
Saudi Arabia	0,66	2,00%	2,00%	1,00%	3,00%
Algeria	0,98	3,81%	3,52%	10,35%	7,80%
Morocco	1,39	18,63%	2,90%	18,42%	2,99%
Egypt	1,60	2,00%	1,42%	2,17%	7,50%

Table 4.1 b): Percentage of Murders and Violent Assaults
Committed by Women and Juveniles in some countries
(Adapted from Interpol — International Crime Statistics 1991-1992.

Tables 4.1 a) and b) show some statistics about homicides and violent assaults for women as compared to juveniles. However, they account only for crimes reported to Interpol by the police of different countries, and the police of each country only report crimes they consider worthy of an investigation or that have been reported to them as such. Therefore the data is not always uniform, accurate or comparable.

It is obvious that many crimes or serious injury may go unreported in some countries or are reported as accidents. Generally, the poorer the country, the less reliable or complete are its statistics (with the notable exception of India). Generally, there is also difference in perception about what is acceptable to report or not. Infanticide usually committed by women may not be reported as murder, especially in countries where women do not give birth in a clinic and the birth is not recorded. People are reluctant to report to the police a crime that will result into the police meddling into what is considered domestic affairs and prefer to settle problems on their own. The murder of undesirable wives or widows is a case in point, especially when the murderer is a mother-in-law as is often the case in say, India. The killing of children, especially girls is so common in a few parts of the world that nobody in the police sees fit to investigate or record these as homicides.

Note also that murders undertaken by women in war-like situations, is not taken into account. The 1980s and the 1990s have been notable for the high number of war theatres where women have taken an active part in combat, ethnic crimes, terrorism, or revenge killing, notably Rwanda, former Yugoslavia, Cambodia, Peru, El Salvador, Nicaragua, Liberia and so on.

Therefore, we must assume that there is a sufficient amount of omission and bias in reports submitted by certain countries to Interpol, that richer countries produce better data than poorer countries and that therefore conclusions may represent better the situation in the former than in the latter. Still, here is an attempt to extrapolate some general conclusions from those figures as follows:

- Richer countries generally have more homicides carried out by women than poorer countries; while serious assaults carried out by women in poor countries are generally more prevalent than serious assaults by women in rich countries, although the difference seems to be narrowing for some European countries and the USA:
- Females are responsible for about 10 % of the murders undertaken in affluent countries, but about 3 to 4 % in poorer countries.
- Females carry out on average about 12 % of most of the serious assaults in a country.
- Homicides by women, no matter what country or region of the world we take, never exceed 15 % of the total homicide rate.
- Males are thus responsible for never less than 85 % of homicides worldwide.

Girls and Women, Boys and Men: Patterns of Assaults and Aggressive Behavior

The Interpol figures reveal another interesting phenomenon. In several countries, the percentage of serious assaults carried out or reported for adult females is greater than that reported for juveniles of both genders combined.

This observation seems to apply more to developing countries. Perhaps this is a function of the fact that many forms of juvenile crime are not reported, either because they are so commonplace or because children are given second chances. Perhaps this is also a function of the wider horror associated with serious physical assaults and murder by women.

We would have expected that for homicides, but it is surprising that in these countries, female adults as a group seem to be more violent than juveniles as regards the incidence of serious physical assaults. Another possibility is that the ages at which women can exhibit physical aggression is much higher in the developing world than it is in rich countries. One is also more likely to find that it is the older women in developing countries who are living alone and who are more free to express themselves because there are no males to inhibit them and fewer social constraints than is the case for younger women. Interestingly, for boys aggressive behavior is more permissible at much earlier ages. It may be interesting to see then how patterns of violence differ by age in both sexes.

Experiments in Finland show that both boys and girls seem to have a peak of physically violent behavior — kicking — at age eleven (Bjorkvist, Osterman & Kaukainen in Bjorkvist & Niemela 1992). Although the frequency of aggression in these children was indeed higher for boys (by a factor of four), peaks were recorded in both genders at that age. Interesting things then began to happen. Boys' aggressive behavior, such as kicking, fell around twelve. For girls, although the drop in aggressivity also began around that age, it was far more gradual and between ages 15 and 18 (when the experiment ceased) the level of such behavior in girls was constant. For boys, it continued to fall so precipitously that by age 18 boys reached the lower level that girls were on. That is, levels of physical violence in boys some four fold higher than in girls, starting from age 8, fell four fold lower to the level of girls by age 18. On the other hand, verbal aggression scores was at all times equal in magnitude between boys and girls; both also peaked at age 11. By age 18 girls' and boys' aggressivity, whether in insults or kicking, was the same. These tests were done on Finnish children. Different cultures will probably show different results, but the example used is interesting in any case because of the technique used as well as the results.

Insofar as the peaks at age 11 are concerned, this may be the time that pubertal hormones are beginning to be produced. With the actual onset of puberty, at around 16 for these boys and around ages 14 for girls, social relations begins to impinge on whatever aggressive tendencies either sex have, and peer pressures and adult cues may then be more important at these ages than before, when children are more free to behave as children. Thus I suggest that at least in Northern European children, socialization and normative type behavior really begin to *mould* children's aggressive behavior at around puberty, and not so much before and that may indeed be because group norms become much more important at these ages so that boys stick to boys' groups and girls behave as they consider other girls with them should behave (Bjorkvist, & Kaukainen in Bjorkvist and Niemela 1992, ch. 5).

It may be anecdotal, but crime statistics lend credence to the fact that younger women are less liable to be violent than women over 40. This is the reverse of what happens to males. It may either be that socially, adult women are more free than younger ones to express aggression in violent acts, or there is the possibility that some biologically determined factors are not expressed until later in life and that this may be a sex-linked phenomena, one that may depend on a rise in female levels of testosterone or other hormones. Probably both *society* and *serum* are implicated.

Increasing Trends

However, from an examination of Interpol statistics for the last 30 years, one notices that in many countries there is a disturbing increase in violent crimes and murder committed by women. While also increasing, the rate for men seems to be much more constant for most countries.

Looking at trends between 1969 and 1992, we can say that on average the proportion of *murders* undertaken by women seems stable for some countries (with notable exceptions such as the USA, Rwanda, etc.), while the proportion of *violent assaults* carried out by women is increasing in most countries.

The fact remains that in many countries females are becoming more violent, are using assaults or murder more often to offset their frustrations or achieve the same political or economic objectives than males have traditionally killed for. Notable exceptions are that there seem to be no women mass murderers (except in fiction) and that women do not kill in the rare instances that they carry out forceful, non-consensual sex with a child or an adult.

In the USA the rate of homicides among youths is reported to have increased three-fold in the past 30 years — FBI data show age 21 to be the peak for aggravated assault (Lore & Schultz 1993). No comparable figures for USA based homicides carried out by women over the past 30 years have been found, but it is reported that the number of women on death row in the US prisons, while small, has doubled over two decades. Since the overall rate of violent death from assault in the USA is some 4 to 18 times what it is in other industrialized countries (due to the large use of guns), the number of such murders by women follows the same trend, so that in absolute numbers there would more women killers in the USA than in any other industrialized country. Furthermore, according to the Justice Department Report,[50] 21% of adults on probation or in prison were women in 1998, up from 18% in 1990 (a record population of offenders). Police in the USA report that in some places, violence by women has increased so much that one quarter or more of arrest for domestic assault are of women.[51] The Report also states that women in the USA commit about 2.1 million violent crimes while men committed 13 million violent crimes. Thus the percentage of women committing violent crime is about 16%. Note that the Report states that three quarters of the assaults by women were carried out on other women.

Moreover, there seems to be an increase among female teenagers of sexually aggressive behavior — at least, in the West. School violence in which girls have been implicated is rising every single year since 1980 in all European, North American and African countries, as el as in Japan, if what one reads in the press is to be believed.[52] Freedom to express oneself whether in hostile behavior or fashion or sexual behavior is therefore as possible for girls today as it is for boys, at least in industrialized countries.

In 1974 the average age for first intercourse among females was 17 years; in the UK today it is reported to be around 14 years. The age of sexual consent and of first sexual experiences (intercourse especially) is becoming lower but it should be remembered that while precocity or promiscuity are not *per se* aggressive, there is all the same an increase in anecdotal evidence that girls are rather more aggressive than before in demanding and having sex. Girls as young as 7 are now demanding to wear sexually suggestive clothing, according to a recent series of articles in US women's magazines.

In a new study by Viemero et al. in Finland, it was shown that overall aggressiveness in girls increased over a decade by around a factor of about 25 percent (in Bjorkvist & Niemela, 1992). There was *no* concomitant increase in boy's aggressivity. In fact, at age 13, girls exhibited even more aggressive behavior than did boys, who overtook them only at age 15. We may speculate as to whether the lack of the outlets for aggression that boys have — such as military activity, gangs and the more violent sports — does not serve to internalize the aggressivity of girls, which thus builds up only to explode under pressure later. The study showed that aggressive girls were more popular among their peers than non-aggressive girls. Not only did their self-image improve but the girls also preferred to consider or identify themselves as aggressive than non-aggressive. Girls with low self-image even saw themselves with regret as not being aggressive enough.

Verbal aggression by females, always a traditional method of female attack and female defense is also more *open*, more crude and more accepted in public in both industrialized and some non-industrialized countries.

In Anglo-Saxon, Hispanic, and French cultures that this author has lived in over the past 40 years, aggressive language has changed so considerably in girls and younger women, that it seems no longer possible to distinguish boys from girls in their use of swear words or those which use scatological or sexual innuendo. Even in the Arabic-speaking populations that I was brought up in, there is more use of swear words by educated and bourgeois females, words that denote vulgar expressions to do with bodily functions, words of aggression and of violence traditionally reserved for men.

As a result will there be more or less violence against females? Could males become less aggressive as males, as a result of increased female aggressivity?

Sex as Violence, Aggression in Sexual Relationships

The sex act of course resembles an act of violence. Penetration of the female is an intrusive, invasive act. Female response is dependent on a complex brain reaction that substitutes the habitual female fear of penetration and physical harm, to a receptivity and desire for this when the appropriate partner turns up and *turns on*. How and why this is developed is not just dependent on secretion of male and female hormones in the young female, but also on cultural cues which reward, condemn or help initiate different forms of sexual and other types of aggressivity in human females. Thus in some cultures, a sexually aggressive man is considered as exhibiting desirable behavior when he makes forceful advances. The degree of forcefulness or of even brutal (or boorish in the West) behavior during courtship or during the sex act is not just culture dependant. It seems also dependant on prior childhood experiences for the women and her feelings of self worth.

So, do human females encourage male sexual aggressivity? And how much of these *cues* affect young children and influence their future behavior? The dilemma for the growing female seems to be how to marry submissiveness with independence, vulnerability with desire, and fear with pleasure.

No woman wishes to be forced into being a victim of male lust. Of the *reported* 32,000 women that are raped each year in violent South Africa,[53] presumably not one has considered this a pleasurable experience, otherwise it would not have been reported to the police. However, about 10 to 20 times more women do not report their rapes, either through fear of humiliation or of retribution, not to mention the trauma of simply reiterating the details time after time to the authorities. Why do men want to *harm* females — and then feel they have given women *what they want*?

Depreciation of females in male-dominated cultures is a complex reaction to fears of feminization of males by female behavior, to exaggerated attempts to bond more with males and to anger, perhaps from previous suffering at the hands of a dominant female or the absence of tenderness from a mother. Unfortunately, too many male groups think it is masculine to mistreat or harass women.

It is paradoxical that whereas women may have a great deal to fear and resent from most men, they would invariably prefer a strong, dominating male as consort over a weaker one. In that sense, two factors oppose one another:

- *Self-protection* — that is, traditional evolutionary female behavior which seeks to choose a strong dominant male in order to achieve maximum protection to herself and to any current or future offspring, and
- *Self-resentment* (for want of a better word) — because she knows that she will suffer since dominant, strong males are usually crueler, more violent and more domineering than weaker ones.

Indeed, the dominant status of males is contingent on acquiring and demonstrating such traits to all and sundry. The logic goes: such are the dangers of women being unprotected that it is better to get beaten and restricted by your own male, than suffer the indignities of rape and mayhem from other males for being proud and alone or for choosing a gentle male.

Sexual passivity in women also probably arose from beatings and other real or implied threats from male consorts, which demanded and sought exclusivity and sole access, thus making it a sin for human females to advertise too much to other males their accessibility[54]. It was not enough for the human male to copulate and then walk away from the female, as is done by dogs or cats — he had to own her, to ensure his own prodigy and his own self- and group-esteem. Indeed, this is a characteristic of all higher male mammals and may be the one of the closest evolutionary links we have to our more ape-like cousins.

The human female has it even worse than female chimps or bonano apes, however. The latter do sometimes wander away from the main patriarchal group for example and copulate with another male, or are sometimes very active in the most promiscuous way with other males within the group. In many cases, according to De Waal, the female chimp decides on her own to join another patriarchal group. In female bonanos and macaque monkeys, female-to-female sexual liaisons are common and evidently tolerated by males, but this is quite taboo in almost all human societies. Other scholar's work also points out to another phenomenon: the less time human or ape fathers spend with their offspring, the more the risk for female infidelity to increase. This may either be because less contact between father and offspring may mean less time to spend with the mother, or simply because the female realizes her offspring will suffer from the lack of male parenting. Thus, once again the higher female mammal could attempt to replace a neglectful male in order to choose the best father/consort for her own or her children's sake. The rage that men could have against women who may be suspected of hiding up or condoning their wives infidelity is well exemplified by the execution in France by guillotine in 1943 of a mother suspected of aiding other women to commit abortion.

Parents and Families and Marriage

Fathers can teach certain kinds of violence that allow their sons to mistreat women. Boys will tend to emulate patterns of violence from the father, such as wife beating, whereas girls will try not to emulate what they consider to be ugly, male behavior, so repulsed or fearful are they. On the other hand, mothers who are violent tend to produce daughters who become violent, and sons who harbor either feelings of violence as well or are masochistic in nature. That is to say, their sons will seek domineering females later on.

Nevertheless, anti-social behavior by mothers, as well as by young women ten years before they had children, seems to be a better predictor of future behavioral problems by male offspring, than equivalent *anti-social* behavior by fathers/young males. This pattern seems to hold especially in poor, high-crime environments, but it should be added that the research has chiefly been done in the USA (Capaldi & Patterson 1991; also Emory, Kitzman & Aaron 1996).

Emory et al.'s tentative results after a mammoth ten-year long study that involved 854 women, who subsequently married, showed that delinquent behavior among adolescent girls significantly predicted separation and divorce up to ten years later. The delinquent girls had almost twice as many separations from spouses as did low or non-delinquent girls. Both Emory et al. and Capaldi et al. independently conclude that children of these divorced or separated mothers had more behavioral problems than children whose parents stayed together. Emory et al., however, are careful to point out that no cause-&-effect relationship was necessarily proven between the behavior of the woman prior to marriage and the subsequent behavior of the male offspring. It seems divorce *per se* affects offspring behavior more; even in mothers who did not exhibit anti-social behavior, children were shown to be more disruptive if the mother went through a divorce or separation.

A boy who grows up away from his father is twice as likely to end up in prison, a girl raised by an unmarried or divorced mother is five times more likely to become a teenage mother than a girl who grows up with both biological parents. A teenager from a single parent or step parent home is more likely to possess drugs, own a weapon or assault someone at school than a teenager from an intact family.[55]

Emory et al. also indicate that the younger the mother, the more the chance for the first-born child, male or female, to have behavioral problems later on. Thus, it seems that the mother's aggressive nature at adolescence, whether in terms of seeking sex or conflict with others, may predispose her later to unhappiness in relationships with both children and consort — at least, in the West and in particular in minorities of the USA. Previous comments about the importance of a father's presence should therefore also be balanced with these findings as regards the importance of the maternal character.

None of the above researchers showed whether the influence of brothers, boy friends, husbands, lovers or any other males might have been a causative factor in these girls' delinquent behavior. The studies also do not reveal whether the male consorts' violent or non-violent behavior was a contributing factor in the children's misbehavior and whether either this or the violent or anti-social behavior of the neighbors, the high crime milieu, or anything else in the child's environment (e.g. school) may have contributed to any part of these findings. One also doubts that an aggressive girl in Papua New Guinea, Peru or Pakistan is going to have the chance to be as *anti-social* or *delinquent* as a Nordic or North American girl.

Thus, the response we see above may be purely a by-product of the particular violence-prone, independent, aggressive milieu of certain modern cultures. There seems to be a relationship between wife abuse and subsequent behavior of a child. This may occur not only because some emotional damage is done to the child but also through mimicry. However, the extent males will copy the behavior of the father or consort is a function of cultural norms that condone or discourage such behaviors.

Wife-abuse in the USA is the leading cause of injury among women of reproductive age. In the whole world it is estimated that between twenty and sixty percent of women are beaten (Heise 1993). About the same percentage of all families surveyed worldwide state that they used an act of violence against their child during the past year. The more frequent or severe the abuse, the more likely the victim will grow to be a violent parent or partner (cf. Stein 1989).

According to a 294-page report by the World Organisation Against Torture in Geneva (1998), more than 200 girls and young women were mutilated in acid attacks the previous year. Dowry disputes, domestic fights between couples and refusal of marriage were the main reasons. In Brazil, 80% of murders against women and 70% of the rapes are committed by the victim's husbands, relatives or friends. From Cairo, Egypt, 30% of married women interviewed reported being beaten every day, 34% once a week. In the Congo, 80% of women interviewed reported being beaten by their husbands in one village. In most countries looked at, even if such acts were on the books as crime, the police rarely intervened. The question of what effect this has on children witnessing such acts has not, however, been answered. One assumes that male children will learn from their father behavior that such beatings are normal and will perpetuate them, while for girls, the fear of males will increase and this may lead to extremes of submissive behavior and to psychological trauma.

Does a Male's Presence Increase Aggressive Behavior?

Another way of looking at the whole question of female violence is to determine whether, in the relative absence of human males, female violence increases or decreases. After all, though females traditionally decry male violence they are clearly just as capable of encouraging it. Female violence in the relative absence of human males is a controversial subject, one in which — no less controversially — animal studies show opposite results from studies done on humans.

It is generally accepted that in humans female aggressivity decreases if females live together in the absence of males. Bring an adult male in, and the females begin to fight among themselves. For instance, in parts of Borneo, Sarawak and earlier in Brunei, men and women lived in separate dormitory houses termed *long-houses*; no anthropologist has reported that women fight more in these long-houses. Quite the reverse, they seem happy, organize their own ceremonies and meals, look after each other's children and mates as required, while their regular 'husbands' remain in the longhouses or go hunting. These are not aggressive females compared, say, to their female neighbors on other islands or within the same island, who live with their husbands and who are reported to fight with other females and their husbands much more often.

Are animals different from humans here? Why does the more vigorous, aggressive male chimp or baboon or kangaroo mate at will with receptive females while the weaker males cannot? Can these animals live peacefully without a male? The evidence is mixed — depending on the species looked at.

An article in *The National Geographic* (May 1995) reports that young elephants of both genders become more violent in the absence of a mature bull elephant to dominate them. Lionesses fight more between themselves if a strong male is not present. Chimps, however, can get along fine without a male; their cousins the Bonano apes even perfect lesbian type relationships and seem perfectly happy if adult males are not present.[56] Gorillas do not enjoy being without a male, however — in fact, there are reports that they pine for them and die or fall sick more often if a male is not present. They certainly don't fight more in the presence of a male.

So, back to humans: we should observe that the number of female-headed households is increasing everywhere, an important new shift in the male/female balance. Such figures would have been unlikely twenty or thirty years ago (see Table 4.2).

Black families in the USA	65 %
Botswana	45 %,
Jamaica	42 %,
Malawi	29 %,
Scandinavia	25 %
Peru	23 %,
Thailand	22 %

Table 4.2: Female-headed households: estimated figures.
Source: "Coordinators Notebook" No. 16; UNICEF Consultation
Group on Early Childhood Development, 1995.

Furthermore, the quality of male-female relationships in marriages and other types of unions is deteriorating, if one listens to the various complaints men, women and children manifest, and if one believes family counselors and physicians. From the same source as above, we learn that the relationship between partners in a union affects children and the interaction between each of the parents and the child also affects the relationship between the partners. Noteworthy, too, that the fathers' relationship with the child is most often dependent on his relationship with his female partner; if the latter is particularly cruel, violent or insulting, male anger will spill over into wife- and child-abuse, just as female frustration and anger also often translates into child abuse.

The conclusion to be drawn from animal behavior at any rate is that for a non-human a dominant male presence enforces peace. If we remove the presence of a predominantly, not to say domineering male culture, would there be a higher incidence of female-generated violence? Many feminists are of the opposite opinion: that males make women fight. This makes sense of course. Competition and insecurity for women would be higher if they had to depend on males. In very male-dominated or patriarchal societies, aggression between females is much more common than where the sexes are more equal (Burbank and Glazer in Bjorkvist & Niemela. 1992).

However, others disagree slightly. Males only inhibit females from fighting because the latter are scared of male ripostes if they are seen to be fighting. What seems to be the most common pattern is that females, rats or humans, behave as aggressively as males, "when they are not in danger of being recognized and hence retaliated against. [...] Women are as aggressive as men, as far as the motivation to hurt is concerned" Bjorkvist & Niemela, 1992, 14). Nonetheless, however violent females can be, it is usually the more violent males who are happy actually to go so far as to kill.

A historically important account of female in-fighting in oriental harems, where a woman's access to the dominant male leads to both power and material rewards, is found in an altogether amusing book entitled *Le livre de Goha le simple* (Ades & Josipovici, 1969). Written in the early 1900s in Cairo, it relates in some detail the wily and aggressive manipulations of women in Egypt (then under Turkish rule) and the way in which they fought both verbally and physically to ensure sexual domination. Those that did not *need* males did not fight.

My conclusion is that children will probably have a better chance of becoming non-violent individuals in an environment where there is little competition between females for the attentions or security of an adult male.

Perhaps all this is not violence in the sense of causing death or grievous bodily harm? Certainly, all this is unlike the injuries caused by male in-fighting. Thus, prison violence, even were it representative of normal society, which it is not, is still much higher for males than females, with the later rarely coming close to male violence in terms of physical bodily harm. But women tend to hurt or mutilate themselves more than men do.

Discrimination Against Women

Some forms of discrimination against women, such as lower salary scales or lack of opportunities, still exist in industrialized nations, but discrimination against women takes a much more dramatic form in non-industrialized nations. In sub-Saharan Africa, for instance, as well as in South Asia and the Middle East, most women today have still not had access to an education that teaches them how to write their name. The UN Development Agency estimated in 1996 that around 70 % of the 1.3 billion people who live in absolute poverty are women and that they represent two thirds of the world's illiterates. About 65 % of women in India are forced to drop out of school after a year or two, or have no access to schooling. About 55 % of the women in Sub-Saharan Africa, and South Asia are illiterate, compared to less than 5 % in the so-called developed world, and in any case even if they could read they may not live long enough to write down the name of their children — almost 30 times more women die from birth complications in Africa and South

Asia than in the West. Under such odds, it may appear inappropriate to talk about problems of violence and women, when so many outside the aggressively individualistic, rich West are dying needlessly from lack of medical and educational care. Clearly, when we talk of *women*, we are talking about two kinds of totally different worlds. And in the non-Western world the phenomenon of secret murders by women, a phenomenon clearly related to these statistics, is common.

When we consider subtle changes in speech patterns indicative of aggressiveness or independence of females in the West, for instance, their sisters in the South have not even reached the stage where they can converse freely with men. While in the West a by-product of greater freedom may be a higher level of serious and violent crimes carried out by women, in such male-dominated societies outside the West women often have to operate *in secret*. British administrators in Ceylon noted the comparative rarity of infanticide because even in the poorest of circumstances men and women were there much more equal than in other Asian societies and women were rarely abandoned (Godnesekere in Alston 1994).

Intimate Mutilation and Secret Infanticide

A puzzling feature of female behavior is the obsession with self-injury. This may be in the form of *anorexia nervosa* — self-starvation and sometimes self-injury which appears only in young women — to female genital mutilation (FGM), a form of injury known to exist in at least 30 countries and which, though done to women by usually other women, may also of course be considered as a form of self-aggression. Anthropologists may argue that it is a respectable ancestral tradition, women and men in cultures that practice FGM may argue that going against tradition will make a daughter non eligible for marriage or more promiscuous, some religious leaders will argue that it is a religious teaching (although nothing in the Koran, nor the Bible says so), nevertheless, it is a very aggressive act to cut off part of the female genitalia and it does represent shame or hatred about an intimate part of the female body. As this practice is mostly perpetuated by women (mothers and grandmothers), it may also be a pathological form of female self-depreciation.

Certainly, the economic value of female children in some cultures is so low that they do become a burden. In parts of the Middle East and Asia, especially in India girls cannot find a husband without a consequent dowry. With one-child policy in China, the practice of female infanticide probably increased in parts of that country. However, with the advent of amniocentesis and the possibility to know the gender of the fetus, female infanticide will be replaced by early abortion of female fetuses. Direct infanticide is found most in societies in which the woman's voice is most suppressed; and where women's activity is kept out of sight.

The health and nutritional neglect of female children compared to male children is much higher in many countries. As UNICEF statistics have constantly shown since 1982, this is a form of indirect female infanticide usually practiced by women in countries as diverse as Brazil, China and India — to mention a few of the largest (Scheper-Hughes 1987, 35-58, 95-112, 187-208).

The killing of female infants, by women, in poorer countries, is almost always carried out by a mother, a female relation or a female birth attendant. A million female children each year are murdered in this way in India alone — a conservative estimate. In a dramatic article by Usha Rai, published in *The Indian Express* (3 June 1995), the different ways babies are killed in various Indian states are described (some half a million in one state alone) and we are informed that each attendant in another state killed around three to four babies a month. In one district of Bihar alone, for every 1,000 male child deaths, there were 1,820 declared female child deaths; in another district the ratio was around 1,570 female child deaths for every 1,000 infant male deaths.

Such surveys have so far been carried out in Bihar and, earlier, in Tamil Nadu by an organization called Adithi. It does not favor criminal proceedings against these attendants or the parents, "for fear of driving the problem underground". That statement alone says a lot!

Is there a different value given by several societies to female-initiated murders of children? Is it almost always accepted that this is a *private woman's domain*?

For many anthropologists, this is almost always excused as *some natural way to regulate births*. I have even read accounts where the observer likens the practice to some mystifying power of women to give and take life. The whole mumbo-jumbo and secretiveness of female ritual is no doubt a factor in the perpetuation and concealment of it all. These crimes do not usually enter into official crime statistics, they are easily obscured and — partly because it is female initiated — infanticide has not been the concern of many men. One must also not shirk from stating, however, that the killing of girl babies is encouraged by men in several societies where this obsession for male offspring is common; women clearly respond out of fear of being abandoned. Even in England, failure to produce male heirs cost the wives of Henry VIII their lives...

Related to this is the discrimination practiced on girls who *do* survive infanticide but eventually succumb to all sorts of maltreatment and neglect, thus reversing the usual biological pattern of most boys dying before girls at a young age. The report singles out 13 countries where more girls die, including Singapore, the Maldives, Egypt, Grenada, Pakistan, Bangladesh, and so on (UNDP 1995, table 2.4.). Since a number of African and Near East countries are missing from the list, I certainly suspect the list to be much longer...

According to the UNDP 1995 Human Development Report (p. 35), in societies in which females are treated more equally there are around 106 females for every 100 males (102 for every 100 males in sub-Saharan Africa), this ratio falls to an astonishing 94 females for every 100 males in China and South and West Asia. Indeed, the report states that in China some 49 million women appear to be missing! Adding to this the shortfalls reported from Mid-East and North Africa and the rest of Asia, the global shortfall is around 100 million women!

Women Abusing Children: Sex, Abuse and Punishment

Clearly murder of children is an extreme case of violence by women. What of lesser domestic or family violence? In the conservative countries of the Arab peninsula for instance, there are other forms of violence perpetuated by women, such as violence directed against female domestic workers, mainly those from the Philippines, Sri Lanka, Thailand and other Asian countries. Beatings of maids is said to occur in several households on a routine basis. In Egypt, during this author's youth, maids also were routinely slapped or spat upon by rich and poor housewives, themselves possibly simply passing on the frustrations they feel in their own oppressed state. In Malaysia, a modern society by most standards, a national campaign has recently started against the beating of maids by housewives.

But of even more concern is the harm that could be done to children who are routinely beaten, humiliated or slapped by their parents. In France and Germany it is not uncommon even today to see mothers slap their children in public. Indeed, child punishment is the only area where an adult human female can usually express aggression in all cultures without fear of condemnation, nor social censure. But discipline is one thing; what must concern us first here is something rather more serious, child abuse perpetuated by women (cf. Chapter 4, p.110).

Most child abuse is carried out by mothers in the privacy of the home, according to Eron (Eron & Heusman 1982, 95). Other studies indicate that most child abuse is by children abusing other children. It is probably true, as Eron notes, that while females who had conduct disorders as youngsters tended to have an increased rate of psychological disorders as adults, the same is not true for males. Girls showing violent character would not find husbands. (The old saying, *boys will be boys,* seems to have no such neat equivalent truism for girls.) Whereas girls seemed to have far less conduct disorders than boys, those that did misbehave or show male-like deviant behavior seem not only to be punished more severely in most cultures, but also to suffer more, with more anxiety and more affective disorders later on. A cruel chain of events is thus set up. Mothers may punish girls more severely and in turn these girls grow up showing less affection and producing in turn more disturbed and less affectionate children. Glazer and Miller and others indicate that female suicide, the extreme act of self-hatred, is more common in women and girls who have been punished unfairly or severely. (Bjorkvist & Niemela 1992, 163-171; Scheper-Hughes, 1987). There are no comparative data for boys, however.

Women perceive more readily than men that aggressive behavior produces harm and guilt and anxiety to oneself (see Rabbie et al. in Bjorkvist & Niemela 1992, Ch. 20). Strangely enough, children of mothers who denied their anger are found to be more aggressive than children whose mothers showed their anger (Ch. 25). Children very much feel a mother's repressed anger and some will even go so far to say that this can be felt by the fetus in utero — so, it is likely that an angry mother who is at the same time inhibited from showing her anger, is a cauldron of furious chemicals and signals that may do more damage to her offspring than had she had a safety valve by which to vent her anger.

Many papers presented at a European Conference on Child Abuse and Neglect (ECCAN) in Oslo, Norway, in 1995 — too many to cite here — report an increase in child abuse throughout Europe, but particularly in the former Soviet and Eastern European countries. In most cases, around 90 % of the children that were interviewed in studies presented from East European countries (ECCAN 1995, 64) suffered such abuse, about double the supposed incidence in West European countries. In around 80 % of most cases reported, it was adult females that inflicted the beatings. In another study, this time from Kenya, child domestic laborers (ayahs) were reported to be routinely beaten, and we may suppose it was their female employers who did most of the beatings (Abidha in ECCAN 1995).

Insofar as sexual abuse is concerned, one third of female physicians interviewed in the Czech republic of the age range 40-45 reported abuse occurring some thirty years ago, but in younger female physicians aged 23-25 years old the incidence (i.e. occurring ten years ago) was forty percent. This is a spectacular increase over a relative short amount of time. In Croatia, a study undertaken by the staff of the Children's hospital in Zagreb also showed a progressive increase in the number of child abuse cases between 1990 and 1994 (Urli et al. in ECCAN 1995, 158). This period coincided of course with the collapse of many mixed Serbo-Croat families due to the war there and it did appear to several experts — and to this author when I was in Zagreb — that many female heads of household in 1991-1993 were reporting many more cases of family brutality and abandonment than what had occurred before. While traveling in Eastern Europe and parts of the former Soviet Union in 1992 and 1993, I was surprised at the frequency with which miserable looking children huddling in railway stations, in the streets. Foster homes and State institutions described the frequency and severity of the beatings they received at home. I am tempted to believe that there is an intergenerational transmission of brutality in Slavic cultures, whereas alcoholic and violent men beat their wives and children and where violent women and men beat their children.

There is also a considerable body of evidence that relates maternal distress to child abuse in children (Gunatilleke in ECCAN 1995, 31). A study from Finland showed that violent youth offenders were much more likely to come from homes where abuse was prevalent, than were youth property offenders (Haapasalo et al., p. 61). Other studies from Sweden indicate the important differences of abusive, neglectful and normal mothers in their techniques of child discipline (p. 45). And from Norway comes a fascinating study of 20 women subject to sexual abuse from their mothers (two from grandmothers) — which not only reveals that mothers can abuse daughters as well as sons, sexually, but also how traumatic this can be to the female victims concerned (Lind p. 106). Other female abusers, such as teachers, can also affect children's futures as is shown by Piekarska from Poland (p. 77); and organized or haphazard child abuse by day-care workers is also reported to be undertaken mainly by adult women (Telford, p. 79).

From the UK comes another paper on children sexually abused by adult females. The authors present a figure for the "extent of the problem" which they "estimate to be one in a hundred males and one in a hundred females in the general population that are sexually abused as children by a woman [...] The majority [...] being perpetrated by the mother or the primary female caretaker." However, of 39 women who had sexually abused their own children, they found that whereas 22 were the sole perpetrators, 17 did so in conjunction with men (Saradjian & Youngson in ECCAN 1995).

Most of the evidence for the extent of this pathology seems to come from Northern Europe. Is there more of such abuse undertaken by women there, because of the more permissive sexual atmosphere in that part of the world? It is sometimes curious to see that friendship can be used as an excuse for sex with a child, even on the part of women such as a middle-aged Northern European woman who told me that she paid very young Sri Lankan boys to have sex with them while holidaying on the island, because she wanted to "be friends to those tender boys."

Insofar as sexual abuse of children by adult women is concerned, this is a phenomenon that seems to occur mainly in instances where an abandoned and often alcoholic mother or female relative is said to be "desperate for affection and physical contact," according to a woman who had been sexually abused by her mother.

Are the problems also not problems of definition? That is, what may be considered as rather odd but acceptable ways of stimulating a child or an adult in, say, a Latin American country or a Middle Eastern one, places where a great deal of child fondling is common and would not be considered nor reported as abuse, may be seen quite differently in the supposedly more *aware* countries of the West. Not to trivialize the problem, let us observe that bottom pinching of women in Italy was until recently accepted and not considered a form of female abuse. It seems to have become less of a joke around the time the women's movement reached Southern Europe...

Female-generated abuse on young children may have sequels that are just as important as male abuse of children. In some cases it might even lead to more traumatic consequences, regardless even of culture, in adult relationships with other women. That violence and abuse in the home is more independent of demographic and economic status than it is of the quality of the marital situation is well borne out in the paper presented by Smith (ECCAN 1995, 84). Atkar and Baldwin reveal that culture or geographical origin is another important variable (p. 153). They report that Asian children in the UK are more under-represented in child protection registers than are white or black children. Similarly, research has found that geographical origin is important in assessing children's problems (Lamb & Sternberg, 1992). But this may not mean the abuse has not occurred. It just means it is not reported or is not considered important enough to be reported — two quite different phenomena. Another paper by Smith (ECCAN 1995, 85) indicates boys are hit more often than girls, a finding consistent with anecdotal evidence from all around the world —but what is most interesting is that mothers also hit boys more than they hit girls. Is this yet another way males are conditioned to be violent?

We should also put sexual abuse in the context of other forms of child abuse. In France for instance, in the city of Rennes, pediatric records reveal that cases of child abuse could be broken down into the following categories:

Home violence	38 %
Neglect	23 %
Assault	6.6 %
Lack of food	5.5 %
Abandonment	5.5 %
Sexual abuse	3.5 %

It is puzzling to note the low level of sexual abuse when we hear of the much higher levels reported from the Czech Republic above (p. 18) or the incidence reported from parts of the USA and Scandinavia and the UK. Once again cultural definitions, values, perceptions and even scientific bias must be looked at closely. There is also as ever in such contexts, the silence created by a reluctance to report. For instance, the level of seduction by homosexual female teachers is far higher than males imagine possible; yet rarely is anything said or done... Not so for males. Another point is that female abuse of children may only rarely be sexual in nature, but whether it is physical or verbal, it may be high in most cultures and a reason for concern just as much as male violence towards children.

Finally, it is interesting to note in a review paper by Gitlin & Pasnau (1989) that even the risk of infanticide is included among the psychotic manifestations related to *post-partum* depression exhibited by some women during their periodic cycles. What is important here as well is the authors' opinion that undesirable life events and marital problems also seem to plunge many women into the psychotic syndromes that are commonly associated with the hormonal fluctuations during the reproductive cycle. Indeed, it is remarkable that the hundredfold drop in, say, estrogen and progesterone during the few days between *antepartum* and *postpartum* does not actually create *more* mood swings and dangerous behavior. We thus must postulate here that criminal behavior by women is not always associated to their hormonal fluctuation, but rather to unhappiness, frustration and male-type influences they may be subject to. Finally, the authors quote from T.M. Johnson that "although premenstrual symptoms are seen cross-culturally, it is recognized, defined and treated as a specific syndrome only in Western, industrialized cultures."

Armed Women, Women at War, Love & Peace

Assassination squads led or composed by women have existed in diverse groups as the German Red Army groups, the Shining Path and Tupamaro guerrilla in Peru, the African armed groups fighting in Sierra Leone and Liberia, and even in India. At the moment, women suicide bombers and Tamil Freedom fighters are particularly active in Sri Lanka. These women have killed one of India's Prime Minister and nearly blinded the current Sri Lanka's Prime Minister with suicide bomb attacks. In the West, particularly in the USA, women bomber- and fighter pilots, policewomen and others carry arms. But these women are not necessarily more violent than embittered or ideologically influenced women in the Third World. Thus, there seems to be no evidence that a *progressive, emancipated society* is a requirement for women to participate or lead in organized, premeditated, acts of violence.

It would be interesting to find out how these women belonging to armed groups were motivated or educated into such violence, and whether this induction process actually took longer, shorter or differed in any way from the equivalent process in males.

In India, female highway robbers & murderers known as Dacoits have informed researchers that they became murderers because of their anger at being raped when young. Similar replies were given by some female soldiers in parts of Africa, but in Germany, Japan and Peru, leftist women guerilleros who kill seem more obsessed with righting a social inequality, than in extracting revenge on men for power and sexual independence. In essence of course, women in *both* cases may become very violent because they feel or have been violated in either the mental or physical sense.

As for peace-loving behavior... At various times recently some countries, notably South Africa, Chile, Argentina, Israel and Algeria, have borne witness to great acts of defiance by large groups of women, against cruel, unjust or fanatical regimes and movements; yet the record so far of women as *active* participants in anti-violence movements, in both West and East, is dismal. Were it not for their much-vaunted individual rhetoric as regards their love of *peace and harmony*, such a statement would not be apt. Women assume that it is male violence that is responsible for so much strife in the world, and then tacitly accept it without much active protest; should they not speak out more?

Of course, feminists and others will argue that years of discrimination have sapped females of collective action and militancy, centuries of submission have molded them into passivity and so on, but this appears a little hollow in countries of Northern Europe for instance, where political participation and equality have been present for several generations. Are Iranian, Palestinian, or even Yanomamo Indian women more aggressive in the political sense than their European counterparts?

A fascinating prediction is that female warriors may be in more demand in the future. Traditionally, the smaller female body and its lesser muscular strength did not allow her to fight males in any systematic physical manner. But with the advent now of electronic and distant warfare, will this change? It is no longer necessary for a non-infantry soldier to be strong, and is this why we are seeing more and more recruitment for female fighter pilots, tank crews and naval personnel?

Role-Models

It has been found that adding violent or aggressive war themes to video games increases their popularity with boys but not with girls (Malone 1981, 333-370). Other games of violence continue to appeal more to boys than girls, even in the aggressive societies of Northern America and Europe. However, if children are first primed with aggressive stories, both genders are more likely to choose toy weapons for play. Furthermore, girls who decide to be with 'macho' males, like motorcycle gangs (bikers) or street fighters, tend to develop physical fighting skills that resemble that of males (Goldstein in Bjorkvist & Niemela 1992, 65-76).

Female rats, chimps and a host of higher mammals seem to prefer the presence or odor of highly aggressive males (Bjorkvist & Niemela,

1992, 375). Obviously, this is because they may be assured of more aggressive offspring; aggressive males may be healthier than non-aggressive ones. Girls and boys most likely 'learn' aggression in the way that reflects their early experience of aggression. Once learnt, these patterns extend to adulthood, so that the more aggressive boys or girls become the more aggressive and anti-social and criminal adults.

Eron shows well how female humans can respond to aggression in male ways (Bjorkvist & Niemela, 1992). He chose 632 children and followed them for 22 years, from grade 3 to age 30 (1960 to 1981). In a second study, he studied longitudinally, between 1977 and 1983, children in 5 countries (Australia, Finland, Israel, Poland and the USA). He and his co-worker Heusman found not only a correlation in *all* countries between television habits and aggression in boys, but also, at least in the first two countries, that girls scored higher than boys in what he called "identification with aggressive TV characters." Boys could not associate themselves to aggressive female characters, but girls could associate themselves to both female and male characters. Eron summarizes it thus: "Aggression is now becoming more acceptable and normative behavior for girls' own attitudes about what is appropriate for them to do, and how they act has changed." An earlier study in the 50s and 60s had not shown this (Bjorkvist & Niemela 1992, 90-95).

Africa Rights has recently published a report entitled *Not So Innocent: When Women Become Killers*, dealing mainly with the fact that amongst the mass murderers of Rwanda in 1994, was a number of educated women whose victims not only included younger Tutsi women — potential rivals perhaps, since they are supposedly attractive to Hutu men — but also children of both sexes. Were these educated women murderers enacting the same desire to purify their country, as men were? Unlike the 1,000 or so poorer women who were arrested for the same crimes in Rwanda, some evidence exists that these educated women managed, initiated or supervised killings *without* the encouragement or orders of men nearby. In a survey carried out by UNICEF in Rwanda on child survivors of the massacres there, some 56 % of the children reported seeing other children taking part in killings — some at the orders of adults, but many without adult participation. A fair number of those doing the killings were reported to have been girls.

Women guards in Nazi concentration camps carried out many murders according to archives of the Federal Government in Germany. Indeed the cruelty and sadism shown by women prison guards in concentration camps was so terrible that a few were executed on the orders of the International War Tribunal in Nuremberg at the end of World War II. But this cruelty in Germany and its satellites by women was in no way limited to concentration camp guards. There is considerable evidence by people who escaped from Germany prior to 1938, that acts of vandalism and physical violence by German, Czech, Polish, Romanian and other Central European women, against Jews, Gypsies and other minorities, took place with the advent of fascism and state sponsored racism as early as the late 1920s. Even to this day, I have come across Central European women who express a most profound hatred of the above minorities and who have stated on more than one occasion, that given the chance they would physically eliminate them. We must never forget that both women and men carried out the murder of Jews and Gypsies in and outside Austrian, German, Polish and Ukrainian concentration camps.

No less fierce, were Spanish women fighters and a fair number of civilian women during the Spanish civil war in the Thirties. Survivors have reported that scores of women pillaged, burnt, beat and killed opponents on both sides.

In more recent times, we have witnessed Cambodian women fighters from the Khmer Rouge, killing and beating soldiers and civilians, during the forced exodus of people from Cambodian cities in the 1970s, and in Mozambique, Angola and Liberia, young girl soldiers also executed opponents. In the civil wars that recently wracked Argentina, Chile, El Salvador and Nicaragua, women soldiers, terrorists and saboteurs also killed people. As did women terrorists in the USA in the 1960s and 70s and women in the German, Italian, Japanese Red Brigades and their offshoots.

But for all these female horrors, they are outnumbered by a ratio of at least 1,000-to-1 by male sadists, torturers and killers. Thus, women's behavior in wartime or terrorism is for the most part a pale reflection of male behavior. Moreover, there is no doubt that women have been a primary cause of reconstruction efforts after most wars and calamities. Indeed, one can ask whether in their absence, men would be as capable of the patient efforts and tasks it takes to rebuild homes, clear rubble, interconnect with others and bury past animosities. From the point of view of children's upbringing, their greater capacity for reconstructing social fabrics are vastly superior to that of men. Were it not for women, and the reproductive urge they bring with them, conflicts may well be extended...

Why shouldn't women then, be as avid or as insecure about power as men? Because we are taught that they lack the stamina, the toughness and the drive that men have. Remove their shackles then, and see what happens... This is the objective of those who demand to be fighter pilots today.

The Biology and Sociology of Why

Why are crimes increasing among women? And why are there more in richer countries?

One reason may be that economic dependency on men or family is decreasing rapidly, especially in the West. Women are thus under greater pressure to *provide for themselves and their children*. In addition, greater independence and a materialistic environment will increase the pressure to compete, although inter-female aggression (not necessarily homicide or violent crime) is supposedly higher where females are very dependent on males (Bjorkvist & Niemela 1992, 3-16). This may be because of competition and uncertainty over their position, which causes more stress and anger.

In biological terms there may be a much higher cyclical rate of substances causing stress in the body, that cause women to respond to anger with rage. Some of this rage reaches very high levels during parts of the female estrus.

It should also be noted that there is always some of the male hormone testosterone in females as well, known to increase in fighting males. Indeed, sexual arousal in the female is partly dependent on it, as is the growth of body hair and the production of certain other hormones. Both sexual desire and aggressivity in females seem to be highest during the same part of menstrual cycle that is around 2 or 3 days prior to the onset of bleeding. Testosterone levels are thus higher in aggressive females. There is good evidence for this (as noted by Benton, , p. 42; Sandnabba, p. 374-376; and Hood, p. 396, in Bjorkvist & Niemela, 1992), but it is by no means the only hormone that could be responsible for male or female aggressive behavior. It may also not be a rise in the hormone, which is responsible for this, but rather sharp fluctuations in the level of other *female* hormones such as estrogen and progesterone. Doctors treat women who complain of great irritability and aggressivity just before the bleeding phase with hormones that *stabilize* the level of these so-called female hormones. Aggression in men may be more constant because they do not have such great fluctuations in reproductive hormone levels.

Withholding Emotions

Another important difference between men and women is also apparent. Women often release or exhibit a great deal of repressed anger, not just by sudden explosions of physical violence as men do, but also by emotional outbursts, sudden changes in patterns of friendship and alliances, or the withholding of sexual and affective behavior. This is traditionally represented as one of the only ways for women to *punish* those they are associated with and have betrayed them. Indeed, various contributors to the book by Bjorkvist & Niemela consider these forms of indirect aggression to be not only be much higher in females than in males, but also that their effect on the recipient of such behavior to be in many cases more damaging even than physical aggression.

Children very much feel a mother's repressed anger and some will even go so far to say that this can be felt by the foetus in utero – so, it is likely that an angry mother who is at the same time inhibited from showing her anger, is a cauldron of furious chemicals and signals that may do more damage to her offspring than had she had a safety valve by which to vent her anger.

Michael Meany and his team at McGill have shown that baby rats who had the most intense maternal nurturing during the first ten days of life showed later on the best resistance to stressful events, with lower levels of ACTH and corticosteroids and quicker returns to normal levels of these hormones after the stress.[57] Furthermore, a protein, CRF, produced by a gene in the hypothalamus, which is the trigger for ACTH production, is produced in lower concentration in rats who had the most maternal stimulus. Thus gene coding, its production of a CRF synthesizing type protein or/and the expression of certain genes of RNA messengers are modified by maternal behavior.

Another study showed that rats who were deprived of their mothers for 3 hours per day during the first two weeks of being born, not only behave with less confidence, appear more anxious and have more of a penchant for alcohol, but they also have altered CRF levels in the brain (Plotsky et al. 1995, 500; Niemela 1992, 81). These baby rats, once they reach adulthood continue to produce higher levels of ACTH and glucocorticoids and more of an exaggerated stress response. Thus, they have an altered gene (coding for more CRF) and presumably they will transmit this trait to some of their offspring. CRF injected into the spinal fluid of normal monkeys produce a reaction akin to desperation. The reaction closely resembles that which happens when they are separated from their mothers at an early age. On the other hand, injection of a CRF antagonist reverses these stress type reactions (p. 82).

Insofar as maternal stress and its effects on fetuses are concerned, gestating rats subjected to repeated aggressions or aggressive displays by other rats gave birth to rats who became particularly aggressive at adulthood. In rhesus monkeys that were pregnant and subjected to repeated loud noises, the offspring exhibited much higher levels of anxiety and stressful behavior (p.81).

In other rhesus monkeys who were reared without their mothers, stress response was also higher as confirmed by higher levels of ACTH and cortisol (p. 81; Suomi 1991, 171-188).

Walker (1995) think that during rapid brain growth, overproduction of stress hormones by the mother can affect either receptor sites for stress hormones or change the sensitivity of fetal brain tissues, affecting in turn the conductivity of neuronal electrical impulses.

Thus, a particularly damaging behavior trait in some women is to withhold affection from their children. Or from birth, never to provide it. There seems to be a more damaging effect on the child when women — especially the mothers — do this, than fathers. In Morris' *The Naked Ape* (1968, 106-110) there is a good account of how an agitated mother will increase anxiety levels in a baby, and how her smile will calm it.

Not only may this lead to violent or unsocial behavior in many such growing children, but on reaching adulthood many such children exhibit anti-social behavior ranging from an inability to show affection or to form stable or affective relationships (in males or females), to chronic feelings of insecurity and rejection and increasing promiscuity (mainly in females), to violent behavior against women by men, including murder and rape. Of course, the absence of a father figure also causes some of this as well, but most experts are of the opinion that absence or withdrawal of affection by mothers is more damaging to the female or male child than the fact of a father showing little affection.

Where women are able to belong to large extended families, where the presence of other women allow for a certain degree of female intimacy, self expression, communication and games, aggressive and destructive feelings may be less likely to explode than in cultures where the female is more lonely. An explanation of the increase in homicidal behavior by women in Western societies? This need for intimacy seems to be far more important to females than to males and is certainly more present today in the poor countries of the world than in the richer ones. There is therefore a fair amount of difference between male and female in exposure and response to situations of conflict, but it seems that it is more culture than gender, which determines aggressivity. This is the view of psychologists such as Adams (Bjorkvist & Niemela 1992, 17-25) and anthropologists such as Rohner (1976, 57-72).

The Role of Culture

Thus, while there may be a gender-linked difference in expressing aggression, this depends more on the relevant prior experience and culture, than to gender.

In the West, females have reached equality with males in many things although discrimination continues to exist. The pressure on women to provide sexual favors when desperate for a job and their difficulty in being taken as seriously as equals is a constant reminder to them of their vulnerability and the need to *prove themselves*. This need to prove oneself in what is essentially still a male dominated world even in the most advanced countries, leads often to exaggerated forms of supposedly typical male behavior, namely aggression and violent speech patterns. For many women in the West, access to alcohol or drugs, or sexual experimentation, is also increasingly free. The result is that women who show or are encouraged to show aggressive type behavior are increasingly accepted. Or are forced to be accepted by social pressures.

If more opportunities for women to join the military were available, would this lessen the frustrations, anger and violence of women? Or simply make for a more *masculine* society in general? Even the great feminist, Germaine Greer, author of a new book "The Whole Woman" now says that women are uniquely capable of providing the world with "steadying and gentling influences desperately needed today."[58]

In another group of countries, the position of women in society and their equality to men before the law is of course variable, with very skewed situations in countries such as Afghanistan, Saudi Arabia, Somalia, Sudan and so on. Yet, while opportunities for violent behavior by women outside the home is difficult in these countries, it can be shown that violence can manifest itself both in the home and outside, in the supposedly women's world they (are forced to) inhabit.

It is generally considered that insofar as women's real equality before the law is concerned, the next tier of *repressive* cultures are the poorest African countries, such as Ethiopia, Niger and so on. Women may fare better as regards their rights under most laws, but extreme poverty and/or illiteracy there condemn women to an even worse situation than the preceding group of countries.

Another group still may be constituted by countries such as Bhutan, Egypt, Iran, Kuwait, other Arab Gulf Kingdoms, Laos, Senegal and Yemen. Widely differing in income, these countries have nevertheless maintained a rigid structure as regards *acceptable* female behavior. Women are however freer than in the above countries to express anger outside the home and even to strike at other women and even men in public — e.g. Egypt, Senegal, Yemen...

Relatively speaking however it is both culturally and psychologically impossible to state that women in one country may be unhappier or happier than in another. Income and improved status do not correlate with lesser rates of violent crime committed by women. If anything, it seems to be that unlike for males a higher proportion of women will commit violent crime in the richer countries than in poorer ones. Is this due to more opportunities or is a question of better statistics?

Media and Women Violence

We may ask if any of these perceived increases in female generated violence are being influenced or even represented by the media around us. Is increased female violence, at least in the West, reflected by the culture of this generation?

A cursory review of the number and content of recent TV programs and films in which females are either killers or are using force and firearms to defend or avenge themselves will show a steep increase, particularly in the United States, over previous years, particularly if we look at the 1980s. Various police reports from that country and also prison reports show that more women in the 1990's have committed violent crimes from spouse beatings to murder than at any time before in the modern history of the United States. A recent U.S. Justice Department report shows that the numbers of women incarcerated for homicide or violent crime have increased several fold in 1997-1998, over the levels twenty years earlier. Reports from Germany, France and the United Kingdom seem to show the same trend although the magnitude seems much greater in the United States.

Films produced in the late 1980s or early 1990s in Europe or the US, such as *Thelma and Louise, Basic Instinct, Diabolique, L'Ange Noir*, to mention just a few, have shown great success in portraying females, as killers of several males or females, not as was the case before. On TV, video song clips as well as several other programs have repeated this trend, showing young women as active fighters, soldiers, thugs, and karate experts.

Popular figures such as the singer Madonna, the female rock group, the Spice Girls, the Slits, the actress Anemone in France and various female rap singers are mainly popular with the young, because they portray aggressive females who are as free, bad-mouthed, and decisive as male figures, if not more so. The demure, hesitant, almost masochistic, female singers and actresses of the past are an obsolete product for young people today, in the Western Hemisphere at least.

In the Southern Hemisphere, there are equivalents too, such as Indian actresses taking up more and more violent roles. But in the South, there are also real women fighters: Winnie Mandela, openly defiant and violent, Palestinian and Israeli women carrying rifles, Latin American women terrorists and freedom fighters, Angolan and Eritrean women soldiers proudly taking part in pitched battles, thousands of brutal armed female Tamil rebel fighters in Sri Lanka and so on. While it may be argued that such women are making it easier for others in their countries to achieve more emancipation and equality, that has rarely happened if anything. Conversations I have had with Algerian Palestinian, Eritrean and Peruvian young women indicate their disappointment that their situation did not change once peace occurred. This has increased their frustration and anger against their society and their ever dominant men.

Generational Transmission of Female Anger

In societies such as in many parts of India, inequalities between human beings, not to speak of between male and female, are considered more in the lines of normal fatalistic events than in Western cultures.[59] Such then would be the greater shock in the latter societies when the little European girl or the young American woman, discovers that she is not equal either in employment or, more commonly, in the eyes of society. A resulting feature of all this, in Western societies at least, may be a greater rage, a greater propensity for female violence, than in a more *traditional* non-western society. This may be a partial explanation for the higher violent crime and homicide statistics by females in the West, not just a question of better reporting or more freedom.

Another factor to be investigated is whether such female resentment at unequal treatment is not handed down to succeeding generations of female offspring by subtle or even overt signals and stories, which serve to keep the proverbial pot boiling.

What one is basically trying to advance here is a theory of cultural transmission of female anger throughout generations, which given the appropriate spark can ignite in much violence against themselves, their children or their partners.

Female resentment and violence against other females is often the result of the discrimination and insecurity they are forced to assume. Thus in India for example, their suffering at the hands of other women or men reach such magnitudes that thousands each year commit suicide, or are killed. Many also become killers of other women or criminals to escape oppression. Added to this is the underreporting in official documents of such actual or attempted murders and injuries of women (UNICEF India 1994). The barter of women in India as elsewhere due to early marriage and the system of dowries is one step removed from other forms of exploitation, but they are all connected.

Protective Mechanisms

If aggression is also a feature of females, we cannot assume that it is *only* the Y or male chromosome that carries the aggression gene — since females do not have a Y chromosome.

Thus whereas the propensity for violence in males may be indeed much higher than in females, we cannot say that they are genetically programmed to be so as far as a *single* chromosome is concerned. Studies in humans and mice show that a series of gene abnormalities affecting the uptake and/or removal of some neuro-transmitters, such as serotonin, dopamine and norepinephrine, lead to abnormal levels of aggressivity in males, but not so far in females (Cases & Seif 1995).

However, recent experiments with prairie vole rodents in the USA indicates that a gene for passivity and nurturing could be successfully isolated and then inserted in normal male mice who are not particularly family oriented with the result that they, too, became more peaceful, more protective to their young and more faithful to their mates.[60]

Nevertheless, whereas experimental studies in animals involving surgery and injections of male hormones does lead to very violent females, a *natural* model of a very violent female with altered or a persistent bio-chemical signature seems to be lacking.

A search of the literature on menopausal or post-menopausal women may detect a propensity for more violent acts as the concentration of estrogen hormones fall, just as more acts of violence seem to occur in women a few days before the onset of their monthly period. This may indicate that an *override* mechanism by a hormone may affect a gene's expression. If there is a gene for violence, then it may indeed be on the X chromosome, giving the same trait to males and females, but the fuller expression of the aggression gene may be more dependent on the release of either male-type hormones or cultural conditioning — more probably both.

However, the recent experiment mentioned above regarding the socialization of mice using a gene from the prairie vole indicates that it is the hormone vasopressine abundantly present in lactating women and women about to give birth that actually turned these mice into calmer, more affectionate and less violent animals. The gene altered or increased the number of vasopressor receptor sites in the brain of mice. Thus, women may have a series of protective mechanisms to guard against overly violent behavior. While most may indeed be culturally imposed there is nevertheless evidence to suggest that genetic controls also operate via the release of certain hormones and the modification of cellular receptor sites to offset a continuous *mode* of overly male type aggressivity and violence.

Newspaper Sources and Other Quotations

50 US Department of Justice Report, according to the International Herald Tribune, 23 Aug. 1999, 3

51 Carey Golberg. "Many wives are Spouses who batter." New York Times, 24 Nov. 1999.

52 Special School Violence Supplement. International Herald Tribune, 14 feb. 2000.

53 BBC Radio; 13 October1995.

54 For example, 33 % of all infant mortality in chimpanzees is due to adult male monkeys killing infants which are not begot from their own female possessions. According to Hrdy in "The Spencer Lectures" given at the University of Oxford, Department of Zoology; 4 December 1995.

55 Jell Jacoby commenting on the National Marriage Project. Boston Globe reproduced by the International Herald Tribune, 28 July 1999.

56 According to Hrdy in "The Spencer Lectures" given at the University of Oxford, Department of Zoology, 1995.

57 Dong Liu et al, Science 277, 1997.

58 Commentary article to the Washington Post, reproduced in the International Herald Tribune, 10 June 1999.

59 A review of a press article that appeared 100 years ago on women's issues indicates that the extent of bottled up female anger may be both understandable and predictive of later behavior. In a 1895 issue of the Paris Herald, an American newspaper, ancestor of the International Herald Tribune, a report entitled "Rights Denied" shows how an appeal to repeal the law that excused a man to kill his wife if she was found in the act with another man to the French Chamber of Deputies was rejected. Only in the 1970s was the law changed. But about seventy countries allow today some sort of mitigating, if not excusable factor when judging a man killing his wife in similar circumstances. Indeed, it seems to be still expected behavior in some cultures today.

60 "Genes Transplants turn Mice into Social Creatures." International Herald Tribune, 20 Aug. 1999.

Chapter 5

Some Biology: Chemistry over Culture?

This chapter deals with possible mechanisms that could effect both an origin and a process leading to violent behavior. Segall, Dasen, Berry & Poortinga (1990) play down genetic or biological influences: "The basic premise is that ecological forces are the prime movers and shapers of culture and behavior. Ecological variables constrain, pressure, and nurture cultural forms, which in turn shape behavior." (p.18)

What, then, of the way some animals possess behavior specific to their breed or species? Why is a Pit Bull Terrier much more aggressive than a Cocker Spaniel — yes, from birth? Ah, they will say, these are not normal animals. They were bred to be that way. Precisely! Their genetic origins were *selected* to make them that way. I prefer Segall's other remark: "Culture by almost any definition, includes the product of behaviour of others, especially others who preceded us" (p.26).

I have noted already that more males commit violent crimes than women in a ratio that is approximately ten to one, *regardless of the culture*. Since we know that biological males[61] are capable of greater and much more frequent bouts of physical violence than females, can we attribute this solely to upbringing? Is it possible that this occurs because of the influence of other males? The short answer is No. Many males brought up in the absence of brothers can be just as violent as males brought up in the presence of other males. Similarly, females brought up alone, with other females or without boys or fathers, can be as violent as females brought up in male-orientated household. Thus, it is not by copying male or female role models that one is necessarily more violent as an adult.

Of course, as children, the presence of aggressive brothers or sisters, mothers or fathers, can lead to more competition, more fighting and more manifestations of aggressive behavior. But there is no evidence that in adulthood, violent behavior is necessarily a function of that, however much clearly facilitated by it. Some children, regardless of gender, can be violent even if brought up in non-violent families.

Boris Cyrulnik, a French psychiatrist-philosopher has recently written about the impact of "sensorial isolation" on violent behavior, that is children brought up in societies in which empathy for others is deliberately (or not so deliberately) minimized by parents, by the greed of increasingly materialistic societies, by poverty or misery, war or ethnic strife. Cyrulnik, like others, considers that genetic factors play a negligible role in violent behaviors.[62]

However, if we admit that certain chemicals in the brain affect our moods then we are thrown back into some aspects of genetics for our internal biochemistry is very much a function of coded sequences arising from DNA and RNA molecules.

If biochemical change came about because there were differences in upbringing, there may not be cause for much surprise. But, if these differences occurred because something happened to the fetus or the baby or the adolescent from an outside *chemical* influence, then we should become much more alarmed. We can expect and indeed regret the influence of parents or friends or siblings on our behavior or that of others, but it is quite another thing if we are told that an exogenous chemical might affect our current or future behavior or that some magnetic or electrical influence might do so, too. Most of us might even consider that a bit far-fetched. However, fetuses can be deeply influenced by exogenous and endogenous electrical or chemical factors, so much so indeed as to affect in some instances future patterns of brain processing including aggressive behavior. Early brain injury in infancy has now been shown to prevent some people from learning normal rules of social and moral behavior in childhood. These children on reaching adulthood showed no guilt or remorse for violent acts and found it difficult to get along with others. There may thus be a "biological origin to human empathy."[63]

In the first sections of this chapter I shall address changes wrought upon the fetus, upon the individual before birth, turning thereafter to biological events in later life.

Some Possible Genetic or Fetal Influences -- Born to Kill?

One theory involving the question of why some humans are more violent than others is that the more violent have less of a piece of genetic material that inhibits violence. This theory of a loss of controlling genes, a loss that liberates our baser, more basic or nasty characteristics, offers a return to Adam and Eve and the Serpent in the Garden — that is to say, to a religious basis of creation. Was Man good, wise, non-violent and perhaps not even interested in sex, before he *bit the apple* and released the DNA molecules that controlled his baser self? Was ancient Man less aggressive than his modern counterpart? Perhaps. But there is no proof for this. I think the opposite indeed, that Man was always aggressive, probably even more so than today.

Some may consider that it is via the male Y-chromosome that violent behavior is transmitted; but since females show violent behavior yet do not have a Y-chromosome, it is difficult to accept that it is the Y-chromosome alone that imparts violence. Nevertheless, there must be a factor in the Y-chromosome that *favors* violent behavior — simply because males are about 10 times as violent as women (as discussed in the previous chapter). And there is some evidence also that a loss of part of the male Y-gene may impart some factor facilitating both longevity and non-aggression (Smith in Bloom 1995, 148).

In any case, it is clear that some *messages* are transmitted via males and not via females. This may hold the key as to why males are more violent than females. Since the ratio of males to females is almost similar worldwide, yet for both genders violence varies according to culture and geography, we cannot say that violent behavior can be attributed *only* to biological factors, to hormones or to male-female differences. Of course, it is just as clear that there is a genetic, biological factor, possibly because something has happened to the fetus during development, quite independent of either parental genes or the way the child is brought up, such as early brain injury. We must look at the influence of environmental factors on fetal development; and where possible, whether these factors act differently on males and females.

It is conceivable that malformation in fetal brain development may predispose a child to abnormal, including conflict-seeking or violent behavior. This malformation can of course have many causes. Such physical alterations to the brain may be of one of the following four general types, which I shall expand upon in this order:

Physical damage to the brain caused by accidents of a mechanical or physical nature, known as trauma.

Malnutrition of the mother, the fetus or both.

Genetic damage — chromosomal damage — caused by chemical pollutants, radioactivity, genetic mutations, viruses or spontaneous, sometimes inherited, factors that in each case lead to:

Psychological-physiological conditions that may cause irreversible structural or chemical damage because of disease or illness such as tumors, high blood pressure and so on.

1) Physical Damage

Accidents at birth or other accidents that cause rupture, constriction, expansion or insertion of outside bodies in the brain, can lead to behavioral changes. Embolisms or *strokes* for instance, or even merely a hard knock, can convert a *normal* individual to a violent, uncontrollable monster. But what may be less well recognized, known or understood are more *subtle* behavioral changes caused similarly.

Individuals vary markedly in their capacity to adapt to a given type of trauma. Mood changes, as everyone knows, can also occur much more markedly in some individuals than others. Furthermore, the statistical chances or probability of certain types of accidents increase in certain income or cultural groups or are more common in certain geographical areas. The risk of being hit by a car as a child is obviously going to be higher where there is a lot of automobile traffic than in a pastoral area or where there is a higher proportion of alcoholic drivers...

The brain of an infant is very sensitive to any types of intra-uterine or extra-uterine occurrences and thus a huge variability of responses is possible, many of which will be transient in nature while others may be permanent. Psychological traumas may also have a transient or permanent effect on the brain, via the sudden accumulation or loss of some of these chemicals or changes in electrical potential that lead to a reaction that produces aggressive behavior. The brain depends on specific stimuli at specific times in order to develop *normally*; thus the absence or distortion of that stimulus may lead to what one calls *mental problems* later on in life.

To be more specific, proteins are now found to store and process information. Proteins are formed from amino-acids that in turn are linked together in a specific sequence that is determined by RNA and DNA containing structures in the cells. (Each protein, including some which are hormones are formed in accordance with the coded (base) message found in a piece of the DNA, many of which in turn form the chromosome. Different "pieces" of DNA are called genes and all the genes we posses are found in our 46 inherited chromosomes, 23 from our father and 23 from our mother). If there is a small alteration in the coding process, some of these proteins may be less or better able to store or carry some of the information they are supposed to process.

Are there some humans more susceptible to this than others?

Magnetic resonance imagery (MRI), a process by which the activity of brain cells can be recorded or *imaged*, reveals that the brain of human psychopaths process information at a more superficial level, than non-psychopathic brains. There is less emotion in psychopaths, less guilt, less relationship with other humans because their brain cells process less stimuli. This idea immediately prompts several urgent questions. Does the process of obtaining a *high* from *thrills* indicate some abnormality? Is it true for example that the gene marked as gene 11 has a longer length in those who seek thrills? [64]

Are any of these brain processing or genetic abnormalities amenable to treatment? Can they be reversed? Are early detection programs useful here? If perception by chronically or acutely aggressive people of what is hostile differs from that of more *normal* people, can they be *trained* to accept or recognize certain human cues better? Several treatment programs have shown that the answers to these may be a very qualified, *perhaps* (cf. Goleman 1995).

In a series of elegant experiments conducted by Blackmoor et al. [65] at Oxford, a specific tactile, auditory or even visual signal such as a smile has been shown to cause more reactivity as well as an increase of groups of cells located in different parts of the brain. This was shown by the method of injecting colored *marker* substances into the areas concerned and also the development of new instrumentation that could photograph areas of the brain where chemical and electrical activity increases due to the stimulus. Perhaps, the absence of signals such as love, a caring smile, and so on, at a specific time during the brain's growth, cannot be compensated for at a later time. In the human infant, the post-partum age when such signals seem to be the most important is 3 months to 2 years. Work on children that are malnourished led to these conclusions.

2) Malnutrition

Poverty or neglect may lead to overt or even hidden types of malnutrition (cf. the Appendix to this chapter). Whatever the causes, moderate to severely malnourished infants be they so at birth or later on, exhibit poorer mental coordination reflexes than well nourished siblings (Chavez, Martinez & Yashine 1975). Research I was associated with in this regard seemed to confirm that if the malnutrition was severe enough and occurred before 2 years of age, the damage to mental intellect and coordination was much more difficult to avoid then if the malnutrition occurred after 2 years of age (Scrimshaw & Behar 1976; Wurtman & Wurtman 1977). Other researchers have also linked physical growth of children to psycho social interventions with the mother., showing that in some cases physical growth from such interventions are nearly equal to nutritional interventions. The amount and quality of attention the mother gives to the child has been shown to compensate for some of the effect of moderate malnutrition, insofar as both physical growth and achievements in mental acuity tests are concerned.

Dasen & Super (1988) summarize this current knowledge about the behavioral aspects of malnutrition. Of the links between malnutrition and aggression, they cite the observations of Barrett (1985) that malnutrition produces difficulties in tolerating frustration — in our animal cousins it produces overt aggression such as the hungry lion syndrome — impairs social responsiveness, leads to withdrawal, absence of *feeling* syndromes (p. 117), poor classroom behavior (p. 118), rejection by others (p. 128), bonding failure (p. 130) (sometimes however a cause rather than a result); and in general, poor adaptation. The great value of the Dasen paper is in its treatment of the difficulties of establishing cause and effect, in the methodological complications of this type of research, and on how malnutrition, presumably outside famine conditions, is basically a disease of dysfunctional family environments whatever the later consequences may be.

Maternal malnutrition is responsible for a high proportion of low birth-weight babies. This and certain vitamin and mineral deficiencies while the child is growing cause neuro-developmental malformations: B-group vitamin deficiencies in particular cause neural sheath malformations; iodine and iron deficiencies cause mental slowness (known as cretinism) and poor motor development; deficiencies in calories and proteins, including deficiencies in essential fatty acid lead to low levels of arachidonic and docosahexaenic acids — important structural material for the sixty percent of brain material which is lipid[66] — and this is said by Crawford[67] to lead to poor brain formation and mental development as well as low birth-weight. Other work related to the influence of key nutrients on brain development are amply summarized in the book edited by Wurtman & Wurtman (1977).

The degree of malnutrition and its timing in the reproductive cycle affect tissues and organs differently. Malnourished mothers give birth to infants who may suffer temporary or permanent physical and mental defects, depending on the severity and nature of the malnutrition. Every year approximately 1.4 million babies are born with, or develop severe neuro-development disorders that stay with them throughout their life (UN Nutrition Bulletin 1993). Perhaps a third of these may be due to different types of maternal malnutrition — or even over-nutrition.[68]

Stressful environments during pregnancy, including events that follow the ingestion of some drugs, can affect the fetus in the womb. This psychological stress or the poisoning caused by ingesting drugs or alcohol or the maternal malnutrition itself, effect brain maturation in the fetus or leads to low birth weights. The incidence of low birth-weight babies is about 25 million worldwide.[69] Infants of very low birth weight are also at increased risk of poor mental development and the same risk is true of babies for whom the home environment and especially maternal contact is poor. This relationship is complex and not always easy to prove but generally, both maternal and early child malnutrition affect the psychological development of the child with some studies showing poor emotional control in the child (WHO 1999) and others that show that malnourished children have less attention and affection or have more distant or neglectful mothers. Work by Chavez, Martinez & Yashine (1977) in Mexico for example showed that infants who had insufficiently reactive mothers — mothers who did not play, speak or cuddle — fared worse in mental tests than infants who were malnourished but who had good maternal contact. Even with enough food they grew less fast and performed worse in mental tests.

Is there a link between the degree of violence in some areas and malnutrition?

Culture, Conflict and Children

Low birth weight gives an excellent indicator of fetal malnutrition, and we may compare it to the geography of violence discussed earlier.

Asia *	21 %
Pacific and Oceania	20 %
Middle East and North Africa *	20 % [estimated]
Africa *	15 %
Latin America *	11 %
North America	7 %
Europe	6 %

Table 3.1: Geographical incidence of low birth weight.
Source: "Safe Motherhood Database." World Health Organisation, 1990
Note: High incidence of violence is indicated by an asterisk.

Violence has been shown to be highest in Asia, followed by the Middle East and North Africa. This corresponds to the pattern of low birth weight above; but this may be a spurious connection. Thus, while the amount of violence and malnutrition around the world seem to be associated, we cannot in truth say they are statistically correlated. Many of us take this association to mean that where there is poverty, misery, isolation, war and internal strife, there will be malnutrition, and therefore violence.

Is there a link between frustrated, hungry families and a later generation of a violent people? This point will be discussed further when the subject of frustration as a root cause of violent behavior comes up. Dollard, for example, states that "frustration if it exists, will always lead to aggression in one form or another" (Dollard, Doob & Miller 1939).

3) Genetic Damage

A paper by Cloninger (1996) reveals that people with an extra long DNA sequence on chromosome 11 show a greater ability for risk-taking and are more quick-tempered. The work, carried out by Richard Ebstein in Israel, may or may not be verifiable, but it does call for a deeper investigation into whether certain personality traits, including a predisposition to violent behavior, may not be facilitated by a certain genetic make-up — be it a gene that is inherited or one that is affected by an outside agent.

Complicating this argument is the question that even if some part of a violence gene is inherited what proportion of that gene needs to be present before violent behavior will be manifested? Some geneticists even doubt that a genetic factor may explain more than 5% of violent behavior (Michel Revel cited in Vaquin 1999), but even that 5% may be significant.

Despite objections to such ideas by scientists such as Rose, Lowentin & L. Kamin (1990), who refute the theory that behavior may have a genetic basis, there is no reason to refute the possibility that human behavior may not at the individual level be affected also by an outside agent that acts on an inside agent; or that an inside agent may determine, through succeeding generations, in response to an internal or external cue, how somebody will behave. While humans are much more difficult to *program* than an insect which receives or does not receive a particular food, it is still conceivable that *outside* factors could inhibit or promote a genetic process. These outside factors then could affect a child's ability to behave normally because they interfered with his genetic development.

There are those that argue that the species as a whole may indeed have a genetically determined way of behaving, but that individuals within that species may not differ much from each other when responding to an external or internal stimulus. That may be so, but all that may be dependant on what transpired at an intracellular level sometime between conception, fertilization and later growth.

We must not assume that poorly developed or damaged brains always lead to more violent behavior. The opposite can also occur, as in cretinism, where an over-slow, passive individual is produced. Both extremes are possible and so, care should always be taken when attributing violent behavior to a specific peri-natal cause.

Experts are also not sure that violent behavior can always prove to be related to structural malformations. Yet experiments on various animals, especially cats and monkeys, indicate that damage of certain parts of the brain lead to a very violent animal. The opposite also occurs. Excision of parts of the frontal lobes, termed Lobotomies, carried out often on violent individuals in various countries between 1920 and 1960, led to the production of catatonic, non-violent and poorly reactive individuals. But these lobotomies were done — and are still being done — to excise structures or parts of the brain which effect violent or irrational behavior. A number of surgeons and neurologists also report that the effects of some accidental surgery on the brain lead to an individual that may be overly violent. Accidental trauma in childhood can lead to a loss of emotion, poor sociability and aggression (Damiaso 1999).

Genetic or chromosomal damage effecting the optimal development of brain or nerve tissues occurs as a result of a change in either a piece of the transcriptional material or even part of a molecule in which the coding sequence is changed by substitution of another atom, or by an electron transfer. This may occur either as a result of chemical reactions that are spontaneous or through exposure to accidental or deliberate radioactive fallout — e.g. an atomic explosion.

Viral or in some cases bacterial infection may also cause a change in the coding of a key molecule, so that a mutation can occur — e.g. German measles or smallpox or certain sexually transmitted diseases. Some drugs, such as the infamous Thalidomide, or so called recreational dugs such as cocaine or crack also cause birth defects that affect the brain. Chronic alcohol ingestion also leads to birth defects and heightened aggressive behavior. Dr. Dennis Viljoen[70] showed that 11% of farm workers' children in South Africa were affected by fetal alcohol syndrome (probably the highest rate in the world). The rate is 0.2% in the USA, where it is the third most common birth defect. On post-mortem, the brain of such infants has fewer indentations and therefore its surface area is much reduced. Children born as a result of this syndrome often suffer from a squint, a flat face and sometimes a stupid or dull-looking expression. We should note in passing that this sort of description is still used by police forces around the world — as a mark of the violent criminal!

Relatively more simple substances, such as lead or carbon monoxide, may also lead to brain damage by blocking oxygen uptake or its insertion in a key molecule and the ingestion of recreational drugs such as tobacco, cocaine, heroin or crack during pregnancy lead to vastly increased probability of smaller infants and stunted babies, damaged brains, and infants that exhibit extreme jerking or irritable type syndromes.

Can this not mean that structures involved with inhibiting or controlling violent response and behavior may not be irreversibly affected?

It also follows that the risk of having a child with these problems is greater in certain groups, countries and localities than in others. Polluted living environments, especially those where toxic waste, factory effluents, poor building materials and paints are concentrated, are geographical risk factors. Slums, homes located near waste dumps, drug-infested housing estates, and some countries such as those in Asia or both Americas where drug-addiction or alcoholism is widespread, are therefore greatly at risk. Poverty and neglect of pregnant women is a major factor, too.

4) Damage by Toxins

What then could be the possible magnitude of mental damage in fetuses and children caused by environmental toxins?

There is much in the literature on these agents and how they contaminate our environment but thee is little on their proven effect on adults and even less in children insofar as violent behavior is concerned?. Nevertheless it is worth presenting some of these toxins to show how they might affect our behavior.

An indicator that this may be important is that the incidence of violent behavior in young people in industrialized countries seems to be rising at a similar fashion as the prevalence of allergies and skin and lung irritations increasingly thought to be associated with pollutants in the air, in water and even in foods. From animal and plant studies, lead, arsenic, manganese, sulfur, nitrous compounds, mercury, tin and aluminum are all known to affect metabolism and, if present in high doses, to cause irritable behavior, malformations and even death.

Some of these, such as mercury and aluminum cause brain damage in humans, the latter being implicated as a possible factor in Dementia and Alzheimer's disease. Oxides of nitrogen, sulfur and carbon block or modify simple molecules carrying oxygen to the brain — e.g. metheglobolin instead of hemoglobin, carbon monoxide instead of carbon dioxide or oxygen, and so on — and their presence is higher in cities, hence in slums, where the problem of violence is also higher. There may not be cause and effect, but there is clearly an association. And what of even more complicated substances, the pesticides, herbicides, insecticides, fungicides and other substances that are used in agriculture and that increasingly enter our water and food?

Hormone disrupting chemicals such as some pesticides, plastic additives, fertilizers and growth enhancers can also interfere with brain development in the fetus. John Peterson Myers, co-author of the book "Our stolen Future" indicates how widespread and dangerous these toxic chemicals can be.[71]

Parkinson's disease, a mental illness affecting coordination, is known to be higher in rural than urban areas and more common in the West than in poor counties where the use of many of these substances is much less than in the West. The pesticide thought to be identified in some outbreaks of Parkinson's disease, is present in rural well supplies, which of course receive run-off from fields. This substance, MPTP, may be at any rate a contributing factor.[72] Other substances such as flour made from a certain palm tree in Guam were shown to be contaminated with some organopeptides and lead to dementia, violent behavior and death in some Pacific ocean inhabitants, while organophosphate derivatives from pesticides are now implicated in brain diseases of domestic animals such as sheep. *Mad cow disease*, which causes dementia and which is now known to be transmitted to humans as well, is caused by a viral agent transmitted from insufficiently sterilized bone meal fed to cows. These diseases are relatively *modern* diseases. They do not seem to have existed before the advent of modern industrial or agricultural chemistry. If only a tiny percentage of such compounds cause malformations or mood changes, could they not also be implicated in permanent fetal brain changes?

France and the USA, large agricultural countries, are now seriously concerned about the 100,000 tons of pesticides that are being applied on their fields and orchards.[73] Sweden and the Netherlands have enacted legislation to cut their use by half. The International Labor Organisation of the UN recently estimated that 40,000 people die every year from pesticide contamination and some 3 to 5 million suffer grave sequelae each year as a result of such contaminants. What of those many millions more who are exposed but show no immediate or overt symptoms? Nor can we be certain how many millions suffer from other contaminants and by-products of industry, such as those from the wood, paper, asbestos, battery, explosives, metallurgic, paint and pharmacological industries.[74]

Certain substances in processed foods could even affect sexual development and moods. Thus, more than a decade after attention was first drawn to the levels of phyto-oestrogens in soy-infant formulas, real concern is now being expressed about the possibility of a variety of hormonal effects from exposure of infants to these substances (Setchell, Zimmer, Cai & Heubi 1997) This has prompted at least one government agency (UK in 1996) to issue statements and recommendations about the use of soy-based infant formulas in early life.

The daily exposure of infants to isoflavones such as genistein, daidzein and their glycosides (bioactive phyto-oestrogens) in soy formulas has now been found to be 6-11 fold higher on a body-weight basis than the dose that has hormonal effects in adults consuming soy foods. Circulating concentrations of isoflavins that mimic the effect of natural female hormones, in seven infants tested who were fed soy-based formula purchased from shops, were 13,000 to 22,000 times higher than plasma oestradiol (female hormone) concentrations in early life. Note the contribution of isoflavins in breast and cow milk is negligible. The authors of this research state that this may be more than sufficient to exert biological effects, including interference with signal-transduction — mood — effects as well as reproductive effects. In adults, modification of hormonal regulation of menstruation occurs and there is even concern that as with diethylstilboestrol (a synthetic hormone given to women), changes in genetic imprinting can also occur (Setchell, Zimmer, Cai & Heubi 1997, 26; also cf. McLachlan 1980).

For simplicity's sake let us take the possibility that in the foods we ingest, there are contaminants of one sort or another that may effect the way a genetical message or piece of instruction is relayed or translated within or between cells. Since these *messages* from our genes are chemicals, they can in theory at least, be affected by other (outside) chemicals. We lack animal models to estimate effects on such subtle things as mood changes and excitability. Our observation of fish, mollusks and other aquatic creatures, which serve as biological sources for our estimation of water-based contaminants, are useless here because these animals are unable to record or mimic the effects on mammalian and particularly human brains of these contaminants. As to the use of rats, cats, dogs and even higher mammals such as chimps, the fact that they are caged and thus under observation in artificial surroundings, probably terrified of what is happening to them, makes it difficult to associate whatever mental symptoms that we observe to spontaneous acts of violence.

And if there are mental symptoms, could we not assume that some of these may in fact lead to violent or aggressive behavior?

Adding all these factors together, is it not conceivable that just occasionally one or more of these thousands, no, hundreds of thousands substances may affect genetic transcription at some level?

If the answer is "Yes" then the next question quickly follows: if our chromosomes or genes can be so affected, can this not also mean that in certain cases these affected structures will in turn change our behavior from an inherited *norm* to something different?

Mooded Stress Reactions: Some Biochemistry

Cortiosteroid levels in a fetal brain that is *stressed* can exceed by 20 times levels found in a non-stressed fetus[75]. Does this lead to permanent damage? What might be the reaction that occurs in the young brain as a result of repeated stress, including violence, or lack of affection. Newer lines of research throw another dimension into the connection between moods and the environment. Departing from the fact that some people's cortisol levels are more easily aroused than others, Martha McClintock,[76] biopsychologist at the University of Chicago, theorizes that whether or not a person actually feels in control of a given situation may contribute to the release of a stress-type hormone such as cortisol — in turn related to the release of both adrenaline and testosterone. McClintock rightfully asks, "How can something as amorphous and difficult to localize in the brain as an opinion or belief trigger something as concrete as a change in cortisol release?"

Interestingly, she based much of her research on observations carried out during her student days, which revealed that the menstrual cycle of herself and female roommates, including eventually all women living together in her dormitory, eventually ended up with synchronous cycles. Signals from one's surroundings *are* translated into bodily changes, just as perhaps mass hysteria or group violence can affect hundreds of people so that they sudden become uncontrollable. Aggression in Man may therefore occur as the result of an environmental cue, originating in one human and affecting many others.

The question has still to be asked: Who starts the process? — why that human and not another? And is there a *primer*? Does this primer denote a chemical, hormonal release, which is the *environmental* trigger that is then noticed, observed, smelt or heard by the others, who in turn then adjust their own chemical or hormonal cycles accordingly?

In other words, can the originator of the signal be a chemical or is it an environmental cue that then releases a chemical?

Female rats and several other creatures including insects have been shown to produce pheromones that regulate sexual function in other animals of their species —this may be in animals of their own sex, female rats for instance regulating, enhancing or suppressing fertility in other female rats, or in opposite sexes, by exciting and attracting the other to copulate. These pheromones are airborne substances. Can we know if humans are also sensitive to airborne pheromones? At least those that give rise to conflict or aggression? Or the reverse, to complete apathy? For if some substances cause mood changes which lead to violence, other substances may reduce it...

Depressed, frightened or very stressed animals and humans are sometimes reduced to a catatonic type state, unable to fight, flee, or have any form of sexual arousal. The regulation of reproductive hormones in some of these situations is affected. Indeed, it was this author's experience while working on mothers who were famine or war victims in 1984 in Ethiopia and the Sudan, that both menstruation as well as breast-feeding had ceased in a category of what appeared to be very lethargic, depressed mothers — mainly those who had recently lost husbands or children or homes — and that they were in such a state of inertia that they were refusing either to eat or to feed their surviving babies, even when food was provided to them (Basta 1988). Was it the *mental* depression that had caused all these symptoms, or was it the *physical* malnutrition, the rapid drop in body weight, the drop in fat stores of the mother that led, as others have shown, to a cessation or diminution of estrogenic hormones?

Probably both. The malnutrition and stress associated with loss of home and loved ones came together for these women. As body weight fell, hormonal functions began to *adapt*. In turn, it may be that this *de-regulation* led to a more depressed state, which in turn led to more shutdowns of some functions.

McClintock has also confirmed other studies which show that rats, deprived of communal interaction, go into a form of un-estrus, or menopause, much earlier than they are supposed to; and that they are also more prone to cancers. The significance of this here is that social isolation, the lack of or introduction of an *outside* or *cultural* event, can be shown to effect body chemistry. Presumably, a *positive* effect on body chemistry may be achieved by maximal social interaction.[77]

I should note here as well some important aspects of what is termed Post-Traumatic Stress Disorder (PTSD) — defined as a psychological response to an event threatening death or injury that entails a sense of re-experiencing the trauma and the intrusion of memories or feelings; a pattern of avoidance, numbing of responsiveness, or reduced involvement in the external world; and a *persistent* state of physiological arousal, reflected as difficulty in sleeping, startle responses and angry outbursts. Previous trauma may lead to an attenuated cortisol level, i.e. the body accustoms itself chemically to a violent event, so that when it is repeated, there is less of rise of stress hormones such as cortisol than the first time the act of violence occurred. What is more, combat veterans with PTSD have alterations in hypothalamic-pituitary-adrenal axis functioning, which may explain why they carry out sudden irrational or abnormally violent acts well after the event causing PTSD has occurred. Low cortisol levels may persist for decades following exposure to trauma and people with PTSD may have specific deficits in the monitoring and regulation of memory information.

It is also worth noting that childhood physical abuse predisposes to PTSD. What this may also imply is that people who have had PTSD may influence or condition others to behave as they do, unless those near or around such a individual are also exposed to more positive outlooks or less PTSD-type behavior from others in a society or group or culture. How does this act to produce more or less of the hormones associated with a violent mood or a depressed mood?

Aggression—Depression and the Importance of Serotonin

"Abnormal aggression" is a term already used by scientists to describe certain types of human behavior and this seems to be associated with a higher production or concentration of the serotonin in the brain neuro-transmitters.

What constitutes abnormal levels or low levels of serotonin still needs to be established, as is the answer to whether there is a linear association between hormone level and graduations in abnormal aggressive behavior. Serotonin may not of course be the only substance involved. Testosterone, whether directly or via the cortico-hormonal release pathways, may act synergistically, or independently, and epinephren, nor-epinephren or other adrenaline type hormones may also be responsible for part of the violent behavior.

What seems certain, however, is that rats, cats and some humans born with an inability to break down serotonin fast enough or sufficiently will exhibit abnormally high aggression. In fact, there is a genetic condition characterized by the absence of the enzyme monoamine oxidase-A (MAOA), responsible for the breakdown of serotonin. In both rats and adolescent humans afflicted with this inability to produce enough MAOA, sexual and other forms of aggression are markedly more violent, irrational and rapid.[78]

Drugs are now being produced in experimental doses to duplicate MAOA's ability to block serotonin production.

Serotonin is also responsible for other mood changes. In depressive cases, its eventual removal once produced is delayed or faulty while its accumulation is thought either to inhibit the release of other hormones or in high doses to inhibit or alter nerve transmission (synapse). Serotonin is somehow necessary for a translation or transfer of electrical impulses across nerve ends. The breakdown and regeneration of the molecule is thought to lead to the changes in electrical potential, which causes a *message* to pass between nerve ends. Depressive people cannot reduce their serotonin levels as successfully as non-depressive people. Evidence exists to indicate that aggressive-depressive states are in a sort of chemical continuum. Depression, which at first glance seems to be the opposite of aggression, may in fact lead to episodes of extremely violent behavior in response to some perceived slight, insult, or frustrating occurrence.

In many societies, people speak of a person being so *frustrated* by a certain condition that he or she *had to resort to violence*. Certainly there seems to be a kind of collective depression or frustration, which afflict most violent societies. This is caused by one of the following:

- a *genetic disposition* towards aggression-depression, first in a few, then many individuals, by a process of *mimicry* or the appearance of the gene in more and more people through intermarriage;
- an *oppressive or difficult environment* that upsets a lot of people and reaches levels leading to a collectively angry or sad society; or
- a historical, culturally transmitted pre-disposition — behavior because this is how it is supposed to be, following expected norms.

Whether it is first a chemical that leads to a behavioral trait in the absence of an environmental cue, or whether in every case serotonin, testosterone or any other substance are only released and affect the brain when some outside stimulus is provided, should not only be seen in terms of either/or. It may indeed be the case that a predisposition to abnormal levels of violence exists in some individuals and that the origin of this is dependant on genetically determined alteration which sets them apart from others. The change could also come about as a result of a non-genetic occurrence at the embryological or later developmental stages. Whatever the cause, a series of social or historical occurrences may then allow for a different response to provocation or other stimulus in these people than in those, which have neither the disposition so described nor the level of the social or historical background.

The reverse may also be possible. If we assume that most of us are extremely susceptible to what our *culture* thinks is *normal*, a particular chemical or morphological abnormality may in theory be *covered up* by an over-ride mechanism that favors group obedience or cohesion. It may then be that if the level of the abnormal substance, or if the normal substance, present in either too much or too little concentration, reaches a certain threshold, the *over-ride* cultural control may not be able to operate properly (we see this type of threshold set-point mechanism operating in electricity, molecular and mechanical, phenomena everywhere).

The next question to ask is whether a cultural or educational *over-ride* in humans can reach a certain level so as to minimize the worst excesses of a predisposition to violent behavior? Studies on animals will not help too much here. The cultural factor cannot have a similar effect on animals as on humans. The interactions in humans are so complex that it is impossible at times to attribute a specific defect to a specific biological cause.

Maybe the better question to be posed is: to what extent can a genetically or environmentally damaged human individual have this violence attenuated, reduced or even permanently inhibited by a strong dose of either affection or punishment or both? I believe that sufficient affection in particular, perhaps more than punishment, can indeed help some damaged individuals to control their violent disposition, as for example in some cases of childhood autism.

The results of treatment of a psychological or educational nature on abnormally aggressive individuals should be more available to the public to see how this has succeeded in over-riding the biochemical or anatomical abnormality. We know some violent men are helped by some of these programs, yet others — notably sex offenders — are less so. Is there a chemical origin to this difference? The public needs to know more.

When discussing treatments, are we sure we are applying these in relation to, or with the full knowledge of, the nature and extent of the underlying cultural or historical origin of the problem? In particular, if it is a case of a combination of poor biology *and* poor upbringing, oriented towards aggressive behavior, we may not be sufficiently cognizant of the enormous historical or cultural precedents, the overlying covers and envelopes, that many centuries of *conditioning* have added to particular groups, cultures or populations of human beings. Each group may be very different in the way it has accumulated such *envelopes*. Thus, from the point of view of treatment, knowledge of the culture of the individual or group being studied must precede or accompany whatever elements one uses in psychiatry and in pharmacology.

Aggression and Fear

Until now the possibility that aggression may be a modification of the fear response has not been discussed. Fearful individuals, as earlier discussed, are capable of an exaggerated aggressive response and some experts are of the opinion that all aggressiveness is but a manifestation of fear. Yet, in a series of neurological experiments in which the amygdala of rats and other animals including man was damaged, this resulted in the loss of learning about fear. Presumably the ability to fight was not affected?

Violent behavior may also be likened to a system in which some aspect of control has ceased to function — fear could lead to such loss of control. A study looking into binge-eating and craving for sweet foods in women concluded that substances such as Naloxone, an opiate blocker, could reduce cravings and *loss of control.*[79] The significance of this is that control in an individual can be removed if the right chemical comes along.

So, I ask: could aggressive behavior, individualistic or collective, be likened to a series of events, which suddenly produce a massive release of opiate-like substances in the brain once the *stimulus* of aggression occurs? Orgasmic release during sex operates in a similar way, so does male sexual behavior. Is it possible that aggressive acts may be but a refinement or extension of the same mechanism? While we associate sex with pleasure, it could be that in some people, particularly, say, sexual psychopaths, violent or aggressive behavior is also a pleasurable act.

The important male-female difference in the tolerance of violent behavior may be likened to the *opposite* of what happens in the classical female, opiate-mediated love for chocolate. In the case of males, it may be that violent behavior produces the opiate-like satisfaction that chocolate produces in females! — and that in females the element of satisfaction in aggression may produce insufficient opiate-like substances!

It has been shown that women's studies tend to reinforce a stereotype, that sentiment and emotion are more feminine traits and that a less emotional type of intellect is more *male* (Patai & Koerige, 1995). Other studies show that in the human female brain, neurons are more densely packed than in males, and that this gives an advantage to females in expression and auditory perception.[80]

If the different brain structure in human females also allows them to be more conscious of outside events and their possible consequence on their safety and well-being, if we also assume that females are more fearful than males about fighting, then once again we may assume that a certain morphological structure in males may favor aggressivity.

Drugs and Violence Control

Drugs such as anectine, apormorphine, bromazepam, chlorpromazine and cytoproterone acetate are used (and are still being used) to induce terror in criminal system aversion therapy (the first two), or to sedate or even to castrate violent prisoners (as in the case of the last chemical above). It is interesting in this regard to note that the use of chemical tranquilizers is far higher in a women's prison than in men's. Thus, in 1979, at Holloway, a London woman's prison, 941 doses of such drugs were given, whereas at Brixton and Parkhurst prisons for men, 299 and 338 doses respectively were administered (Rose, Lowentin & Kamin 1990, 174). Thus, while violent behavior can be chemically controlled, it does not necessarily follow that all violent behavior is a result of a chemical imbalance, or that it is amenable to the action of a drug on a specific diseased site, since the latter may carry out its effect only by inhibiting a large area of the brain.

The claim also, that certain drugs, such as Ritalin, may help calm hyperactive or violent children, is murky (p. 182-185). Some are helped, others not, signifying a complex etiology to this whole question of violent behavior. Also relevant here is the possibility that there are not only different forms and origins of violent behavior, but that outside events may modify the action of drugs and chemicals in the brain. Even some food, such as cheese, yogurt and the like, will modify the effect of MOA inhibitors, with often-drastic results. Parents' moods and behavior also influence a child's propensity for violent behavior (p. 184). So, too, teachers' attitudes (p. 187).

Surgery, Training and Shocks

Brain surgery or electrical shocks also seem to be cruelly effective in the control of violence. Some experiments carried out on violent animals and humans showed, however, that this is not always effective, unless large areas of the brain are destroyed. The age of the human or the animal is also a factor (Rose, Lowentin, & Kamin 1990, 190).

In some higher and lower animals some sections of a destroyed brain can be taken over by another part of the brain — a fascinating finding that is not only function-specific to some animals but also a result of training (reward and punishment conditioning). This points out to the possibility that *feelings* may be affected by training.

There may also be little in common with the idea of empathy in a cat, or that of a higher ape, and that of a human being. For example, it is believed that when confronted with a mirror, only the great apes and humans are capable of recognizing themselves. Scientists such as De Waal (1996) and others think this may be the reason that empathy, reciprocal behavior and a sense of obligation are present in these *kinder* species because, so the argument goes, they and we can distinguish ourselves from others, thus put ourselves *in others' shoes*. Affective behavior (love?) can also occur in some pets and not others of the same strain or species. Is this because the *affectionate* ones have copied such behavior from loving masters or is such behavior a learned response devoid of *real affection* that will bring a food reward or an outing? I doubt that it is the latter. I believe that dogs and apes are genuinely affectionate to their kin or to the leader of their pack.

Higher mammals such as apes and humans may also be much more easily influenced to behave in a certain way by the mere power of mimicry or *suggestion*. Thus, when told that an individual in one group of people was to be given a drug that would make him or her behave in a certain way or in the same way as the others, a human subject given an inert substance (a placebo) will tend to behave in that way. The placebo effect in most controlled, double blind, experiments can typically account for around 30 % of an observed effect (Basta 1974; Rose, Lowentin & Kamin 1990).

That others can convince us of our feelings and moods is frightening. What is even more frightening is the contemplation that recent rises in hospital admissions as well as in out-patient treatment of mental problems, including admissions for violent speech and behavior, could in part be due to suggestive influences from others, as well as from the current media hype. One in 12 men and one in eight women will visit a hospital now in the US and Britain for treatment of mental problems. This is much higher than any other time in our history (Rose et al. 1990, 197-8). How much of this increase is due to real illness, how much to easier access to hospitals, how much to better health care and how much to the influence of people close to the patient? But how much also due to changing concepts of *unacceptable behavior*? The whole concept of what is *humane* or *liberal* can change drastically within 3 generations!

In the 1920s, the "merciful killing" of the "hopelessly insane" was seriously considered. After a series of visits to the State mental hospital by legislators who were shocked by the behavior and language of the inmates they saw, a bill to that effect was submitted to the Connecticut Legislature in the USA, in February 1921. Fortunately, the Bill did not pass, but the example is given to show how unforgiving people were of others who appeared to be different. Connecticut today is supposedly one of the most liberal states in the USA, if not the world.

To give another example: it is increasingly more frequent today to treat and then free male rapists after three or four years of treatment with substances like Androcur, than to castrate them (Androcur drastically lowers testosterone levels.) This is not only because the technology makes it now possible to do this, but also because previous obsessions with *punishment* are now being replaced by concepts of *recycling humans via treatment* — at any rate, in parts of the West! Not all are so *enlightened.* In the USA today, some anti-abortion fanatics kill abortion workers and are supported by others in the movement. For some of us, anti-abortion fanatics that indulge in such behavior are suffering from mental illness, nothing less.

Perceptions regarding violent behavior, punishment, the freedom to express oneself and beliefs in supernatural events seem to change relatively quickly. What may be related to that, chemically, in the brain, is that molecules are re-arranged in response to a new set of stimuli. Out goes the previous arrangement or configuration, the old ideas, and in comes the new configuration. Presumably, this is then *set*, as we do with a digital clock, until the next series of stimuli come along. If the intensity is strong enough, the next series of stimuli will replace this last *setting* with a new one; if not, then either a partial re-arrangement of the molecules will take place, giving a partial or a portion of a new setting, or if the stimulus is too weak, if it is inconsequential, then no re-arrangement of the molecules take place. Cultural cues may operate via such pathways. Perhaps then this indicates that even the most violent societies can be "re-set" if the right stimuli come up!

Emotional Intelligence Quotient

In its briefest definition, emotional intelligence can be called *empathy intelligence.* It means the power to read into one's feelings, relate this to others, understand their feelings and phobias, to control much of one's more hostile and destructive impulses, and to maintain a better kind of self control in the face of adversity. A very *mature* kind of individual would no doubt have these characteristics — and maybe could combine it with aggressive tendencies, to achieve a definite advantage over other human beings.

Let us look first at the work of T. Achenbach[81] at the University of Vermont, who has assessed thousands of American children's behavior over a decade and a half, starting in the mid-1970s. He found that anxiety, depression, impulsiveness, disobedience, aggression, mean behavior and emotional deficits were increasing. Scores were lowest for poorest children, but the rate of decline was the same for all, privileged and impoverished alike.

This may have graver consequences for society than a drop in IQ scores, because an emotional deficit may lead to much more anti-social or disruptive, even violent behavior, than a low intelligence. Studies show that boys who are impulsive and disobedient at schools are 3 to 6 times more likely to pick fights and have later criminal records. For girls, this type of early impulsiveness is translated into a 3-fold increase in pregnancies in comparison with less emotionally immature girls. Eating disorders are apparently also more common in those girls that have a low EQ.

Neuroscientists have found that the prefrontal lobes, which control emotion, are among the last parts of the brain to reach full maturity, some time in late or mid-adolescence. Thus, it may be possible to effect more positive behavioral changes even by teenage years. Both Achenbach and the Gulbenkian Foundation (1995) study imply that such positive changes did occur in children treated for "Emotional Literacy" or "Emotional Education". Thus it seems that the neural circuitry can be re-shaped even at relatively late ages.

Here we must also examine whether emotional intelligence is related to control of impulsive behavior and whether this in turn is directly linked to violence. Is there, for instance, a relation between the number of nerve connections between the limbic system (emotions) and the neocortex (reason), in violent and non-violent children? Does one have more and the other less or vice-versa? Moreover, is it possible that regret or shame is not felt in people who have an injury (severance) to the connection between limbic and neo-cortical structures?

Another possibly related concept is the ability or chance or opportunity for some to be able to shift more easily from one state of arousal to another, less aggressive one — to change mood, so to speak. This may also be a function of opportunities that may or may not be present. Does an inner-city delinquent have the choices that a sports-loving rich child in the wealthy suburbs has? And why do optimists and pessimists differ so much? Is there a connection between pessimistic children and violence later on?

Empathy may be the reason that high EQ people can be less aggressive than people who show little or no empathy to others — a characteristic of the typical violent psychopath. In turn whether one is *sufficiently* emphatic or not may depend on the parents' relationship with the infant. For instance, public school No. 75 in New York City apparently began a program for "emotional literacy" five years ago, and they claim that fights at lunchtime decreased from 2 or 3 a day to none at all, because the children were taught to manage anger and frustration.[82] Some scoff at this notion that children can be so conditioned. Others point out that the difference between a criminal and a non-criminal, both of whom could have brilliant EQ scores, is that the latter may have obtained "more moral education than the former".

What is *moral* is of course culture dependant. In Victorian England, there was not necessarily less violence than there is today, despite the *moral* atmosphere of those long ago times. Did the criminal class in Victorian England receive the same *moral* education, as did the bourgeois class? It did not.

To return to clinical studies, isolation or the absence of affection leads to increased mortality in adults and children (cf. Bloom 1995, 60-5). The same occurs in animals as in humans. Thus, affective behavior is such a necessary input to adequate growth and survival that even children who were moderately malnourished, but received attention and affection seemed to do better in intelligence tests than those with mild or no malnutrition, but who did not receive parental affection (Chavez, Martinez & Yashine 1977).

From my own observations of many malnourished children in Africa and in Latin America in the 1970s, those who were rejected, whose parents were ashamed of them, who were hidden or kept in isolation — in some cases because they were thought to be cursed — exhibited abnormal affective behavior, clinging to strangers, seeking eye and body contact, and crying when left behind.

During a visit to a famished village in West Africa after the 1970's drought, a 3 year old child ran out of a hut where he had been kept hidden because his hair had turned orange due to protein malnutrition (kwashiakor). He clung to me during my visit, and when I left, his cries and tears were a reminder for years to come of the need to comfort sick and malnourished children (not just to give them food).

The point here is that some sort of trauma is or has occurred in these young children, and if they survive, it might be reasonable to inquire whether they become *damaged* adults, capable of paranoiac, psychotic behavior. Are some of the world's most cruel psychopaths, adults who were deprived of love and affection?

As a corollary, could there be a link between maternal or paternal, affective child-rearing behavior and violent cultures? Do the more violent peoples, those from South Asia, Latin America, North Africa and the Near East have less affection when they are babies? The answer is of course "No"; maybe quite the contrary, as anyone who has observed the difference in at least the maternal show of affection in these parts of the world, as contrasted to some of the Northern European cultures. On the other hand, individuals also exist in these parts of the world, where affective behavior is overt and open, who may have been deprived of such behavior for any reason, and who may in fact suffer more precisely because they can more easily see how *different* they are from the majority who do receive affective attention.

In cases of isolation or deprivation, is there a resulting failure of production of neurons or neuronal synapses in the child's brain, or is there a failure to produce or eliminate certain chemicals, and so on?

Those who are severely depressed are risks to society and themselves, because they could be accused of courting death, whether via increased susceptibility to traffic accidents, or to sudden acts of murder and mayhem. Such individuals may either be losing the ability to be afraid --loss of control from the amygdala? (Goleman 1995) or may be producing substances whose production or removal from tissues is impaired. Since people deprived of early affection (or frustrated in receiving or providing it) are said to become depressive adults, we can hypothesize that these will have a higher tendency for sudden acts of extreme violence than those who were loved and protected. Is it any accident that Timothy McVeigh, the accused in the Oklahoma bombing massacre of 1996, as well as countless other American and European murderers, seem to come from homes where the mother has absconded, died or been replaced?[83]

If the brain is not being fed properly emotionally, defective structures and chemical reactions will result, as in *any* case of malnutrition. Nutrition therefore must include love.

Appendix to Chapter 5

Fats and Cholesterol

There is recent interest on the role of polyunsaturated fats, cholesterol levels and mood, particularly depression and/or violent behavior. A review article on these interrelationships by Hibbeln & Salem (1995, 1-9) demonstrates that fatty acids of the n=3 polyunsaturate type, if deficient in the diet, can cause violent impulses. These fatty acids are a major component of nerve membranes. Their presence is essential for signal transduction and for the necessary changes in the biophysical properties of the membrane when a nerve impulse passes.

Other authors, cited in the article by Hibbeln and al. show that brain function and behavior, particularly in primates and rodents, are so dependant on a certain level of both cholesterol and essential fatty acids (such as those present in certain types of fish), that even dopamine, serotonin and epinephrine mediated nerve transmissions are affected. I have previously discussed the possible role of these hormones in aggression but this is the first good review that shows that dietary intake may also be a major determinant in the concentration of these hormones. Others also show that repeated pregnancies may lead to a depletion of certain fatty acids such as those of the 22: 6n-3 type and that this could be the reason that post-partum depression occurs for such women. At the same time it is probable that if the fetus is also depleted of these fatty acids, impaired nerve or brain function may occur leading to behavioral abnormalities later on.

Other relationships discussed in the above article relate to alcohol-mediated depression and violence, which may operate through alcohol's oxidation of the unsaturated fatty acids, thus making them relatively unavailable for the behavior they were supposed to affect. This may be why breast-feeding causes less chance of a low IQ in infants than formula feeding — the breast milk of humans has higher levels of 22: 6n-3 than infant formulas, several of which are indeed totally devoid of it.

These authors try to show that fish-eating populations such as the Japanese and Chinese have much less depression than those where fish consumption is low, partly because the latter have lower intakes of n=3 fatty acids. This may seem a little far-fetched; still, the authors do cite the results of the intensive cross-cultural collaborative study conducted in 1992, which revealed a clear cultural difference in rates of depression between different nationalities. Of course, this is *cultural* but could the *cultural* also not include the *dietary*? Incidentally, this same study and others showed that females had in general more than double the rate of depression that males had, and that this difference was true in all populations studied; although female rates are always higher, the magnitude of the difference did change according to population. For example: St. Louis, USA, has 8 % of the females classified as major depressive, compared to 2.5 % of the males, and in Japan the corresponding figures are 0.46 % and 0.35 % respectively.

Sugars and Amino Acids

Insofar as simpler substances such as sugars or amino acids are concerned, there was much discussion in the 1970s on the relationship between sucrose and both hyperactivity and aggressive behaviors, as well as work that indicated that amino acids such as tyrosine, tryptophan and glutamate could affect mood.

In the case of sugars, the experimental designs left something to be desired either because impurities may have not been ruled out or because the psychological tests sometimes proved that other factors were at work. One set of investigators even claimed that aggressive criminal offenders were essentially hypoglycemic and that sugar could affect this, by decreasing or increasing motor activity (Virkkunen & Huttunen 1982, 30-40). But all these studies either failed to determine whether it was because people were hyperactive or aggressive that they consumed more or lesser amounts of sugar, or whether the normal diurnal and other patterns in blood sugar or insulin or glucagon could have confounded the results. Still other investigators flatly refuted these findings, showing no effect whatever of sugars on hyperactivity or aggression (cf. White & Wolraich 1995).

As to the amino acids, in theory they can raise the amount of serotonin and dopamine in the brain and do seem to be able to pass the blood-brain barrier. Studies by Dr. Richard Wurtman, the leading authority on this, as well as work by others that I had the privilege briefly to be associated with at MIT in the 1970s, did not show any effect on mood or behavior, certainly as far as non-epileptic humans were concerned (Fernstrom & Wurtman 1972, 414-16; and Wurtman & Wurtman 1977). Newer work however indicates that carbohydrate increases brain serotonin by causing changes in the proportion of different amino acids going to the brain — another variable that may affect previous experimental results.

In any case, this field is so complex that all we can say with any certainty is that behavior can be influenced by nutrition, but we can only hypothesize about the effects or mechanisms. In addition, we are still not certain that some of the effects so described are the results of brain metabolism, or whether they cause brain metabolism to change. The proverb: "Tell me what you eat, I'll tell you who you are," may not be so far off the mark after all. One thing is however certain. Providing love and security affects the brain positively and this leads to happier, less angry people.

Newspaper Sources and Other Quotations

61 *"Biological males"* is used here for all males with the xy inheritance, independent of errors in external sexual organ morphology or errors in upbringing as male or female.

62 "La violence, réalité, obsession, fantasme." *Le Monde des débats*, Paris, Nov. 1999.

63 Cf. work by Prof. Anthony Damasio, University of Iowa College of Medicine. *International Herald Tribune*, Oct. 1999, 6.

64 According to Prof. Robert Hare, Department of Psychiatry, University of British Columbia, in an interview, CNN, 23 March 1996.

65 Prof. Colin Blackmoor, Lecture at the Department of Experimental Psychology, Oxford University, November 1996.

66 Personal communication by E. Pollit, San Diego, 1982.

67 M.A. Crawford cited in *SCN News* No. 10, 1993

68 For instance: too many calories cause higher blood pressure, toximias, big babies that have trouble clearing the neck of the birth passage, and so on.

69 One newborn in six weighs less than 2,500 grams, which is the limit reckoned for normal weight at birth. *Safe Motherhood Newsletter* No 12, 1993.

70 "In South Africa Vineyards, a Tragic Legacy." *International Herald Tribune*, 15 July 1999.

71 "Toxic Chemicals and Public Health." *International Herald Tribune*, 16-17 Oct. 1999.

72 From a lecture given by Dr Marsden of London University at Oxford University, 30 November 1995.

73 Indeed, a forthcoming report from France, indicates that for Brittany alone 72 % of its inhabitants are exposed to water which contain pesticides in quantities well over the 0.1 microgram per litre level recommended by the European Union.

[74] (*Le Monde*, 30 Nov. 1995, 22).

75   Program about fetal transplants, Arte Channel 5, France, 11 April 1997.

76   *New York Times*, 30 May 1995.

77   Thus, the swaggering and fighting or boasting that accompanies male behavior in, say, some soccer matches continues despite public dismay, because it creates a good deal of pleasure for the males concerned. This male *bonding* is probably preceded by massive secretion of chemicals such as pheromones in all the males nearby.

78   Personal communication, September 1996; cf. Isabelle Seif, Institute Curie, Orsay, France; and Science, June 1996.

79   Editorial. American Journal of Clinical Nutrition 61, 1995, 1,206-1,212.

80   *Courrier International*, July-August 1995.

81   *New York Times*, 10 Sept. 1995.

82   *Time Magazine*, 16 Oct. 1995.

83   In McVeigh's case the mother left him in the care of his father at 10 years old, in order to run away to Florida.

Chapter 6

Environments

Man has often claimed that ugly environments breed crimes of violence. Some may argue that it is not the physical environment itself which leads to this, but that the poor and the unemployed, the desperate and the outcasts from society have no other place to go in any case, than to the cheapest and most rundown environments. Thus the argument goes, it is not the place itself, which influences the propensity to violent crime, but the social condition.

Yet what about the places we live in, the foods we eat, and the air we breathe? Do they have an effect on behavior?

Surely they do. Kagan and Levi are of the firm opinion that we may fall ill faster and more often if our physical environment is not to our liking and that aggressive behavior will also be exacerbated in these conditions (Levi 1975; Kagan & Levi 1975). Cities provide the most evident test-bed, of course. Urban style living is affecting more and more human beings as more move to the cities. In a space of the mere 60 years from 1920 to 1980, the proportion of the world's population living in cities has more than tripled and over 59 cities now have more than 5 million people living in them. By the year 2000, around 70 % of the world's population will be living in cities (excluding China, where rural to urban migration is not as rapid) — up from 14 % in 1920. From a purely epidemiological point, we will expect more of the violence and occasional mayhem that affect human beings to originate in cities. However, in rural areas as well, crime is on the rise. The purpose of this chapter is to look at the factors, other than purely sociological ones that exist in our geographical and technological environment that may contributing to this rise in violence and which are both figuratively and literally poisoning a young child's mind.

Living Space and Styles

Environmental stresses affect our health and behaviour. We may fall ill faster and more often if our physical environment is not to our liking and aggressive behavior will also be exacerbated in these conditions (Kagan & Levi 1975, 11). Our tolerance of environmental ugliness, noise or any other discomfort we have to put up with will depend on culture, upbringing and present mood. What appears to us to an intolerable high rise slum in the Bronx or in Wolverhampton, may appear to be wonderful accommodation to someone sleeping in a cardboard shack in Bombay's slums, or in a damp, insect-infested corner of a room in Lagos. Similarly, while the noise of people shouting, the TV blaring, children playing or couples making love may disturb a German or a Swiss, this is not only normal noise to a Roman, an Athenian, a Mexican, a Chinese or an African, it is indeed good or desirable noise, noise by which people communicate and live. As with everything, there will nonetheless be limits to tolerance.

There are some *givens* in all this as well — unwelcome or unwanted as they are.

Air pollution and toxic vapors affect both the fetal and the adult brain negatively, as we have seen. Lead contamination from household paint, piping or automobile fuel lead to brain seizures and in turn, behavioral abnormalities including increased hostility. The World Health Organisation estimates that only one in five of the world's town-dwellers enjoy acceptable levels of non-polluted air, as pertains to nitrogen oxides. About half the world's cities have unacceptable levels of carbon monoxide emissions — and this includes 42 cities in the USA. Chromosomal and other types of genetic damage occur from high doses of radioactivity — perhaps even the radioactivity from natural sources, such as radium seepage in homes built on certain types of land.

Just as important are the body toxins and psychological pressure that could accumulate from a lack of physical space. Rats, apes, humans and other animals kept in close confinement become very aggressive to one another even if food is plentiful. Thus a *minimum space* is needed for all living creatures, not just to avoid aggressive encounters but also to *ventilate* in the more literal sense of the word. A high concentration of carbon dioxide inhibits respiratory movements and where too many congregate in a small space, there is an excess of carbon dioxide (and other gases) and less oxygen.

The availability of hard drugs and alcohol is higher in cities than in rural areas. Ingestion of alcohol in some cities is so high that we can reasonably ask whether it may not be responsible for group violence on a large scale. According to a longitudinal health survey in the Russian Federation for instance, the average annual consumption of alcohol for August 1993 was 23.1 liters *per capita* for adult males, 4.3 liters for adult females and 2.5 liters for teenagers (note the large discrepancy between male and female intakes). There has since been a decline, but only for females and teenagers; indeed, adult males were drinking 45 % more alcohol in October 1996 than they were in 1992 (Zohoori et al. 1997). There is some evidence, cited earlier, that excessive levels of alcohol consumption damage DNA and RNA structure in sperm cells. Alcohol also damages brain and liver cells and in large quantities inhibits the transformation of some vitamins to active substance needed for the functioning and integrity of nerve cells. Could this be related to high levels of insanity, malformations and violence in young Russians? Do people drink so much in Russia, because they find their environment depressing or because of cultural and even inherited physiological factors?

Part of the mechanism of some depressing environments and, let it be said, of our make-believe response to it, concerns tragic news and the seeming obsession for and reliance on it that we have. In many newspapers and on TV news programs, violent events are trivialized or treated in a way that limit the capacity of people to understand their causes. This increases the "them versus us" phenomenon and increases the isolation and hostility of some people.

Pollution and its Possible Effect on Aggressive Behavior

A recent study seems to show that noxious substances in our environment can change or affect brain chemistry. The specter of lead pollution has already been raised as one of the elements that could account for the increase in aggressivity seen in some urban areas.[84] Now, a study on 800 boys attending Pittsburgh public schools by Herbert Needleman (Needleman, Riess, Tobin, Biesecker &

Greenhouse 1996), a psychiatrist at the University of Pittsburgh Medical School, confirms that high bone lead levels are predictive of aggressive behavior in boys. Controlling for socio-economic variables such as maternal intelligence, economic status, child-rearing patterns, two parent families, race, and so on, Needleman's team found that teachers, parents and the children themselves predicted which students were aggressive and these predictions correlated with increasing bone levels of lead. Lead is a poison that interferes with the ability to restrain impulses. Since bone levels are much better indicators of a substance's accumulation over time, compared to blood levels, it is clear that those exposed to a significant substance accumulation will have more of that substance in bones than others.

More than 50 years ago, Randy Byers, a neurologist at the Boston Children's Hospital, linked acute lead poisoning in children to "later violent, aggressive behavioral difficulties, such as attacking teachers with knives or scissors."[85] Studies in Edinburgh, in New Zealand and in the USA, carried out six to eight years ago by different investigators, all seem to confirm this effect of lead on aggressive behavior or on attention-deficient disorders, which many consider good indicators, or predicators of later aggressive behavior (Needleman et al. 1996, 363). Interestingly, some of the above studies show that such effects are more or only pronounced in one of the sexes (males) and in certain ethnic groups.

Is there a code in our cells that needs an outside catalyst such as lead in order for it to be unraveled and a certain concentration must be reached for this to happen? In any case, high lead levels are still found in household paint used in many countries, in gasoline, in several factory type effluents and in some beverages made with water that is contaminated with lead. Children, especially infants who eat peeling paint or who live in environments with high atmospheric levels of lead are at high risk. Lead and similar substances could produce their effect not only by physically interfering with the blocking of a critical reaction in the brain but it may also allow other substances to be released or inhibited.

Needleman proposes that a toxic metal such as lead could affect a child's social adjustment by a neuro-chemical alteration such as one affecting nor-epinephrine inhibition or stimulation. This could result in what (quoting from Taylor et al.) an "unmediated rapid response to stimuli" — in other words, uncontrolled or overly rapid response to a cue or cues affecting aggression. Certainly, the way aggressive or violent children over-react to the slightest provocation is indicative of such a lead or non-lead mediated response.

Another, more anatomical explanation is put forward by Goldstein, who hypothesizes that lead could affect the normal pruning of nerve fibers that occurs around 2 to 3 years of age, which then leads to "over-responsiveness" — too many nerves being stimulated to fire at the same time (Needleman, Riess, Tobin, Biesecker & Greenhouse 1996, 368). It is interesting to note here that it is at these ages that maximal lead exposure peaks occur and it is at these ages that we have hypothesized that aggression begins in babies (or at least, that is when they start to behave less passively).[86]

The fact that violent criminals have also lower verbal IQ scores, that they are often more hyperactive as children and that they sometimes suffer from attention deficits indicate either that a neurological or chemical imbalance may have existed early on in life, or that they may become *unsociable* or *uncontrollable,* because they have suffered from discrimination as a result of these problems (Wilson & Hernstein 1986). Whatever the mechanism, we are now fairly sure that it is at an early age that something occurs to tip the balance towards aggressivity.

Another recent finding concerns the effect of a chemical contaminant (substances termed phtalates) present in processed milks, which were found to cause testicular shrinkage as well as disturbances in mental development of experimental animals, and disorganization of the female reproductive cycle. This shows how susceptible we may be to what was once thought to be a relative harmless substance used for softening plastic wrapping.[87] Tests undertaken for the British Medical Council and the Ministry of Agriculture in London show now that nine popular brands of processed baby milks have concentrations of these phthalates high enough to kill sperm, which may explain one of the causes of lower male fertility — a phenomenon on the increase in all industrialized societies, as noted earlier.[88] While this may have little to do with behavior that is violent, the fact that sperm cells can be damaged by substances contaminating a food product allows for several hypotheses concerning damage to other type of cells, including those in the brain, by other contaminants in substances that we ingest.

While such research is still in its infancy and those should not be a cause for alarm, there is room for concern. The recent controversies regarding beef that is contaminated with chemicals containing antibiotics, hormones and even the virus that leads to mad cow disease shows how by adding some substances to our food, we can alter some aspects of human well being and resistance.

Living Spaces

Not less important as transmission factors that affect some aspects of behavior are the physical condition some people live in and the environment present in some schools. A very interesting report on eight French low-income suburbs, the equivalent of inner cities in the UK and USA, shows how negative it can be for a North African immigrant to move from a farming area, where daily work had to be undertaken in a relatively spacious familiar environment, to one in an urban slum environment where no work was found.[89] The report draws the following picture: poor housing, tiny rooms, little privacy, especially for the young, unemployed parents who don't get up in the morning, and when they do, soon go back to sleep, kids who go to bed hungry, who are lonely. There is also a penchant to *ethnicise* all problems, which can be confusing for a child. Some people, including parents can create a deep mistrust of everything and everyone around them. Some religious or ethnic associations have ideologies opposed to the efforts of more liberal type associations that try to integrate children and to encourage open discussion.. It is a sad state of affairs. The gloomy outlook and thin chances of getting ahead in life are further exacerbated by an environment of graffiti, broken down hallways, tatty corridors, the lack of shops and exercise facilities. Is it any wonder that the crime rate in these French cities is some 80 % higher than in middle-income areas of the same cities?

The absence of play areas and their distance to the home are important factors of both parental and to child stress and aggressivity. This is not only because both parents and children need some respite from each other, but also because a parent needs to know where his or her child is and with whom. If the play area is inadequate, inexistent or far, there is also more likelihood that bored youngsters will play in the streets, that they will revert to acts of vandalism and violence and that they will be exposed to violent individuals, who will exploit them and so on. There is also a positive biological and physiological effect to sports and playing (Bjorklid 1982). Play areas and open spaces are important not just to *breathe* properly, but also to exercise the body muscles (to oxygenate them) and to reduce stress (which is also a form of inadequate psychological and physiological ventilation). Vigorous physical exercise is clearly associated with positive emotional well-being in adolescents (Steptoe & Butler 1996). Plasma endorphin concentration increases during and after exercise and this changes the concentration of opiates that may be responsible for combating depression. In this way, exercise centers and playing fields, sports facilities and dance or drama centers may well decrease the number of potentially unhappy, suicidal or violent youngsters. On the other hand, lack of play space is said to affect children's physical and mental growth, causing children to become more aggressive.

Not only are family fragmentation and strife augmented by inadequate living and sleeping space, television, cinema and video also constitute a new type of environmental *contaminant*. Even if for most the effect is temporary, these media can be extremely effective stimuli in changing mood and affecting attitudes and behavior. Long hours in front of a screen may cause daytime behavioral disturbances, not just because of the content of programs, but also because of the noise, speed of images, eye strain, different types of electromagnetic radiations and sitting in a fixed position for a long time.

The importance of sports, meeting places or youth facilities where youth can meet with mentors, is revealed in another study, this time from the USA. Researchers studying the "Big Brothers/Big Sisters" program in 1995, showed that of 959 youths of 10 to 16 years of age, followed up for a year and a half, those with mentors were 46 % less likely to start using drugs than those on a waiting-list for mentors. For minorities, the effect was even greater, with 70 % less likely to use drugs. Those in such programs were also 27 % less likely to start drinking and a third less likely to hit someone. They skipped half as many days of school.[90]

Learning Spaces

How much aggression in schools is due to poor physical condition of the school and its surroundings? It is very difficult to answer this in any scientifically acceptable manner. The confounding variable here may be the fact that poor physical conditions are found in poor income areas; while the converse may not necessarily be true, richer areas tend to have more pleasant surroundings, better school maintenance, more motivated teachers and better equipment, play and sports areas and more spacious buildings. But it should be possible to correct for some of these variables by investigating whether better run, modern, pleasant-looking schools in lower income areas have higher or lower or similar rates of school violence as run-down schools in the same area or a similar one. Perhaps going to work in ugly areas increases the chances for teachers to become more hostile to their students.

One should also briefly mention that the fear, loathing and unimaginativeness of some teachers in the run-down schools in blighted — or even not so blighted — low-income urban areas, themselves contribute to the hopelessness and violence. John Devine, a counselor to the New York City Department of Education, believes that:

> atrophy in the role of some teachers there, in response to violence in the schools, has led them to relinquish their supposedly traditional obligation of caring but firm moral tutelage, of challenging inappropriate adolescent behavior, from rude language to actual physical violence..." Instead, "the deportment of students has became the responsibility of squads of especially hired security personnel supplemented by a technology of metal detectors, walkie-talkies, and magnetic door locks..." Thus "in one school, the internal security force comprised no less than 17 guards, 4 deans, 18 para-professional assistants and several teachers on corridor and cafeteria assignment, plus one permanently assigned city police officer... On 'scan' days, 40 extra security guards, arrive to set up the weapons detection devices (Devine 1993, 21).

However much one sympathizes with teachers about this sorry state of affairs, it remains a probability that this environment of policing by guards heightens the already charged atmosphere of aggressivity. It may mean the uncovering of weapons brought to school and thus perhaps a lessening of the number or severity of fights, but is the teacher's traditional role of guidance and moral tutelage not gone for ever? What positive, admiring role does the teacher have? As for the students, can they ever forget the violent world they come from with such an array of security personnel and devices? Is it even possible, as some prisons studied indicate, that an environment obsessed with security actually leads to more repressed or overt violence, and certainly to less *rehabilitative* concerns?

In several cities around the world a life of drug-dealing or extortion brings not only the rewards of the *exciting* sights of revolvers and corpses, but also a life of sports and luxury cars, clothes and women, all readily advertised as symbols of material success. In the bleakness and ugliness of slums from Lagos to Los Angeles, these are powerful messages. A policy of checking on the source of funds for such purchases is of course difficult and smacks of repression of personal freedom, but do the authorities and private businesses attempt to locate the source of income for these purchases and perhaps, at least for automobiles and other expensive articles, limit or refuse their sale if the source of money is suspect?

The importance of changing value systems in highly materialistic cultures is no easy matter, but it seems likely that advertising directed towards the young may increase competition between them. Thus, drug dealing is on the increase in the young because it is a relatively easy way to make money to buy the goods that allow for better status.

Schools have become one of the main physical locale for teenage and youth violence — in the West at least. It was not always so. As little as twenty or thirty years ago, in most parts of Europe and North America, schools and schoolteachers represented authority and discipline. Fights, fisticuffs or scuffles did of course break out between students. Physical attacks on teachers were rare, however. Today on the other hand, not only are physical attacks on teachers often reported, but also the killing of students takes place in and around the school. In France alone, aggression on teachers rose by 21.5 % between 1993 and 1994.[91] The rate in USA is 11 % of all students having been threatened or shot with a firearm[92]: so, if the 29 cases of students shot in school in France in 1993 were to be extrapolated to the rate of firearm aggressions in schools in the USA, the number of such incidents in France would be 300,000.

The statistics for the USA reel forth frighteningly: homicide is the leading cause of death for Afro-American youth and for all American youth it is the second leading cause; a child growing up in Washington D.C. or Chicago is fifteen times more likely to be murdered than a child in Northern Ireland; FBI figures show that between 1985 and 1994 there has been a 75.6 % increase in juvenile firearm assaults and a 113 % increase in juvenile arrests for weapons violations. Every 3 minutes gun-related violence takes the life of an American child, every 5 minutes a child is arrested for committing a violent crime...(Wartella, Olivarez & Jennings 1998).

No less important is the situation of school education in developing countries. The contrasts between higher and lower income areas in terms of schools and other facilities are of course more extreme. What is often overlooked is that school violence may be much less here because schools even if compulsory are attended by proportionally less. In these countries only the most motivated families will ensure that their children attend schools throughout the ten to twelve year educational cycle. Thus, in poor income areas, schoolchildren must like or be motivated to go to class, more than their cousins living in Western countries, simply because dropping-out is so much easier and socially acceptable in the former than in the latter. Ironically therefore, the upshot in class may indeed be a healthier attitude to school and to discipline in the poorer countries! Additionally and perhaps even more important is the fact that group norms, peer respect and role modeling in poorer countries are more directed towards *respectable* adult hero's than to other youngsters. The younger boy wishes to be a civil servant say, while girls may want to be like their housebound mothers, albeit more educated and more free to choose her eventual spouse. This wish to conform ensures that students take their studies more seriously.

Urban or Rural Aggression

It could easily be assumed that the more aggressive societies come from urban environments and the more peaceful from rural environments.

This is not always so, however.

In urban areas it may be easier to hear of, or observe crime, than in scattered rural areas, but there is evidence from studies done on Pacific Ocean inhabitants (Solomon Islanders and inhabitants of New Guinea) that despite low densities and comparatively unpolluted and beautiful environments, violent crime rates are higher than in major cities of the USA. Also, in the USA and parts of Britain for instance, rural violent crime rates are rising faster than in large urban areas. It is important to note that whereas blighted environments perhaps cause more despair, rural ones may cause more violence because they are too quiet for some and people get bored. Indeed, there may be evidence that stimulation and enhanced psychosocial functioning may occur in response to urban noise and stress; and that the opposite — too much inward contemplation or a pathological like depressive state — may occur in places where there is too little challenge or stress.

But by the year 2000, the majority of the world's human beings will be living in cities — up from 5 % in 1900 to around 70 % today excluding China. More than 3 billion people. In less developed regions, the proportion went up from 25 % in 1970, to 37 % in 1994, to 57 % in 2025. For more developed regions, the figures were 67.5 %, 74.7 %, 84 % respectively (UNFPA 1995).

In other words: the urban population is growing at a rate of 170,000 people a day. People are flocking to the cities of the developing world from rural areas. The move to poor urban areas has negative effects as it pertains to health and nutrition status of these people. Since the malnutrition and stress will increase in the newly arrived rural migrants, then we will expect also a greater chance of children being born with malformation, that might contribute to dysfunctional behavior (Basta 1977). In addition density will increase so will friction. Acute water shortages are now being felt in some of the biggest cities — Beijing, Bombay, Cairo, Lagos, Los Angeles, Mexico City, Shanghai, and Sao Paulo. Their crime rates are soaring. On a visit to Paris not so long ago, the Deputy Mayor of Shanghai indicated to me that her major concern was not so much housing or hygiene, but keeping the peace between increasingly demanding and difficult inhabitants whose resort to violence was rising in a modern China unaccustomed to unruliness. As densities increase, intolerance is bound to follow. Animal studies referred to earlier indicate that a vital, minimum space is necessary between animals of the same species and even parentage. People are no different.

But here is an important point: different cultures have different thresholds for this minimum vital space. It is not so much a question of density of habitation as of cultures. People *can* live together in tight spaces. They may not be too happy doing so, but they don't automatically go out on a violent crime spree when they are packed close together. Violent crime rates in the denser cities do not seem to be much higher than in others.

What seems to be occurring in the more violent cities, also increasingly true for rural areas in these countries, is that family, kinship and neighbor alliances break down. The more violent urban areas are those where poverty and greed, insecurity and deteriorating physical environments, loneliness and family isolation are worst. The influx of drugs, alcohol, gangs and so on become secondary events, invading as much as invited to a core which has already began to rot; as if the delicate, insecure web binding these inhabitants together can no longer extend itself but breaks and, with the connivance of corrupt or simply indifferent municipal authorities, develops into an insecure mess. I call this the *infective process* for violence, for, as in the body, the infection only takes hold when the body's defenses — in this analogy, qualities of solidarity — break down or are insufficient to counter the outside threat.

In developing countries there is another phenomenon involving violence and the environment. This is tension caused by a struggle over agricultural and mineral resources between people who have lived on the land and those wanting to exploit it but who come from the outside. Nowhere is this more apparent than in the current widespread violence, including wholesale murders, taking place in certain parts of Brazil

(Amazon and Northeast regions), Indonesia (Irian Jaya, Borneo), India (tea-growing and other areas of Assam and North-East India), Sudan (South and West), Burma (opium, teak and mineral areas of the North and East), and several other countries in south-east Asia, Latin America and Africa.

A series of violent clashes also takes place as environments become degraded and people want to move out. This is happening in parts of Albania, parts of Russia and China, Ethiopia, Northern Kenya, Mali, Niger, Peru, Somalia, Ukraine, Zaire and so on, where either man-made or natural disasters lead to the spoilage of land, resulting both in migration and in resistance by those who contest the entry of migrants into their own areas. Livestock migration in search of water or grassland has led to the most terrible wars and conquests: the Mongol invasions in Europe in the first centuries AD; the range wars between sheep and cattle farmers in the US in the 1800s; the near extermination of Aborigines in Australia and of the Maori in New Zealand in the latter part of the 1800s and early 1900s; the conflicts between Touareg and settled tribes in Mali and Niger; and the massacre of the Dinka and the Nuba in Southern Sudan in the past decade.

The conflicts over land in Israel and Palestinian territories is another example. More grief and violence results from the confiscation of Arab lands and the degradation of their water and land resources for the building of Jewish settlements, than any other issue in the volatile Israeli-Arab struggle.

How many people have died for the control of land is something yet to be calculated. It may be that in the future we will see less urban strife and more collective strife in rural areas because of land, water and other disputes relating to them.

GEO-Biology

A new science, Geo-Biology, is in the process of being born. This is the study of how physical shapes, sizes, electrical fields and the like, affect not only our overall health, but also subtler body rhythms and moods also.

Electrical Fields —

Rates of depression or hostility may be increased or decreased, for instance, depending on a building's exposure, its view, its layout and even its height and shape. People who live near high-tension electrical lines are known to suffer more from certain types of afflictions, than those living far away from them. This is true for many diseases including forms of cancer, especially in children. Nobody has as yet provided a reasonable explanation for this, in my view; but it may be that ions discharged from these electrical fields hold more than a *normal share* of negatively or positively charged particles, which would alter nerve conductivity or the proper release of some neurotransmitter molecule. Electrical fields give rise to more free radicals, the type of ions that lead to altered reactions, which affect our brain and body chemistry. A large number of educated people consult architects today as to the emplacement and orientation of their future homes so as to minimize depression and hostility resulting from the homes location in an electrical field (such as the "Curie" field) or from rooms orientated in a specific way or that are located too near electrical meters and other types of transmitters.[93]

New European industrial law protects machine-to-machine interference more than machine-to-human interference. For instance, EC directive number 89.336, effective from 1st January 1996, goes at length into safeguards needed to protect equipment from other equipment's electrical fields; nothing is said about human sensitivity to these electrical fields. Yet, we are occasionally told that electro-magnetic radiation from computer, video and TV screens affect the behavior, physical development or mortality of rats, chickens, and flies — and humans.

There is a lot of controversy here. Research results differ. A 1996 report from the US National Research Council[94] states for instance that new research has not found any link between electromagnetic fields and cancer, nor with developmental, reproductive, learning or behavioral problems. The study does however indicate that some forms of childhood leukemia may be increased in areas where high voltage lines are placed. So, why wouldn't overall cancer rates go up? And if they did, could those molecular effects not affect some brain reactions as well? Electro-magnetic radiation has a probably equal chance of penetrating any body area.

A 1997 advertisement from the UK Department of Health[95] invited bids for a large research study to "determine the risk of both ionising and non-ionizing radiation" includes "EMF fields such as those from power lines, cell phones and radio transmitters." The ad asks whether people with "undue genetic susceptibility may be at risk as well as the foetus or child." Twice, it raises the possibility that some people may be more sensitive than others to such forms of radiation.

Ozonoff (1997) of the Boston University School of Public Health raises the possibility that there are health effects from high voltage lines. Ozonoff states that there is a 1.5-fold incidence in leukemia among children whose homes are very near high voltage power lines Others disagree. The nervousness associated with all such speculation may in itself contribute to disease, including a heightened degree of stress and in turn, violent behavior. Fluctuating levels of hormones due to either stress or to real effects from physical phenomena may even show up in breast milk, for instance thyroid hormone levels.[96] In turn, low or over fluctuating levels of thyroid hormone not only affects learning ability in children, but is also responsible sometimes for higher levels of aggressivity in adults and children (cf. Lindsay & Toft 1997).

Green Fields

It is important to assume that there are indeed two facets to this physical environment problem. One, is the direct influence on the brain's metabolism, of electrical or physical or chemical elements that may influence heightened discomfort or even aggressivity; two is the effect of psychological reactions we may have because of overcrowding, because we are unhappy or superstitious about a location we live in, or because our senses are disturbed by the shape, size or sound (or lack of it) of our habitat. Both facets affect the brain's chemistry — affect our *nerves*!

We are told people are unhappier in round buildings, in buildings beyond a certain height (usually ten or eleven stories), without a view — or with a view but of cemeteries or railway tracks. People are said to be more nervous if living on reclaimed swamp land or by certain lakes, and more unhappy if living near certain mountains or living in environments where animals, including household pets, are absent. The site of major battles, containing presumably the remains of the combatants, have also been shown by some geo-biologists and architects to lead to hostility in some people so much so that certain buildings located on them have been abandoned or have had to be relocated. Redlich, Sparer & Cullen (1997) have also summarized much of the research that has been done in the past 5 or 6 years on how certain buildings cause not only mood changes, but also quite often debilitating physical symptoms. Most of these symptoms stem from problems of ventilation, especially in modern buildings, although other factors such as their emplacement, clustering, and so on may be factors as well.

Simpler to visualize or understand are the possible effects on our moods of a badly built school or office, a run-down apartment block, a damp house or a smelly and excessively noisy neighborhood. The tension, the high degree of excitability, hostility even, one feels in noisy cities like New York, especially with their constant sound of police and fire sirens, may be responsible for the nervousness, violence and aggressivity, so well known in that city; as may be the lack of friendliness, but not necessarily close densities and view of so many human beings moving about so rapidly. Recognizing this, some cities in the West have therefore created noise ordinances and in one city at least, Geneva, a special police brigade has as its main function to answer citizen's complaints about excessive noise and to monitor noise levels in that small, still relatively quiet city of some 300,000 inhabitants. In 1995, police had to quell noisy neighbors 1,193 times, issue 473 summons for excessive noise and intervene 157 times solely to control loud TV and radio noise. Imagine the task in cities like Lagos or Cairo or Rome or New York!

Migration and Emigration

Movement and relocation causes stress. Are such feelings a result of psychological or chemical factors?

Studies are showing that changes in body chemistry can occur, when people change countries and even places of residence within the same country. More interestingly still, this is independent of expected dietary changes or new foods that are eaten. In one example the incidence of heart disease increased when Asians moved from India to the UK, but this could not be explained on the basis of a change in diet, since little changed in their diet when they arrived in the West. We cannot assume that it was more cholesterol or saturated fats or tobacco that may have led to the increase. Was it the stress of moving and settling down in a place where people were less friendly or more work conscious? (cf. McKeigue, Miller & Marmot 1989).

If this can happen to the heart, what happens to the head that rules the heart?

We also hear that in the USA one of the many characteristics of men convicted for armed crimes and murders is that they moved a lot from home to home when they were little. Of course, it may not be the fact that they moved that is important here, but rather the reasons for so doing. However, Ekblad (UNICEF 1993, 34) finds that:

> pathogenic mechanisms are likely to be elicited when an individual experiences an unfamiliar social situation or has no recourse to natural or cultural protection.(...) the process of urbanization or migration with the accompanying rapid changes in child rearing practices may be a latent health hazard, regard less of whether such changes may be beneficial or not.

Income and Violence

Moving from one place to another may be to obtain better material rewards. But as the possibilities of material rewards increase, so do competition and the likelihood of corruption.

If it occurs on a significant scale, corruption may hasten the aggression process for it leads to an intensification of greed and the breakdown of rules that govern human behavior. The more an economy is based on market forces and hence business competition, the more will there be a need for rules that govern the accumulation of influence, capital and the processes, which enable a rich minority to rule over a resentful majority. Some competition is essential of course, but if there is a process in which the wealthy and privileged restrict access to upward mobility of the less fortunate, the latter may increasingly fight among themselves for the share of a very limited pie. So stagnation or lack of advancement can also lead to people becoming violent. Certainly, the much higher crime rates seen in the London working class or poor of the last century, compared to today, must in large part have been due to a sense of fatalism as regards the difficulty of getting a share of the benefits the better off were accumulating (cf. Leapman 1989, 232-5).

Equally of course, a sudden surge of income or a rise in living standards in a population may be a cause for more violence. In the USA, crime is supposed to have actually fallen during the Great Depression and raised again when the Depression ended. Groups who lose out in a war have less violence between them than those who won, because in the latter competition for the spoils will increase and because violence is shown to be rewarded (Wilson, 1975). On the other hand, the work of Jane Goodall (1971) and Frans De Waal (1996) on apes and rats show that an ape or rat that has been aggressed by another will vent his aggression on a weaker one. In 1939, the classic studies of Dollard & Miller (in Bloom 1995, 289) and others in the USA showed that when cotton prices fell drastically (the study was done in 14 Southern States over a period of 48 years), lynching and beatings of blacks by poor whites shot up. This is an instance of the so-called *frustration-aggression* hypothesis.

An editorial in *The Economist*[97] makes the point succinctly that neither economic growth on its own, nor a "firm hand at the top", constitute the main reasons for a country's equitable development; but rather, "primary education for women, effective local government, an egalitarian outlook, an open economy, a degree of personal liberty, and patience." The article also argues that "democracy" does not only amount to the freedom to discuss or to oppose a country's leader, but rather the ability (as in Cuba) to complain freely about the services of the state.

Indeed, it is also noteworthy that the rise and freedom of trade unions in a state such as Kerala in Southern India, the freedom for discussion allowed by past rulers there, and the relative absence of an elitist British colonial administration dominated by landowners, made that state more peaceful, better fed, more educated and democratic than its more northerly cousins such as Bihar or Utter Pradesh, where income inequality, poor educational facilities and little investment in social services have created more violent, more unhealthy and more corrupt environments.

In Political Science, a great deal of ink has flowed about the question whether the State has primacy over the individual or vice-versa. If states have a responsibility over the individual, then it should follow that the rights of all citizens should be guaranteed by that state. If states allow a great deal of social injustice and relative poverty, then it may be that a certain disrespect on the part of the ordinary citizen to that state will also be found. The state can be considered as the *home*; if all sorts of unfair things happen in that home, violent behavior will occur. The income gap between the poorest and richest segments of society should therefore also be a predictor of the amount of violence in that society. There must be a correlation. An examination of this reveals that indeed societies such as Colombia, Lebanon, Pakistan, Russia, South Africa, USA and Venezuela have huge income differentials between the top and bottom segments of society. Is it therefore a coincidence that they are some of the most violent societies in the world?

Another way of looking at this is to see whether geographically and culturally neighboring states that differ mostly by the economic or social system they have adopted, where such income differences may be much less, the degree of violence is also less; and this is indeed so — Botswana, Canada, Jordan, Belgium, Chile or Argentina have lesser degrees of violence than their more non-egalitarian neighbors, respectively, South Africa, USA, Lebanon, France, Columbia, Brazil.

For the United States, several studies link poverty to violence, rather than race to violence. One study even looks at violence in toddlers, related to low income (Keenan 1994); another links economic hardship to adolescent aggression (Skinner 1992; and another, studying American Indians, finds that the poorest are the most violent (Young 1991). Clearly, we have to bear in mind that the link between poverty and violence only refers to recorded violent crimes, not to violence *per se*. Thus, conceivably, rich men may beat their wives and children as much as poor men, but since this is rarely reported it does not enter into crime statistics; let alone polite conversation!

That social silence is one manifestation of a phenomenon that embraces equally the way in which some sociologists talk of *cultures of poverty* as *cultures of shame*; for instance, Sinclair Lewis in Mexico and the USA, Saad Eddine Ibrahim (1995) in Egypt. One can predict that poverty in some societies gives rise to such intense shame that it becomes an element in explaining violent behavior. Indeed, some may go so far to state that unless this feeling of shame and inferiority is removed, certain societies will not be able to embark on the road to democratic and peaceful behavior. (Khalifa 1995). Saad Eddine Ibrahim has outlined how trends and contrasts of demography and income help to explain why violence is bound to be more endemic in the African Mediterranean countries and the Middle East than in European Mediterranean countries. One third of the urban population of Morocco, Algeria and Egypt, for example, live in shanty towns that "are a Hobbesian-like existence of vice and violence of *bellum omnium contra omnes* (all against all)". That Islamic fundamentalist groups must find it easy to recruit their most violent people in these conditions of poverty, shame and hatred.

The Price and Dangers of Upward Mobility

It could be that innate human desire to achieve a better status in society or in a group has a reproductive advantage. Dominance hierarchies in animals determine the pecking order. There are countless studies that reveal how posture, testosterone levels, sperm counts and so on are raised once an animal and even a whole group betters itself or rises to the top (cf. Bloom 1995, 195-200). There is thus a reproductive reward to be obtained when rising to a higher status: females have been shown in countless studies to prefer higher status males. Naturally, this will increase resentment and hostility in inferior status males! This doesn't lead to fighting in most humans today, but the profile of many psychopaths is that of a male suffering from various forms of inferiority, including lack of economic or social advancement.

In humans, however, ratios of female-to-male are such that even very poor, low status males have access to females in their own class. Nevertheless, since the promise of riches brings with it power and more choice, an aggressive, even violent, but poor low-status male has more reproductive choices and the chance of a more varied, healthy offspring, than one who is poor but non-aggressive. Removing oneself from poverty through any means, including violent ones, is thus to be expected.

The rich and not so rich middle class know that. Their fear of the *parvenu*, the aggressive hustler from the *other side of the tracks* is such that behavior and structures have been developed to keep him and his brood in place, ranging from outright repression and violence (as occurs for instance in and around the slums in India, Brazil and Venezuela) to snobbish disdain — as in the United Kingdom and other parts of Europe — to religious indoctrination and promises of a better after-life — as has occurred everywhere in Catholic and Hindu/Buddhist societies. Hinduism with its caste system helps to keep certain classes of people in a subservient or poverty stricken states. It is not open to those born into the lower castes, the Shudra, to achieve the riches and purity of a high-caste Brahman. Is it then a coincidence that Brahmans seem to have a much lower crime rate than the lower castes?

Prejudice is connected to this. Any family or individual that has suffered from the stigma of racial or religious or even social discrimination is bound to harbor a great deal of overt or latent hatred. Italian, Irish, Jewish youths in turn of the century New York were extremely violent. Was it a coincidence that as each of these groups was *assimilated or accepted*, their rate of juvenile crime went down?

Thus, if it is a more *normal* behavior for poor Irishmen to drink and beat their wives and children, than it is for rich Irishmen — who are more frightened of what their well-to-do neighbors may think. It was thus *expected* of you to be violent and to use violent language, if you are living in a poor neighborhood and are Irish.

There is nevertheless a linkage between the perception of one's position in society, the chances of upward mobility and the use of violence. History and culture however play a large part in determining whether a particular group remains docile or decides to fights its way out of a submissive role. If there is no other alternative to displace a dominant hierarchy, then it is an open window on revolt. Nor is it always necessary that within a country, the poorest are the most violent. If that was so, we would expect rural Africans, most of whom are very poor in terms of income, to have a higher crime rate than urban Africans, whose income is generally higher — but who suffer from a higher crime rate. The same is true for most of Asia and Latin America. If income was the main parameter, then the poorest societies in the world would have the highest violent crime rates. That is not so. Calcutta's or Cairo's slums are far less violent than middle-income areas in parts of the USA and Britain.

What is important is, of course, relative income within a fixed and delineated area and the density of habitation. The more oppressed or confined people feel they are, the more the potential for violent and non-violent crime.

Some researchers, at times using all sorts of bizarre methods, have attempted to infer that poorer ethnic groups or countries have more criminals. For example, Furukawa (1930) in Japan devised a " National Temperament Scale", in which, on the basis of some spurious correlation involving an equation based on the ABO blood grouping and crime statistics, he came to the conclusion that those with O and B blood groups were *more active* and ready to commit crimes than were races who were *more passive*. Of course, since Filipinos, American Indians, Gypsies and Hindus were supposed to have more of these blood types than did Japanese, Norwegians, Swedes and Italians, among others, they were supposed to be more violent. A closer look at his scale reveals an almost linear correlation between these nations or people that are the darkest and poorest with crime.

More recently still, politicians such as Haider in Austria, Jean-Marie Le Pen in France, Blocher in Switzerland and various other right wing politicians in the USA and Britain have insinuated or stated that immigrant races from poor countries commit more crimes than those from countries that are ethnically closer. But if adjusted for income and employment, this relation does not hold. This type of racist propaganda leads to the ridiculous conclusion that rich and educated immigrants carry out more crime than rich and educated locals; the opposite is true! Employed, educated immigrants are in any society, the least violent people. The violence of some of the rich whether it is hidden or whether it takes the form of exploitation of others, especially in developing countries, must be mentioned. It is even more reprehensible as they know that they will usually go unpunished.

Sickness and Poverty

One of the tragedies linking violent behavior to social class is the inability of poor segments of society to afford or to gain access to the medical or psychiatric treatment that richer segments of society have access to.

Statistics on violent crime will usually be biased towards people living in inner cities or their equivalent, since more people will go untreated for say, schizophrenia, paranoia, alcoholism and so on, simply because they cannot afford such treatment either in a monetary or social sense. There is also more stigma attached to such treatment in poorer than richer societies. In addition, police enforcement, juries and judges in most of the world will tend to favor the rich in terms of lenient or *look the other way* decisions and punish the poorly dressed and dirty more.

Brown & Harris (1978) showed that, in the UK, some 25 % of women of working class background suffered from severe depression, whereas the equivalent incidence in middle-class women was only 6 %, but more middle-class women have the money and access to experienced psychologists. Being poor entails not only more stress, but also less chance for treatment, less chance of compensatory environment.

Sagan (1987) gives several indications that mental illness is much higher in low-income groups than middle- or high-income groups in the UK. For instance, schizophrenic psychosis is some eight times more frequent in poorer classes than in the richer classes; psychosis due to drug addiction or alcoholism, twenty times more common; and affective psychosis, some two-and-a-half times more common (p. 159, 161-163, 176-183).

Various studies also seem to point out that subjective feelings of being in good health are about twice as common in the rich as they are in the poor. Coping strategies are of course far better in the richer segments of society than they are in the poor. Note also that it is not the income, which correlates best with some of this, but rather the education level. The longer a person goes to school, the better read or more literate he or she is, the greater the chance that they will surmount any of the mental health risk factors associated with being poor, and that includes mental illness associated with violent behavior.

Class and Competition

War, in some cases, may be associated with a desire to improve the economic conditions of large groups of people. Is there an association with the horrific death toll in the 20th century, which could amount to 100 million war related deaths (as calculated by Rhodes 1998), or even 200 million (UNICEF 2000), and the loosening of class and income barriers at the beginning of the century?

A condition that seems to be present in the war of what Hobbes so pin-pointingly called *all against all* is that social need and interaction are a form or a condition of competition. If social interaction is of a positive nature, the resulting behavior presumably reflects a positive, forward-looking type of action. If on the other hand the interactions are stagnant and negative, the resulting behavior will presumably tend to reflect that. So, in higher income groups, the chances of meeting someone who will help, advise, attract, innovate and be more able to create things are usually greater than in poor income groups. This *Access Factor* is an important determinant that may protect higher income groups from the violent, frustrated behavior which will perforce characterize someone whose chances of moving anywhere are limited, whether it be up, down, or merely sideways.

Knowing that your fate is *sealed* does terrible things to a psyche.

Entrepreneurial activity, capitalism in its true sense, will tend to favor the rich over the poor and the weak. Thus, in *laissez-faire* societies, the richer elements have varied outlets for their aggressivity and competitiveness — golf, tennis, polo, racing, sailing, skiing, bridge and so on — which in turn rewards them with more money or/and more things to do. Movement is forward. In the poorer elements, the outlets for aggressiveness are much more limited, with little choice other than sex or fighting or contact sports — or watching the rich at *their* play! And in poor income groups it is the male who will have more access to these than the female. We would therefore expect not only to find more crime in these types of societies, but as stated in Chapter 4, more women who suffer from an inability to *channel* their aggressiveness and more women with depressive symptoms.

The *winner-take-all* mentality has repercussions on societies' development. The gap between poor and rich is widening. In OECD countries, between 1979 and 1989, the income of the top 1 % doubled in real terms, middle-class income stagnated and the income of the lowest 20 % fell by 10 to 20 % in real terms. Today, the income gap between the richest 10% in the USA and Europe and the poorest 20% is around twice what it was a decade and a half ago. About 97 % of all salary increases benefited the top 20 % income group. In 1974, top US business executives earned on average 35 times the salary of a middle-level worker; in 1996, it was 120 to 150 times more! (Frank & Cook 1996).

On a worldwide basis: between 1960 and 1990, the incomes of the richest 20 % of the world's population grew three times as quickly as the income of the poorest 20 %. Thus, that richest twenty percent now earn 85 % of the world's money, compared with 70 % three decades ago; while the share for the poorest twenty percent has dropped from 2.3 % to 1.4 % (UNDP 1996).

Yet paradoxically, in the USA and the West, the existence of distinct social and income classes may *protect* against widespread mayhem and violent civil disturbances, because there are opportunities for many to go from one class to another. The boom of the 1990's in the USA has enabled many millions to *graduate* from certain types of cars, homes and neighborhoods to more expensive ones, the young find plentiful jobs and the advertisements offering the better life and the more expensive clothes and cars are no longer dreams for the few. Thus, everyone is running around in a work and spend frenzy and there may indeed be many less youths ready to go into *fighting frenzies* (drug and ghetto's individuals excepted).

In most of sub-Saharan Africa, on the other hand, poverty and hopelessness are so widespread, and distinct social classes so rare, that people turn against their own and only class. The slightest difference in residential or ethnic origin is sufficient for a dispute; hence the terrible civil wars we witness every year in one African country or another. Class differences may strangely enough lead to a diffusion of tension or aggression. If there is no class-consciousness, no social classes, there is no class competition — and so, people compete against one another.

Poverty, Violence and Racial Stereotyping

People are not created biologically equal, but nobody has yet shown conclusively what the best genetic or even cultural make-up might be — if that makes sense even to postulate. Methodological difficulties involved with imputing genetic, as distinct from economic, cultural or developmental, origins to aggressive behavior in children and adults are well summarized in papers such as that of Allen & Futterman (1995).

According to the Center for Criminal Justice based in San Francisco, in California, in 1995, nearly 40 % of all black males are said to have either been in jail or to have appeared accused in criminal court, once in their lives. The corresponding figures are 5 % for white males and 11 % for Hispanics. A large proportion of the 135,000 inmates in the State are black.

Does this indicate that the black population of the USA is more inherently, even genetically, more violent?

It does not.

It indicates that the level of frustration for blacks is probably much greater, the *access factor* is lower and so, the poverty more crippling and the social interactions more limited.

Just how ridiculous it is to impute a certain race with genetic characteristics linking it to crime and violence is illustrated by a survey done on three groups of blacks in the USA : 1) those newly arrived from Africa and the Caribbean, 2) those who are first or second generation Americans, and 3) those that have been there for many generations.[98] Crime rates for the second group is over three times that for the newly arrived and superior to the third group.

If crime was linked to race rather than social or income group, we would expect crime rates for all groups to be similar. This is not the case. We would also expect an ethnic group to be more violent than another regardless of where they were born or how many generation they could count as American. However, both whites and Hispanics have higher crime rates than blacks newly arrived from Africa or the Caribbean (group 1).

Employers that were interviewed almost all said that they also preferred to hire Africans or Caribbean blacks than those born in the US. African born blacks make more money than do American-born blacks: $30,000 *per annum* as compared to $21,000 (1990 figures). Around 60 % of the African and Caribbean blacks have two or more members of their family who work, compared to 40 % for the US blacks. Family stability and structure also differ. At least two-thirds of Caribbean families are headed by a couple, whereas it is less than half for long settled black Americans. Children of immigrant blacks also do much better in school than the US-born ones, and those who are of one or two immigrant generations do less well than newly arrived ones, but much better than the black children whose ancestors have been in the country several generations.

Since violent crime statistics for these groups seem to be inversely correlated to income and education, and the latter in turn to origin and length of stay in the US, we can see that it is not race per se that links with crime, but rather poverty, poor education and lack of work. The *shame factor* referred to earlier is by extension much higher for US-born blacks. They are as a result more bitter, more violent and charged with much less optimism for the future than the newly arrived or even longer established African and Caribbean blacks who have maintained more of their cultural and family traditions — and identity.

It is also noteworthy to conclude from all this that various forces in American society undermine those blacks who remain too long, or those staying long enough and whom absorb the violent, racist and bitter experiences of US-born-&-bred blacks. American society dislikes losers. The minute you are on an upward role, the more likely you will be rewarded. On the other hand, if you sink into poverty and the resulting self-pity, your chances of being appreciated diminish considerably. Not only that, but if you take to drink or drugs to forget your misery, as most will, then you will need to steal, perhaps kill, to get your *fix*. With the abundance of dealers, pimps, con-men and the like in these poorer strata, it is easy to end up in ghettos where you will be typecast because of your race and poverty.

As far back as 1900, the American public was being told that the annual expense to taxpayers caused by crime was $600 million, which in today's figures must be not less than $600 billion (Allen & Futterman 1995, 12). It was therefore imperative to find a scapegoat. The easiest and most popular one was to claim that the cause was the large numbers of Eastern and Southern Europeans, which had begun to flood into America in the late 1800s. A considerable and well-meaning science developed around all sorts of archaic statistical methods, involving blatant error-filled conclusions blaming the foreign hordes for these crimes. The main *inventor* of these types of statistical extrapolations was Charles Davenport, a New England scientist, and his assistant Harry Laughlin, who presented the results of several years of study of demographic immigration and criminal records (Davenport & Harry Laughlin 1913). The sampling base was skewed to certain penal institutions and not others, nationalities were sometimes counted twice using different names, such as separate entries for Serbian, Balkan, Romanian, or by being lumped together as *all Asia* or with Russia, Finland and Poland under one title; nor were any attempts made to calculate and adjust for densities, socio-economic background, length of residence... But at the time none of that bothered the Anglo-Saxon and

Germanic public and politicians, who eagerly welcomed a study which confirmed what they felt all along. Naturally, the most "socially adequate populations" in the USA turned out to be the Swiss, Germans, Irish, British, Dutch and Scandinavians — all the first settlers in NY and New England — and the "least adequate" turned out to be the Serbs, Mexicans, Bulgarians, Chinese, the Greeks, the Turks and Italians.

It may also be but a coincidence, but two factors come to mind from Davenport's conclusions. Firstly, that there seems to be a correlation with darkness of skin and crime, and secondly, that the most violent seemed to be the most recent immigrants. A third and fascinating conclusion one could make is that the *more expressive* the population — the loudest and the most spontaneous or friendly, say — the worse they become. Like his colleagues in Germany and Britain, Davenport ascribed this to the "feeble inhibition" and "moral degeneracy" of these hapless people, people who included the very religious Jews and Italians, who were not after all Protestants. Later, in 1928, eugenicists such as Popanoe and R. Johnson (in Allen & Futterman 1995, 13) were less harsh, calling them populations with a "lack of emotional control" and, better still, more prone to "epilepsy".

In all fairness to Davenport and his school, he did recognize that what constituted a crime in some cultures may not be so in others and later on, around the late 1920s, he did acknowledge that it was not only a case of "bad heredity" that made certain nationalities behave in unacceptable manners, but also that environmental circumstances, such as poverty, could also be implicated. He thus concluded that whereas criminality is indeed biologically based, schooling, religion (but which?) and training could affect the expression of the trait. In around 1928 and the early 1930s, forced sterilization of prisoners, female and male, including emasculation, become common in around half of the then United States as a result of these studies; in order to "segregate and sterilize the anti-social and the mentally unfit" and "the economic ineffective and generally stupid." (Booten; Olsen & Laughlin, cited in Allen & Futterman 1995, 21).

Finland, Sweden, Denmark, Germany and other countries followed suit with 65,000 women in Sweden alone being forcibly sterilized between 1935 and as late as 1976.[99] In 1936, Laughlin and Olsen claimed such steps were necessary, because these people were "born and not made ... they are not the products of slums. They are incurable because they are not suffering from external stress and strain but from an inherent defect in protoplasm." (Allen & Futterman 1995, 22)[100]

Laughlin's earlier testimony to the US Congress in 1922 as to the need to restrict immigration, and to base it on the relative genetic merit of different populations, may be unacceptable today, but in his day it was all too understandable. What is puzzling is why he and others then could not have been more understanding of the possibility that even if certain (violent) tendencies could be *inherited*, this would be more on a direct parent-offspring basis, and not necessarily on a nationality, racial or ethnic basis. There is no more likelihood that intermarriage, co-sanguinity or interbreeding would be greater in the "colored", Chinese, Asian, Serbian, Slavic, Balkan or any of the broad groupings or nationalities, than among Irish, English, Scandinavian or German populations. Indeed, those who come from countries with small populations, like the Swiss or the Scandinavians, (*desirable immigrants*) would have more chance of hereditary disorders than a huge population like the then Russians or Balkan or "Asian" people.

If these scientists were claiming to be disciples of Mendelian genetics, they did not apply it very well. Of course, proponents of Davenport and Laughlin may use precisely the same point to state that people like the Swiss and Scandinavians should have more *inheritable* criminality but do not because they are genetically superior! However, the extent of bias by these early American geneticists is so glaring that they conveniently forgot that Switzerland in the late 1800s and early 1900s — in fact, even until around 30 years ago — had one of the highest *per capita* incidences in the world (especially in Europe) of *sick citizens* because of the widespread presence of Goiter, in other words the Iodine Deficiency which often leads to what was then called "feeble-mindedness". As to the Scandinavian countries, then as now, alcohol-related dementia, suicides and a host of inheritable forms of schizophrenia and depressive illnesses were and are still more common there than in most Southern European countries!

Even if the fact that some nations seem to have more violent citizens than others — I myself maintain so — can be found in cultural patterns handed down from generation to generation, Serbs living in Canada or the USA are not particularly violent people, whereas those living in the fired-up climate of Bosnia or Kosovo are. The new environment demanded an adaptation. Similarly, an Afghan or a Lebanese or a Zairian immigrant in Europe is a tame and pale reflection of the violent image of Africans or Lebanese or Afghans are supposed to be in their countries.

It is therefore not wrong to ascribe certain violent traits to certain populations, but what is to be rejected here is the genetic certainty and genetic form of transmission. Are we taking into effect, poverty, culture, shame induced by being at the bottom of a group? The best statement on all on this is the one ascribed to Borogaonkar and Shah:(in Allen and Futterman 1995, 42):

> In certain environments some persons with particular genotypes will respond by developing certain behavioral problems more frequently than others. However, this does not preclude the possibility that in some other environments, persons with the very same genotypes may well manifest socially adaptive behaviors.

Ecological and Environmental Catastrophe Case Study: Russia

In "The Ecological Catastrophe in Russia," Iouri Cachine, a Russian journalist, highlights the inability of humanity to concern itself sufficiently with the physical and the mental consequences of poor surroundings.[101] Cachine claims that around 10 % of all Russian children are born today with physical or mental handicaps compared to 1 % to 2 % in the West. Of these, 50 % are said to be because of genetic causes, and 20 % are due to ecological reasons — mainly, she claims, pollution of air and water resources, radioactive fallout, and alcoholism in the mother. These malformed infants are increasing at a rate of 1 % to 2 % a year, a terrifying statistic. Furthermore, the president of the Russian Ecological Commission, Andrey Iablokov, claims that around 5 % of the Russian population is suffering from sorts of genetic malformation, whatever that may mean.

What on earth are the Russians doing about it? How is it that such terrifying figures are not a cause for immediate mobilization, for scientific meetings worldwide, for political debates at the highest levels and for lots of international appeals for funds and for technical assistance?

One of the most tragic new phenomena connected to this situation is the increase in violence in post-Soviet Russia, particularly in the major cities and nowhere more than in Vladivostock, St. Petersburg and Moscow. It was expected— axiomatic indeed, at least to liberal thinkers — that freedom from communist bureaucracy would spawn such a corrupted, aggressive and nihilistic generation of young people, so many of whom join the so-called Russian Mafia, or become muggers or even hit-and-run killers, or who prostitute themselves. The speed with which all this occurred leaves one amazed all the same. In just the three years 1989 to 1991, a huge new society and class of thieves and swindlers mushroomed. Today, the violent crime and homicide rate in Russia is not simply the highest in Europe, it is higher than all of Western Europe put together!

Some people in Russia hold the opinion that most of the rise in youth criminality was caused by sudden pauperization of large segments of the Russian working class (Helen Agisheva & Evdokia Kholostova in UNICEF 1995, 159, 163). However, it is much more likely that as friends and neighbors observed how quickly and easy it was to sell oneself and steal and obtain the material goods and status all craved for, the increase in violence really began at the post-poverty level. That is just at that level where some needs could at last be satisfied. In addition, the now so prevalent flaunting of wealth was a further inducement to become more aggressive. The sudden rise to economic power of some suddenly privatized factory managers and the ease by which some who managed lucrative industries became rich, such as in the minerals sector, left others envious and bitter.

The huge drop-out from some pre-school, school and college systems which now began to charge fees, caused another schism between those who could afford them and those who could not. Drugs also began to flow into the country with much greater ease, claiming even primary school children as their victim. More young students began to attack others and we know of the tremendous but also sudden increase of juvenile rapes and drug addiction (Cachine, op.cit.). Some children can now earn as much as $500 a day working as prostitutes or drug couriers in a country where the average daily wage is less than one twentieth of that. As alarming as anything is the statistic that in the first 9 months of 1996 alone, thirteen thousand heavy machine-guns, rifles and assorted firearms have been officially listed as being stolen from arms depots in Russia, by soldiers desperate for cash.[102]

Cachine blames "apartment swindlers, unemployment of parents, de-ideologisation of the population, collapse of national culture" for the worsening problems. Indeed, in Russia of the Cities there has been a collapse of "national culture". Cultural values have been quickly transformed from one in which hard work and social cohesion was paramount, to one in which the quick buck and leaving others in the proverbial Russian dust became more important.

We must not forget however that Russia has always been a violent society. Alcoholism alone reached such proportions that during various eras sale of vodka was restricted, the last being under Brezhnev, a decade ago; but not since the revolution of 1917 has it been a non-egalitarian society. Now suddenly it is and —perhaps this is it — the imbalance between those who have, those who can get and those who may never get is the biggest reason for the violence one sees now in Russia. In other word, nearly all the conditions one discussed earlier for a truly violent country...

Case Study or Sadly General Pattern

Eventually, Russia may settle down, but what of many African countries where similar phenomena (although not as rapid) occurred in the past twenty or thirty years? It is a certainty that post-independence black Africa has had the largest and most rapid rural to urban migration of this latter half of the century and along with it, a rise of a corrupt elite and an increase in relative poverty. This increase in size of a corrupt elite has occurred to an extent never before known in these societies. The result has been a huge increase in violence, petty thievery and insecurity — as any long-term traveler to Africa will attest.

Some even ascribe the recent massacres in Burundi and Rwanda to primarily the economic imbalance, which put different sections of their societies at loggerheads against each other. Poverty was always there, but since independence many of these countries not only saw the formation and institutionalization of a criminally corrupt class for the first time, a separate class in the true sense, but more significantly, access to it became so limited to certain groups, that graft increased tremendously in order to accede to any form of service. The absence of democratic institutions whereby to voice protest, the infusions of ready cash to the groups in power by past colonial masters and their industries and the rise in degrading demands by those who had it on those who did not, became a further cause for friction between ethnic groups.

Africa today represents the most glaring case of social and ethnic discrimination in the world. No wonder the violence! Yet Russia, so polluted, so powerful, so ambitious and so unstable in its envies and remorse, is perhaps so much the worse for us since it is so close.

Newspaper Sources and Other Quotations

84 Lead inhibits the release of neuro-transmitters, while dietary deficiencies of calcium, iron and zinc enhance the effect of lead on cognitive and behavioral development. Mercury toxicity increases if selenium intake is insufficient (Editorial, "Nutrition & Metal Toxicity." Journal of the American Medical Association 275, 1996, 646S).

85 "Boys Delinquency Linked to Lead in Bones." *International Herald Tribune*, 8 February 1996.

86 Needleman also found that as early as 7 years of age teachers could predict with some accuracy which children would show maximum aggressivity 4 years later. Farrington, often cited earlier, also showed that children labeled by teachers as "troublesome" at eight years of age, were significantly more likely to be adjucated as delinquent at 18 years and to have been convicted of a violent crime by age thirty-two. Such judgments may normally be made by hunch or instinct but are no weaker for that; indeed, there is even evidence linking facial features as an index to personality, especially violent criminals. Milunski (1996), of Boston University School of Medecine, shows that a cellular defect in a sub-region of the cranial region, caused by folic acid deficiency, may influence cranofacial development.

87 *Le Nouveau Quotidien*, Lausanne, 29 May 1996, 19.

88 An account of the effects of environmental toxins on sperm counts, and mobility on reduced fertility, penile size and on the possible concept of abnormal sexuality (*gender-bending*) due to chemical contaminants (Colborn et al. *The Economist*, 3 August 1996.

89 Published by the Institut Banlieues and summarized in *Le Monde*, 2 March 1995

90 "Is Summit Asking Too Much of Volunteers?" *International Herald Tribune*, 28 April 1997.

91 *Tribune de Genève*, 7 February 1996.

92 *Le Figaro*, 17 July 1996.

93 D. Petry Amiel, La Gaude, Personal communication, Jan. 2000.

94 *The Lancet* 348, Nov. 1996, 1305.

95 *The Lancet* 348, Nov. 1996.

96 According to J. Nagayama of Kyushu University, Japan. *International Herald Tribune*, 28 April 1997.

97 "Different Roads to Development." *The Economist*, 19 Aug. 1995.

98 "Black like me." *The Economist*, 11 May 1996.

99 International Herald Tribune, 27 Aug. 1997.

100 By 1970, 60,000 people had been castrated or sterilized in the USA, about half of this number before 1940 when over 30 states had adopted the legislation for this (loc.cit. p. 33). Note that as recently as December 1996, some congressmen were calling for sterilization of certain people on welfare,

claiming them responsible for the 46 % increase in violent crime between 1980 and 1990.

101   Iouri Cachine "The Ecological Catastrophe in Russia." *Tribune de Genève*, 12 June 1996.

102   *Asharq al-Awsat*. London, 15 October 1996, 24.

Chapter 7

Some Aspects of Religion and Violence

The Language of Religion and Violence

The language of religion can be very violent. That is not only because fear is a tenet of all religions: the culture from which that religion emanates determines its choice of language.

Thus, when the Islamic Jihad authority announced in response to the assassination of one of their leaders in Malta: "We will explode Israeli blood and travel with it to Heaven..."[103] The language used at the extent of the hyperbole is in keeping with a culture where emotions are allowed to flow freely. Such phraseology in Arabic speaking cultures will help to ensure new adherents and maintain a nostalgic tradition of "holy war" that is borrowed from the past.

It is also a tenet of Middle East culture that revenge is expected and strenuously sought out. It is both Biblical and pre-Biblical in origin. Also noteworthy is the dramatic effect of a threat. Whereas we know from our studies on apes and other animals that threatening behavior can achieve much without the need actually to fight physically, we sometimes forget that humans also use verbal and attitudinal threats a great deal. The more bloodthirsty is the threat with all its attendant imagery, the greater is the fear that may be obtained. Since all religions use fear — *you will burn in Hell...*— it is of course necessary for maximum effect to upgrade and increase the implied threat.

It is thus necessary to create new and more frightening threats — and then the deeds to go with them — to keep up the fear. An oft-repeated phrase can with time become a little jaded. No self-respecting religious zealot wants to be heard as *jaded*; if he wants the flock to increase or even to continue to believe in him, like any entertainer he must say and do new things. Religion is thus not only salvation and piety, but it can become a form of entertainment, especially for a public that has little entertainment. It is based on love, suspense and violence, like most entertainment – with the added ingredient of Revenge. Yet, as will be discussed in these pages, cultures have substituted their values and much of their violence in religions that were for the most part peaceful attempts by sincerely holy men to bring order, cooperation and enlightenment to man.

Salvation from Violence...

Whole regions of the world are so tied up in the religions of yesteryear that some children will continue to be brought up thinking of revenge as a requirement for some fuzzy notion of salvation — personal salvation as well as group salvation. The early theologians of the Christian church and even some of those today believe that Salvation was the chief object of human beings, not *well-being*. Note how modern Buddhist, Jewish and Islamic thought also reflects this.

The history of those who chose to ignore or resist conversions to other religions is also rife with brutal imagery. The Spanish conquest between the 15th and 16th centuries is one of the most glaring examples of this. It is the epitome of barbarity in the name of religion.

Bartolome de las Casas quotes an Indian King about to be executed by the Spaniards, as saying during a final attempt to convert him to Christianity, that if the Spaniards were going to heaven, he preferred not to go there (cf. Collard 1971).

The Japanese on first contact with Christian missionaries, were reported to have been so shocked by the fact that the Christian God could become angry, that some thought he was unlikely to be a God. In China and Japan, impolite behavior, and that includes shouting, was not thought to be God-like behavior; so, angry missionaries and officials from the Christian powers could not really possess a *good* God.

Thinkers in the Christian tradition have not been blind to similar discrepancies. More succinct, drier too is Montesquieu: There has never been a kingdom with so many civil wars as the kingdom of Christ[104] (Lettre XXIX, Rica à Ibben, *Lettres Persanes*, 1721). Montaigne placed Red Indians on a higher moral plane than the Europeans of his time, openly stating that the cruelty, torture and massacres perpetrated by Europeans in the name of their religion made them inferior to *noble heathens* such as the American Indians.[105] One could also note here that both Montaigne's disbelief in the moral superiority of his fellow Europeans and his courage in stating that they may be inferior to Indians and other *barbarians* indicates that fear of the Church in the mid-1500s was, for some, refreshingly absent, at any rate in parts of France. The tremendous suffering and brutality there as a result of religious wars may have led thinkers to reconsider man's allegiance to religion. Thus, religious wars may in fact have eventually led to a *turning away* from religion. Montaigne may have also been the first to state that no excuse could be made for a man's cruelty under any circumstances, an unorthodox view then as now...

It is however easy to confuse a religion with violence, when the connection should be between a culture and violence. The Christian religion was not the problem in the above examples, it was the men who were associated with Christianity and Christian powers[106] Similarly, when we talk about Jewish or Islamic fanatics we should be very careful about not confusing them with the Jewish or Islamic *religions*. The majority of Moslems and Jews all over the World are not violent or fanatical; that is self-evident.

Fanatics come from cultures, not religions that are violent. Insofar that a religion reflects the culture from which it comes, there is of course a connection. But the culture, which gave rise to the religion, may and will change. As it changes, it may not be able to adapt the religion to its new values — for example Catholicism in Western countries today; or, as in the case of Shintoism in Japan, it may become flexible and non-confrontational, adapting well to the change in values, *moving with the times*.

More pertinent still: what happens when a moral code, be it religious or social, dwindles and evaporates, with no authoritarian dogma or set of clear guidelines to take its place? Uncertain moral values, as some religious zealots say, may contribute to a kind of dissatisfaction, which in the young may in turn contribute to disenchantment, a lack of direction in their lives that in its turn translated into violence and an anarchic mode of behavior. For some, discipline in religion is synonymous with the security of the group — and of the State – hence, with many different forms of violence.

The Confusion between Origins and Religion

Perhaps the most important and dangerous result of youth disaffection and militancy today, on a global basis, is their taking up arms in the name of Religion, particularly Islam, and to a lesser extent, Judaism, Buddhism, Hinduism and various sects and religions of the Christian faith. Not a month goes by that religious zealots murder large groups of people in Algeria or Afghanistan. But they are not fighting for religion; they are fighting for political power. Similarly, the conflict between Tamils and on-Tamils in Sri Lanka is not one between Hinduism and Buddhism, but one for independence of the Tamil minority. In Northern Ireland it was not Catholics and Protestants fighting for their faiths that kept the conflict alive for so long but rather, which of the two groups was going to succeed to obtain more power to dominate the other from Great Britain. Fanaticism occurs everywhere, but it is nowhere as visible as in the Islamic world, where the greatest potential for fanatical movements exists and where probably the greatest numbers of opportunistic interpreters of a decent and modern religion exists.

Sometimes devoid of any true religious component, Islamic militancy also exists as an *ethnic* movement in a number of European countries, justifying violence because of unemployment, *host prejudice* or a sense of inequality. Here, it may be interesting to study a little closer how the fuse of ethnic and religious belonging mixes with the explosive powder of exclusion, youth *disaffection*, unemployment and prejudice, to create the newest and most potent crucible of youth violence in Western Europe. The violence it may cause comes not from the religion but from an inability of both immigrant and host populations to accept cultural differences.

Moslem immigrants form the most substantially growing non-Christian religious community in Europe. They number about two million in France, mainly North Africans; two million in Germany, mainly less "religious" Turks and Kurds; and around two to three million in the UK, mainly South Asians.[107] Poverty, alienation and domestic violence are relatively high in these communities, certainly proportionally higher than in the host population. The extent of criminality, domestic violence, youth delinquency varies according to the make-up of the host country and the origins of the immigrants, from a high for the Moslem communities in France, Switzerland and Sweden (where on a relative level violence is high) to a lesser figure for the Turks and Kurds in Germany and the North Africans in Spain and Italy. Lowest of all is the incidence of violence by the Pakistani and other Moslem migrants in the UK — where it is less than in native Britons.

In terms of mental health the problems and conflicts for girls in these traditional Moslem communities is a lot worse than for boys. There is probably no other community of young women that suffers so much in Europe from conflicts having to do with sexual freedom, religious practice and tradition. Like that of earlier mostly defunct Christian dogma, Islamic tradition today puts such a premium on modesty, conformity and virginity in girls that they are constantly torn between having to conform within their communities and having to conform to the outside — to groups where freedom for women is flaunted and admired.

No less a cause of misery and alienation that Moslem men and women, girls and boys, feel in these European countries, is a prejudice they sense in native-born Europeans that to be a Moslem, let alone to be darker in skin as well, is somehow to belong to a group that is "unclean, inherently violent and dishonest." This prejudice dates in Europe from before the Crusades, when in the ninth century the Moors (as they were then called) were by force of arms beginning to settle in areas that had been animistic or Christian.

Understandably, this sort of discriminatory behavior has spawned a backlash, with many people and associations linked to the Islamic faith calling for a renewed pride in the past. But disagreements must henceforth and naturally exist as to the methods and degree of piety that is to be followed. Disagreements spawn in turn, conflict and even violence, directed against their own or others, with · further consequences regarding identity and ways of expressing it. For example, there are 300 Islamic associations today in France alone. Disagreements abound between them. This increases tension and conflict within families and friends and the children increasingly resent and reject the uncertainty and contradictions of what they hear, see and feel. The biggest contradiction, whether it is in Islamic communities of Europe or those in Moslem countries, is the uncertainty of whether to blend into traditional cultures or to break out and embrace a Western culture. The biggest malaise may be their thwarted desire to belong to a society that accepts them despite their differences.

In order to put Islamic militancy into context, it may be worthwhile to illustrate how even fundamentalist Christian and Jewish groups today urge violent ripostes to perceived slights. Taking Christian groups first, we note that many fundamentalist groups in the USA are openly allied to both the National Rifle Association as well as to militant and violent Anti-Abortion groups — which have recently been responsible for the assassination of *seven* separate abortion clinic workers in the USA and Canada, in the space of two years. Furthermore, the vehement, openly aggressive language of such groups during political campaigns and the use of blackmail to unseat *morally unfit* candidates create more hysteria and violence.[108]

In Northern Ireland, the continuing mayhem between Protestant and Catholic groups draws hundreds of violent youths to either side and in Lebanon in the 1970's — barely twenty years ago — Christian militia, using young men, convinced that they were out to protect their homeland, butchered hundreds of Moslems and even rival Christians, including the Palestinian Christians that found themselves in the Shatila refugee camps of Beirut. Finally, in Russia, Armenia, Serbia, Bosnia and Georgia, we find youths drawn to fanatical Christian groups, whose avowed aims are to take power by force or to butcher any non-Orthodox group that happens to reside or claim some of their territory. As to Jewish fundamentalist groups, they continue to draw into their ranks thousands of Israeli and other Jewish youths, even after the shameful murder two years ago by a Jewish religious fanatic, of Prime Minister Rabin. Their hate literature and campaigns against other Jews, non-orthodox, liberal or secular, because of questions of dress, music or the keeping of the Sabbath on weekends polarizes many young people in Israel and adds to the tensions and uncertainties the youth in that country suffer from.

In short, whether it is poverty, immigration, religion or racism, the world of the young today is surrounded by contradictions and opposing symbols, such as the wish to conform to a differing culture and the fear of assimilation and loss of identity. Assimilation of another culture could destroy the unity of religion and cause youths to adopt differing beliefs or even for some threaten the geographical borders. The Israeli newspaper *Hachavoua*, mouthpiece for the ultra-religious *Haridim* in Jerusalem — the sect "that fears God" — has described how the Haridim beat women in public if they are not adequately clothed and also that "fear of Americanization" (which is to say, ultimately, modernization) is one of the principal fears of this large and important group of Jews. This large and important group also called for the putting to death of Judge Aharon Barak, Chief Justice of the Supreme Court of Israel, for authorizing or confirming that road traffic can take place during the Shabbat on Bar Ilan Boulevard. (This same freely published newspaper had earlier called for the assassination of Prime Minister Rabin, who was in effect murdered on November 4, 1995).[109]

Boundaries, threats and revenge are Darwinian responses to the risk of species or group annihilation. Thus, we may even dare to the hypothesis that religion is a *further method* to propagate and defend a species. Religion reduces the risk of disorderly, chaotic child-rearing patterns and outer-species reproduction.[110] Religion also fixes agricultural and geographical boundaries, seeks to maximize the reproductivity of human beings by ensuring all females are fertilized (within a marital union of course). Disproving of divorce by females also ensures the male prerogative of keeping females, so that every male will in turn be able to find a female (and they do not all flock to one powerful lead male). Finally, the selection of the fittest for species multiplication is best ensured in very religious societies because those who will follow the lead male's teachings the most faithfully are assured of the greatest group protection — and presumably the best spouses. In this way of looking at it, religion is the human response to the highest forms of evolution.

And violence must be *sanctified* since religion is so important to the human species that it must be protected at all costs.

The Invention of Stories — and Histories

The power of the *lead male's teachings* may sound primitive but it is basic.

According to several African experts, violence in Africa increased rapidly in the 19th and early 20th centuries not only as a direct result of colonial occupations and manipulations but because these manipulations also led to the rise of several religious leaders or *shamaans*. In times of stress and uncertainty such *magical* or *blessed* leaders arise naturally; it is not just that a patriarchal figure is needed but also a prophetic leader, to look into the future, to advise on wars, to placate the restless spirit of the dead and to organize and lead the various ceremonies —for both the dead and the living. They employ powerful imagery and blood-curdling pronouncements to impress both their followers and their enemies.

"My eyes are filled with blood, my only friend is the vulture," declared a New prophet in Southern Sudan, one hundred years ago

(Johnson & Anderson 1995; Johnson 1994). Much of the fighting that resulted from the rise of the Messianic leaders was also to establish who would be in the best position to negotiate peace terms — thus to gain considerable political and material advantage. Even in so-called primitive settings, the quest for power is the *raison d'être* behind many a shamaan's actions. Since they had to avenge the death of their kin and tribe by battling those who may have brought about direct or indirect deaths, African religions also conveniently *invented* a number of bogey-men, such as those living in dark forests: any tribes living in dark forests were fair game since that was where bad spirits dwelt. The inventions linger and even today forest tribes are feared and hated by many African people.

The intolerance and violence practiced by so-called religious zealots in other parts of the world is equivalent to the blind yet easy hatred of enemies labeled as *forest tribes*, which if allowed to get what they want would swallow you and your land... To return from the jungle, listen to Yigal Amir, the murderer of Prime Minister Rabin of Israel, as a case in point: he followed 'Jewish law'. This required him to kill Mr. Rabin who was threatening to extinguish Jews by giving their land back to Arabs; there is an ancient Jewish prophesy that anyone who threatens the existence of Jews can and must be killed and so, Mr. Amir felt perfectly justified in carrying out the necessary sentence.[111]

Similarly, in recent Serbia, Milosevic raised the specter of Moslem Kosovars about to annihilate Serbia's so-called Christian roots in order to justify his hold on power over what was left of the Yugoslav federation.

Cultures produce stories and legends to justify someone's quest for control over others. This perhaps is how religions evolved after the first awe-stricken primitives began to wonder about the cosmos above and the forces of earth below that swallowed their dead. An *interpreter*, a wise-man or woman began to organize the changing and praying and then began to *translate the messages* from above and below. Soon he or she began to relish the power and awe vested in them and in keeping with human nature used violent language to stay in power through fear. Skin color, place of residence, idiom, sexual differences, act as further links to a particular *interpreter* or shaman and soon religion may become confused with the cause of tribal purity. Legends then become the stuff on which religions are built and fearful language and imagery do the remaining rest.

It continues, sometime seemingly blindly as the world goes on. In *Vie et Liturgie*, a church magazine put out by the Protestant church in

France, a vitriolic article in praise of the Jewish prophet Moses and condemning the way ancient Egypt had treated Jews appeared in 1996; entitled "Rites de passage et passage du rite" and written by one David Banon, a Jewish lecturer at the University of Geneva and Lausanne, it purports to explain how and why "memory and Jewish liturgy" operate.[112] It also serves to illustrate how religion keeps the fires of revenge warm... Yet a new book plays with the possibility that Moses may in effect have been an Egyptian priest and an opportunist who decided to oppose the Pharaoh for personal gain and then move to Palestine... (Assman 1997, 38)

It is well known that the manner, in which the distinction between true and false is made in religion, has led to untold violence and bloodshed in history.

There is after all little difference between an African *shamaan*, a National Front leader like Le Pen in France, most of the Muslim and Jewish and Christian and Hindu fanatical groups and the very ancient old prophets of yesterday. It is in fact quite remarkable that after all these centuries and millions of deaths, the language and justifications for religiously sanctioned murders remain so much the same. It can even be said that if looked at cynically this similarity is a reason to *unite* people of varying racial and religious backgrounds: after all, if Jewish and African and Muslim fanatics behave in just the same way, are they not brothers all the more?

If my exasperation seems too facetious or too humorous, let me observe that in fact this is *exactly* what occurred in international forums such as the UN Population Conference in Cairo and the UN Women's Conference in Beijing in 1994 — disparate groups such as the Vatican and the more extreme Muslim nations such as Iran got together to stifle moves to facilitate women's access to contraception. In all fairness to the new Catholic Church, Pope Jean Paul II has been instrumental in calling for better justice for all, for respect of human rights and for a halt to violent behavior. As early as 1979 his first Encyclical, *Redemptor Hominis,* was directed at the defence of Human Rights around the world. His calls for an end to intolerance have been tireless.

Morals and Moralities

Most wars between the 4th and 17th centuries, in Asia, Europe and most parts of Arabic-speaking Africa were fought using religion as the principal rallying cry. That most of these main religions frowned upon cruelty and aggressive behavior did not make much difference. Morality reduced everything to one principle: "Get what you can using any pretext."

Bad enough at the individual level, the use of such a principle in order to massacre hundreds, indeed thousands, indeed tens and hundreds of thousands of innocent men, women and children, is extraordinary. Was there a period when man ever began to wonder whether this was worth it all? In Europe in the 16th and 17th centuries, some isolated voices calling for a reassessment of the benefits and cost of war, whether for religion or any other cause, were beginning to be heard and were indeed allowed to publish their viewpoints. Notably, in France, England, Holland, parts of Italy — even Arabia. This was tied up with the burning argument (almost literally...) as to the inherent nature of Man, whether he could indeed control his nasty side, or was he doomed to always behave as some sort of aggressive animal?

In my view, two schools of thought about man's inhumanity and cruelty eventually emerged: in the first — most readily identified with the *French school* — Man was at least born an innocent creature but because of the influence and machinations wrought upon him by others, including those of the then Church, he could be manipulated to become a killer of others. However, in the second school, from the palace of the Vatican and oddly even in the more dour, slightly earlier *English* (and also German) school, comes the view that man was an evil animal to begin with, and little could he do to escape that inheritance, unless he fought and begged for religious salvation; as in the animal world, everything in Man was predatory in nature.

Hobbes's tellingly prescient phrase, the *war of all against all,* sums up best the gloominess of the latter school. Unlike Dante, however, and other religious philosophers before him, he did not believe that hell was just around the corner because of our innate evil, but rather that we were made more violent and aggressive — inevitably — because of a social life that led to competition and because of the way in which we try to maintain ourselves in a world of finite resources. Unlike the French and Florentine and Dutch philosophers, Hobbes and his school could see no escape out of that, no remedial system.

I doubt that even earlier historians, philosophers or wise men believed in such a *gloom and doom* philosophy. Certainly, there were cynics amongst them, such as some of the Chinese, Greek or even Roman statesmen and elders who recognized that Man was very frail when it came to resisting the siren calls of ambition and acquisition; but all seemed to believe that a strong education in the learned sciences, forms of martial or non-martial arts, and loyal behavior towards rulers and gods were insurance against unreasonable behavior. Obviously, you had to defend home and hearth, become a soldier when it was needed and even obtain slaves from the savages that surrounded your nation, but essentially, if you were *moral* in the above sense, people like you could live in harmony. It was the collapse of such a moral code, the absence of guidelines that led to trouble. Even today Man as always still holds that it is essential to believe in the pacifying influence of a higher order.

In some cases, that higher order need not be, a god, or gods, but also a ruler or a wise person. Cynicism, atheism, rebellion were all-dangerous, as Socrates found out when he was condemned to death. That was nothing new. In probably one of the most ancient texts reflecting man's disappointment with the violence of fellow man, Ipu or Ipu-Ur, a writer of sacred texts in the service of Egypt's pharaoh, around four thousand years ago, warned against the cynicism and violence affecting an Egypt that had problems paying its laborers and farmers, due to a decline in the public treasury from overspending on monuments and wars. Disenchantment had reached such levels that one of the first mass revolt in Egypt's long history erupted, with the butchery of several aristocrats. Ipu or Ipu-ur, who witnessed these events, was shocked and he wrote a long poem known as the *Lamentations of Ipu* (cf. Bresciani 1969, 65; Lalette 1994, 211).

Ipu lamented such terrible disorder whereas "brother killed brother, servant turned against master and people became wicked and bad." The moral order had broken down, the common man had ceased to believe in the old values and there was no more respect for the old religo-legal system. Thus Ipu, long before any Eastern or Western sage, attributed uncertain morals as the cause of violence and mayhem, a position not far removed from today's religious opportunists and fanatics. Note that it is the absence of morals that is given as the excuse for violence not so much economic or political oppression.

That uncertain morals may be a principle cause for violence is nonetheless perhaps dubious. Obviously, people who are subjected to rule by superstition will be more docile than those who are not – but not necessarily less violent. Contrast for instance the fearless, violent Shiites of southern Beirut or the fanatical hate-filled ultra-orthodox Jews of Jerusalem with the placid, largely atheistic, peaceful, hedonists of most Western cities today. The ancient Egyptians that revolted in Ipu-Ur's lamentation did so because they progressively became poorer — not because they became *less moral*. If you are hungry, you may just become *less moral*. You will certainly become more angry and violent!

Those responsible for the killing of the 55 million dead of World War II did not all come from the world of cynical and irreligious leaders such as Stalin and Hitler. The British RAF, who deliberately chose to create mass panic in one night of bombing Hamburg, killed some 42,000 civilians. The same approach was used for Dresden, Berlin and a host of other cities, including some in France and Italy, where on the express orders of their nations' *wise leaders* the RAF and the US Air Force killed around a quarter of a million civilians in two years of high altitude aerial bombings. The British and Americans were very moral people and had very moral leaders, such as church-going Winston Churchill and nice Franklin D. Roosevelt and even nicer General Dwight D. Eisenhower; but war is war, so away with morality — even if it is of the best *Christian* sort. The Japanese, also a most moral people with a most moral, upright (much more so!) living god of an Emperor and a 'clean, superior' religion, enslaved 300,000 Korean, Dutch, Indonesian and Filipino people as sex workers in their military brothels; and executed hundreds of thousands of innocent civilians during their rampage over Asia and the Pacific, and in China perhaps millions.

That the USA partly responded by killing 130,000 Japanese civilians did not make things *more moral*. I have heard stated that even Hitler believed in a *morality*, because he really believed he was saving the Germanic races. Hence, the problem!

We have seen that *morality*, insofar as it is used to define adherence to a particular religion or a moral philosophy, may in fact be a method whereby Man's baser, more violent impulses find a readily acceptable outlet. Moralists may be the worst fanatics, the most ruthless killers and the greediest oppressors. The Islamic radicals in Algeria between 1992 and 1999 are believed to have killed 75,000 people and kidnapped over 3,000 girls to be sex slaves — a process that is still taking place today. These are people, who consider they are disciples of the most supreme moral and religious order in their country! Any *moral person* can turn out rightly to be suspected of hypocrisy, spiritual blindness and uncompromising intolerance...

There is always an opening for fanaticism, when a leader or a group insist on creating a nation-state based on a national identity that is exclusively defined by language, race and religion.[113] Myths are created to enhance belief in such nation-states (cf. Thiesse 1999). They serve to reinforce the cohesion of the group. All others are potential threats and old humiliations are re-interpreted and reinforced (Catholics and Papists in the 17th century New England, Jews in 1930s Germany etc.).

It is interesting to note that often intolerance and a heightened sense of morality seem to go side by side. Thus de Toqueville in the early 1800's noted that in Puritan New England things seemed to go from bad to worse as communities began to codify laws regulating morality. The code of 1651 stipulated that use of tobacco was illegal and that any expelled Catholic priest was to be put to death if he returned to Massachusetts. Nobody was allowed to worship in any form of service other than that which met local Protestant norms and in Connecticut anyone who believed in another religion was to be put to death. A liar was to be publicly whipped; kissing in public was outlawed as was lazy behavior and drunkenness. This from a people who said they fled Europe because of intolerance!

The Goodness of Religion

The above has mainly dealt with the way religions have been used as an excuse for several ends. Yet against that it will be argued that the human abuse of the morality and momentum of a religion should not be used to condemn the supposedly divine goodness of the teachings of the religion. We should not condemn the message only by scrutinizing the messenger... And it has to be said that the major modern religions — Hinduism, Buddhism, Christianity, and Islam — were originally inspired by very moral, upright and essentially kind and tolerant men. Violence, in these religions, even aggressivity, was not tolerated.

The confusion of the Old Testament for Christians and Muslims, even for some Jews — it is essentially a Jewish and pre-Jewish series of gruesome stories — made it difficult for them to follow the non-aggressive dogma of figures such as Jesus and Mohamed. Many elements in the Old Testament clearly contradict the messages of tolerance, hope and love that these prophets were espousing. The Bible is composed of some 66 books, written by at least 40 different writers over a period of some 1,600 years, from around 1513 BC to AD 98. It is an important record of how in the space of that time Man's concept of revenge, hatred, brutality and violence evolved from the Old Testament's "tooth-for-a-tooth, eye-for-an-eye" to "turn the other cheek" and "love thy enemies" of the New Testament.

In Islam, the Zakat system of making it compulsory for everyone to set aside for the poor around 10 % of their income did much to buttress the poor from hunger and deprivation. Similarly, in the religions that descended from Buddha, alms, humility and penance were so institutionalized that no man, rich or not so rich, could escape from passing some time of his life as a wandering novice priest equipped with only a begging bowl. Not only did this make him familiar with the problems of the poor, but it also ensured that he would help them always. In that sense, religion could and did serve to reduce inequities; and hence reduce the potential for some violence.

The Morality of War

The morality of war is still being debated today by the judges of the World Court at the International Court of Justice in The Hague. Of the 14 judges that presided in June 1996 over a debate on the use of nuclear weapons, three decided that these were "illegal *per se*", four that they could be used in certain circumstances, and seven that they could only be used "in extremis" or when the "very survival of a State would be at stake."("Small but significant step towards disarmament" (UN 1996). Note that the first three were all from very poor countries, the second group was from industrialized countries, three of which had the bombs — and the fourth, Japan, is protected by the US — while the seven came from middle-income countries, including China. So, perhaps there is a morality for the strong and one for the weak.

At least these people are indeed meeting, talking, debating...

International Humanitarian Law is a body of rules drawn from many sources, including "codified laws" set up by multilateral treaties, "customary law" developed in accordance with accepted behavior, and general laws applicable in most countries. Many of these stem from earlier religious practices and dogma, involving acceptable or non-acceptable behavior by Man. But all is not good in the legacy left to us by past religious leaders. We have constantly abused and interpreted and manipulated religions and its followers to baser ends. On balance, can we say that more people have been harmed by religion, even morality (they are not the same thing), than *saved* by it?

On balance, I would say that Man's use of religion has contributed to more violence between groups than lessened it. In December 1941 (the month was appropriate) the leadership of seven regional Protestant churches in Germany issued a proclamation that declared that owing to their putative racial constitution the Jews were incapable of being saved by baptism and that they were the "born enemies of the world and Germany". It urged that the "severest measures against the Jews be adopted".[114] They were.

In the 16th to the 18th centuries the Inquisition blessed the massacre of Jews and Moslems and their expulsion from Europe. They had already blessed the massacres of South American Indians (cf. Collard 1971, 46 & notes 57, 58). From the Protestants, we have the various pogroms, terror and violence induced by figures such as Calvin, the non-involvement of the US Baptist, Lutheran and other Protestant churches during the mass transfer and killings of American Indians as late as the early 1900s. In the Middle East, we note the Islamic regimes intolerance of other religions in Iran and Saudi Arabia and the torture of their adherents when necessary and in turn the silence of most Jewish rabbinical leaders regarding the terror raids and mass expulsion and killings of non-Jewish Palestinians in the1940s and 1950s. After all, according to Maurice Stroun of the University of Geneva, "Zionists from Jabotinski to Begin to Shamir believe that the rights Jews have over Palestine proceed from God." (Stroun & Harsgor 1996)

And on the other front, we note that some Moslem leaders' relative silence regarding discrimination against minorities in their own countries, the actions of some of their more ardent followers in the killing of Christians in Algeria, Egypt and Lebanon in the past 15 years, and today the complicity of Shiite clergy in Gaza regarding the massacre of Jews in Israel by bombing campaigns. Even Buddhist and Hindi clergy — these high advocates of non-violence — are noticeably aloof when it comes to terror killings in Sri Lanka and other Asian states and are perfectly capable of violence and vengeance themselves. In Burma in March 1997, Buddhist monks went on a violent rampage against Moslems in Mandalay, burning mosques, beating up Moslems and behaving in a most un-religious manner.[115] It seems that a Moslem had molested a Buddhist girl.

To try and laud the virtues of religions, which all preach love in some form or another, is relatively easy. To try to reconcile religion with the *excesses* described above makes us defensive. It as if Man wants to justify mass killings, oppression, cruelty, using a moral green light, called religion. It all serves to belittle the notion that Man has risen far beyond his *animal self*. Indeed, some would argue that Religion has done no more than to wrap us in some sort of respectability, when we desire to avenge ourselves against some ill. Perhaps, even allow us to return to our tribal roots long after it removed us from them. Suffice for the moment to quote from Desmond Morris's *The Naked Ape* (1968) that, "religious activities consist of the coming together of large groups of people to perform repeated and prolonged submissive displays to appease a dominant individual" (p. 156).

Newspaper Sources and Other Quotations

103 *International Herald Tribune*, 30 October 1995.

104 «Il n'y jamais eu de royaume où il y ait eu tant de guerres civiles que dans celui de Christ.» Translation by the author.

105 Was he perhaps the first great thinker of Christian Europe to dare to speak on behalf of *the savages* ? This is also one of the first example of the secularization of intellectual thought in Europe (cf. however Montaigne's "Essay on Cannibalism")?

106 Nietzsche was succinct: "There really has been only one Christian, and he died on the cross." (Nietzsche 1968, § 39).

107 Lesser numbers are found in Spain and Italy, a growing number of Albanians and Kosovars now live in Switzerland and Italy. In Sweden, until recently a homogenous bastion, we find Somalis, Kurds, Albanians.

108 Operating from Texas, the Dravidian sect was one such group. Another was the group that encouraged and probably financed the horrific Oklahoma bombing in 1996, which killed scores of innocent people.

109 *Tribune de Genève*, 28 August 1996.

110 This includes the remarkably strong prohibitions on sex with animals in all religions.

111 *International Herald Tribune*, 21 Nov. 1995.

112 Banon, D. «Rites de Passage et Passage du Rite.» *Vie et Liturgie* 26, 1996.

113 Ann-Marie Thiesse "La lente Invention des Identités nationales." Le Monde diplomatique, 12 June 1999

114 Goldhagen D. J. "It Took 100,000 Willing Germans To Carry Out The Holocaust." *International Herald Tribune*, 19 March 1996.

115 *International Herald Tribune*, 20 March 1997.

Chapter 8

The Influence of Mass Media

Introduction

A study about the transmission of violence to children must take into account the power of mass media. In modern society, the mass media, especially television and films, has become a major factor in influencing children's behavior, sometimes as important as school, family and peer groups' pressure. Many parents, teachers and researchers discern a relationship between the rising level of violence and crime in everyday life committed by young children and the scenes of violence shown on television, cinema, videos, as well as by child-manipulated games of violence in video and computer games. Nevertheless, there seem to be conflicting evidence how children will become violent just by watching television or films, however much the cartoons and action plays they look at may seem violent to us. On the other hand, it may be that those children who are already primed to become violent will be the most affected. For such children, the small screen, be it via television or the Internet may teach and provide them certain ideas and the tools to solve problems through violence.

Acting out Violence "for Real"

Some very gruesome crimes committed by youth and ever-younger children seem to point out to a direct influence from the media. Some of these children admitted that they were acting out what they saw their heroes doing on television.

In 1997, a token-booth clerk in New York lost his life after being severely burnt by thugs who squirted an inflammatory liquid into his booth and set it afire. Mr. Kaufmann's death came a few weeks after the release of a Hollywood box office hit in which this scene was shown for the first time. Since Kaufmann's death, 5 other booths were set on fire in NY — thankfully with no casualties — but the movie studio concerned denies responsibility.[116]

That same year, an adolescent couple in Paris killed three people including two policemen. The boy was killed but the girl, who survived and actually shot the policemen, said they had undertaken this spree of violence after repeatedly watching a recent Hollywood-made movie that glorified young adolescent killers. In another case to be tried in March 2000, two French boys admitted that they knifed a girl 26 times and tried to decapitate her after watching a similar episode in a US made film entitled "Seven." One of the boys said he wanted to be a serial-killer like those he had seen in "American films."

Even more worrying are crimes that have been committed by extremely young children in the past few years. In the UK, in February 1993, two boys 10 and 11 kidnap a 2 year old and deliberately killed him. In France, in October 1993, three 9 and 10 year olds participated in stoning to death a homeless man. In the UK, in December 1993, two 10 and 11 year olds were arrested for torturing a 6 year old. In Norway, in October 1994, three 5 to 6-year-old boys beat a little 5-year-old girl unconscious and leave her to die in the snow. From Oakland, California, in 1996, came news of a 6 year old beating to death a neighbor's newborn baby. In Littleton, Colorado, in 1999, two 11 and 14 year olds massacred more than a dozen schoolchildren and a teacher. In Michigan, in February 2000, a six year old came to school with a gun and killed a six-year-old girl. An official said the boy thought it was, quote, "a game like on TV."

Long before the advent of television or the silent screen, long before Columbus discovered America, cultures have complained about *undisciplined* children. Children, young boys especially, have *always* been attracted to violent combat, have always been fascinated by weaponry, war toys and war games. Young boys have always challenged each other in daring to transgress their physical limits and the limits set by society for their games. Dramatic injuries and even death occurring in such games are usually assumed to be accidents, consequences of games that went too far, of fights that degenerated into serious injuries.

The Controversy

Adolescents account for 24% of all violent crimes leading to arrest in the USA. This rate of youth criminality has seriously increased in the past 25 years, in all industrialized countries. In the past 25 years, modern mass media has developed tremendously offering an ever-increasing choice of violent material. Is there a link between television exposure from birth and high criminality among the young? Is television a liberating factor that led potential criminal to act at a younger age than they did a generation ago? Did the six year old, who killed a schoolmate in Michigan by shooting her with a gun, create a precedent that others might follow?

Children need to know who they are and learn how to behave according to the world around them. The media is a main source of information today, especially as regards physical aggression and crime. Has violence in the mass media influence ever-younger children to commit serious assaults and murders?

There is much controversy in the field of research on an association between media and child violence and there seem to be no easy answer.

Most children, at least in the West, are exposed to violence in TV, film and video, yet most children are well balanced and most children can separate reality from the make-believe world of facile violence of the most popular action series.

Still... What of the child who is rooted in front of the TV for long hours each day, who is an unhappy, insecure child, a child who begins to live more and more in a make-believe world, a child who is bored and one whose keepers, friends or siblings have been capable of great cruelty to him or her? How many episodes of violence does that child need to see before some connection will be made about a manner of treating a real or imagined victim in the way the villain or the hero of the episode has done? What of the "Exterminator" or "Rambo" hero-types he has seen, armed with the latest contraptions that can vaporize or kill their enemies with one or several quick shots? Indeed, maybe the speed and efficiency with which these pseudo-heroes dispatch their enemies constitutes the biggest danger — not only it is fast but it is rather guiltless, without too much real suffering and the hero does get his rewards fairly quickly... Children who live within a dysfunctional family, or those who suffered from serious childhood trauma could thus be more ready to act out or copy screen behavior, than those living in more happy and secure environment.

Many factors interact to affect anti-social behavior, such as poverty, racism, drug abuse, dysfunctional families. The mass media may reinforce any negative perception of hostile world, where a child has a difficulty coping and he or she may learn that venting anger and frustration through violence is satisfying and even rewarded.

Furthermore, research shows that children under the age of 7 have difficulty distinguishing reality from fantasy on television (Morison & Gardner 1978 cited in Carlsson & Feilitzen 1998, 67). In other words what seems unrealistic to a mature viewer may appear to be quite real to younger children.

It is assumed that a child with some psychological damage — still not very well defined — can be pushed into acts of mass violence (such as the Littleton massacres in Colorado) by being exposed to weapons, especially firearms and that he or sometimes she will be influenced to act out their violent fantasies by seeing certain films, internet messages, computer games or even listening to rap songs.

In other words, while most children in most cultures may not be influenced into solving problems with extreme violence, a small but as yet undefined percentage that already suffer some personality type of disorder may do so.

Television, the Number One Source of Entertainment

With at least one television set for seven out of every ten households on the planet, television has become the number one source of information. The television set is also the biggest selling consumer item in the world (Lamb 1997). Even in very poor countries, as soon as materially possible, a family will invest in a television set. Where there is no electricity, television will run with a generator and many families will gather around it. Where there are no means of getting national broadcasts, the VCR will be used to run cheap copies of imported movies.

In the West, there are hardly any households without at least one television set – 98% of the 95 million American homes have at least one television set and the television is on for more than 7 hours per day in the average US home (Carlsson & von Feilitzen 1998, 56). In

Australia, the figure is 100% and Europe is not far behind. But the most astonishing figures are from countries labeled poor only a few years ago. Vietnam's ownership is predicted to reach 70% by the year 2000, while over a quarter of Chinese household own one television set. Sales in China are up to 60,000 a day! India's ownership is one television set for every three households and it is estimated that 400 million people watch the Hindu series, the *Ramayana*. Only rural area and shantytowns of Africa are not expected to be as well served by the year 2000 (Lamb 1997).

However, television is not the only source of media entertainment.

In richer countries and among the privileged in poorer countries, children are replacing time they spent watching television with interactive electronic activities such as computer games or surfing the Internet.

Going to the cinema, usually in groups of friends, is still very popular and films often make long-lasting impression. We should note also that violence has entered the world of music, with some types of music directly calling for violent behavior, video clips that use violence sometimes completely unrelated to the song itself and the use of these video clips in rave parties that sanction the use of drugs.

Parental Guidance

Television, VCR and Internet are wonderful tools to spread information and educational material, notably among communities where a large majority of the population is illiterate or has little access to books. Images are, however, very powerful transmitter of messages, and the impression they give can be long lasting. Indiscriminate viewing can possibly have very negative consequences on children, especially the visualization of violence.

Should the blame for the so-called violent mass media effect be laid down squarely on the shoulders of *neglectful* parent, as the mass media industry would like us to believe, or do other factors play a more significant role?

The argument that neglectful parents allow their children to view more TV than non-neglectful parents is persuasive. Neglectful is taken here to mean parents who provide little home discipline. Neglectful parents may also suffer from more problems than non-neglectful parents.

There may be parents who are very neglectful because they are themselves heavy consumers of television. There are parents who have not been brought up in this environment and may not be aware of the influencing power of television. Parents who allow their children to spend too much time in front of the small screen may create conditions that facilitate access to too many violent programs.

The more time the child watch TV or plays on the Internet, the more chance he or she has of absorbing violent imagery and language. Children watch an average of 3 hours per day worldwide, according to a study of 5000 children in 23 countries rich and poor and on every continent. In Australia, another survey on 500 children indicated that they spent 3h10 minutes each day on electronic activities, 2h30 minutes on non-electronic leisure activity and 41 minutes on homework. A total of 33% of available time for leisure and homework was spent watching television – at least 2h30 per day (Nugent in Carlsson & von Feilitzen 1998, 224).

Educated mothers seem to be more discriminatory than poorly educated ones about what their children watch and the time they spend watching TV and are more willing to engage them into doing other things than watching TV. According to a study among Flemish households in Belgium, where average viewing is 15 hours a week for a child, children of unskilled fathers and less-well educated mothers watch for longer hours and stay up later watching television, while children of university-educated mothers watch the least and stop watching the earliest (Roe in Carlsson & von Feilitzen 1998, 242).

Nevertheless, in these richer countries with more than one television set present in a household and often one in a child's room, TV becomes a solitary activity. Thus, there is often no interaction with parents about what a child has seen and there is usually no positive criticism about scenes that may have disturbed the child.

Computer games and the use of the Internet are also activities that take place with little or no supervision from adults, sometimes a completely solitary activity, only occasionally with friends. Parents may feel their children need to become *computer literate* – the most successful businesspeople today are perceived as computer wizards, so the pressure in many households is to leave these children alone to learn about the intricacies of the selling and buying that goes on in the Internet. How many parents know which kind of world their children are spending their time on and what kind of individuals the child is connected to?

Parents, who show indifference to violent media imagery or who glorify weapon ownership or are entertained themselves by violent behavior, sow more confusion in the right-wrong messages children receive, because they will be even less opportunity for such children to obtain a clear vision of limits set by the rest of society.

Many children spend more time watching television than time spent on any other activity. There is ample opportunity for TV to become not only a great source of influence but also an addictive pastime, where the socialization process connecting them to children and adults in their neighborhood will be reduced. Children who do not learn how to solve problems dealing with relationships are probably more likely to adopt confrontational attitudes, even violence, when faced with a sudden problem or else take refuge in silence thus repressing feelings, which one day may explode into violence.

Other Effects Connected to Too much Time Spent in Front of a Screen

Too much time spent in front of a screen may has negative effects unrelated to even what is watched.

Hours spent watching television or sitting in front of a computer game thus robs a child of more important activities, such as socializing and playing with other children or spending time on creative projects.

Hours spent on a computer games and Internet may also have health and psychological consequences that we do not know yet. Quite apart from the choice of available violence on the Internet (internet is not violent in itself of course, it is the choice made by the viewer that determines which sites he/she will visit), there is the chemistry resulting from merely *surfing*. People who spend even only a few hours per week on the Internet have been found to have higher levels of depression than non-users. A two-year study on 169 subjects in Pittsburgh carried out by the Carnegie Mellon University showed that the people who used the Internet more were not the ones who were depressed or lonely at the start of the study, but those who were healthy; the decline in psychological well-being was highest in the latter. One hour per week on the Internet led to an average increase of 1 % on the depression scale.[117]

A newer study by Prof. Norman Nie at Standford University has implied that those addicted to Internet and e-mail also show less opportunity to emotion, have less time to interact with others and become more "lonely" despite more interactions with others on the screen.[118] It is precisely those who are or become *anti-social*, *lonely* and *depressed* who are at risk of becoming violent individuals.

A recent article on scholastic failure in the USA indicates, not surprisingly, that the amount of time watching TV is inversely correlated to the amount of time doing homework. Such studies show also that the longer immigrant children have lived in the USA, the less homework, they do, and the more TV they watch. "Recent-migrant" children watch less TV, do better at school and have higher aspirations. For example: 88 % percent of recent Mexican immigrant children thought school was "great," compared to 20 % of native-born Mexican-American children (whose parents presumably did not put as much emphasis on school results as did recent migrant, but would also let children watch more television).[119]

Scholastic failure or success has a direct effect on a child's self esteem and his/her hopes for the future. A child that does badly at school is more likely *to get into trouble*, to be drawn into gangs or undesirable groups of youngsters or even to drop out of school and spend time in the streets.

Watching something for too long on a screen may have some other medical effects as well. Several parents, scientists and physicians have come out in support of the theory that pulsating electromagnetic radiation, of the kind that television and computer screens give off, does lead to heightened aggressivity in children (among other symptoms) but this evidence is, so far, unconvincing. The radiation is supposedly more penetrating the nearer the person is to a cathode screen. Fifty minutes of exposure per day are sufficient for a one third decrease in scholastic test results among youngsters, a five-fold decrease in memorization and a three-fold increase in nervous or aggressive type behavior.

The Loiret report, published by a combined team of occupational health scientists and physicians from France, in conjunction with the report of Johansson & Aronsson, published by WHO,[120] confirms that after 4 hours of watching TV or playing on the computer, adrenaline secretion is modified and increased stress symptoms manifest themselves. According to these researchers, for every eight hours sitting before a computer screen it takes twelve hours for an adult to return to a more normal adrenaline pattern.

Parents' Choice of Programs and Conditioning

It is important to note that people, on the average, prefer to watch television program without violence," therefore "what drives media violence is not primarily popularity but global marketing... Products need a dramatic ingredient that requires no translation and fits as many cultures as possible. That ingredient is often violence (von Feilitzen, in Carlsson & Feilitzen 1998, 46).

The export market for violent films produced in the USA seems to be more lucrative than the internal market as it is. In addition, program production and purchase depend on advertisement revenues and advertisement fees are calculated according to the time of airing – *prime time* being the most expensive. In order to ensure the highest advertising fees, channels will prefer to show what they think will attract the largest audience and in order to make sure people zap to the required channel they will develop programs with characters that are easily recognized and liked by the public, such as soaps and action series. *Trailers* or advertisement for these coming action movies will be shown at different times of the day. They will contain a condensed version of the enthralling scenes and might appear to be even more violent for children who will see them out of context.

Even in countries where children's programs exist for part of the day, it is very likely that these children will also watch *family programs,* which are likely to depict scenes that are developed for an older audience.

Proposing less violence on television is a huge subject of controversy, not least because one can argue that real choice is no longer possible and that an objective answer can no longer be obtained, because the public in most countries around the world has already become conditioned to soap opera's and, more important here, to action series showing a great deal of violence.

So, do people watch what they like or are they conditioned to like what they see?

Globalization and Cultural Differences

Films, electronic games, television and music distributed largely by the USA, Europe and Japan reach to every corner of the world today. This globalization of information is bound to increase with a potential universal access to Internet. Welcome as all this is, especially for the less technologically advanced societies, some of this media content raises important questions, especially when imported products are brought in countries where individual violence is less common or fashionable.

A study by UNICEF (Lamb 1997) finds that home grown programs are successful in holding on to the majority of viewers. However, when production budgets are reduced, national broadcasters have to import products from outside, among them soaps but also action series, with a great deal of violence. Some of these are an incitation to copy the behavior of other people perceived as leading a more desirable lifestyle. Is the increase in violence now seen in European and Japanese schools a result of youths copying the more confrontational attitudes seen in many US programs?

Another phenomenon of globalization is that even when national broadcasters develop their own programs, they need to compete with the attraction of US made programs. Rather than developing original programs, they copy the program characters and adapt their attitudes to their cultural environment, hence more profusion of action movies with violence in countries where perhaps such depictions of aggressive behavior were not common. Thus, when the gurus of globalization speak of bringing light to others they may also be bringing imagery, which may increase copycat behavior of another country's television inspired violence.

News programs

We need to differentiate real violence for purpose of information from violent fiction that feeds the imagination. Newscasters have a duty to inform people about events that are happening in the world or among their own communities and the violence that is tied to these events.

However, it is also true that many news programs are manipulated by despots, to create hatred, intolerance or subversion. The use of the news media to incite people to violence was well illustrated in Rwanda and Yugoslavia (cf. Chapter 1, p. 31-33). In Rwanda, Radio-Television des Mille Collines was funded by an extremist Hutu. It became and essential propaganda tool for the onset of massacres of Tutsi, even stating in April 1993 that Tutsi cleansing should be done with by May 1993.[121] Serbian leader Slobodan Milosevic and Croatia's Franjo Tujman took over their media to broadcast reports of atrocities, months before the actual fighting and atrocities began. They fought their war first in people's mind. Hitler used the media with even more mastery. His appearances in beautiful surroundings were transmitted through the cinema to maximize the message of order, serenity and all bright

German future. Everything ugly, on the other hand, was juxtaposed with caricatures of Jews and other minorities.

Hate groups will increasingly use the Internet to spread messages in countries where they are not allowed to do so in the open. Children will surf the Internet to find them for first amusement and then maybe to join them.

The news business is also torn by two paradoxes: one is to report objectively on say, violence in a community and two is the fear that such reporting may actually incite people to more violence. Thus, in some countries, news on killings because of ethnic or religious differences are limited to short, bland broadcasts with no imagery (Algeria, Egypt in the 1990s). Perhaps they are not wrong to do so. For speaking and showing too much of violence, especially ethnic, religious or youth violence, may lead to more of it.

Take the following situation: the French Ministry of Education chose to promote 20 September 1996 as a day in which every school in France held a two-hour debate on school violence. It was so heavily promoted by all five French television channels that children and teachers who spoke on camera about the problem became, in turn, victims of violent acts by adolescents wanting either to show off or to punish the *snitchers* who complained about them. The news project thus created new violence.[122] In the USA, several youngsters accused of firing on fellow students have also implied that they wished to be on the nightly news.

Children copy other children, especially if this may allow for a few minutes of fleeting fame. The dramatic rise in school violence in most industrialized countries may be partly due to this. School violence in France has doubled in a space of 5 years according to the National Education Ministry officials and the number of children expelled from classes in the UK for bad behavior rose from about 2,500 in 1990, to 12,000 in 1995-6. The number of teachers retiring early doubled in the same period.[123] While this may partly be due to tougher new measures and an educational reform introduced in 1990 that led to bigger classes (of some 30 students), the vast majority of teachers complain that *the environment* has become more stressful and violent, pointing out that even girls now resolve disputes by engaging in physical violence and that offensive weapons are being increasingly used. Many decry the violence in the mass media as the main influence for this type of bad behaviors. The young choose schools to act out their violence because that is where they meet for most of the time. Since the small screen is now the only other place they find themselves, the school and the small screen are linked as playground arena and entertainment center.

In Japan, the situation of school violence has become even more dramatic, because the traditional image of orderly, disciplined students has been shattered in the past five or six years with an explosion of school violence. In 1998 alone, cases of school violence rose 25.7% compared to the year before. A total of 29,685 cases of school violence were reported from all three tiers of the school system (primary, junior high and middle schools). Many of the incidents were between students but even the much-respected Japanese teacher has become a target of violence with a 19,2% rise in aggressions against teachers in 1998.[124]

A balanced paper by Kodaira, quoting the results of research on media violence in Japan, relates this increasing violence seen in Japanese schoolchildren to a number of causes. "Many TV programs feature at least one scene that use *ijime* (bullying) as a source of humor." Personal and mass media seemed to function as sources of learning bullying behavior. It was concluded that controlling bullying behavior on television was necessary (Sasaki & Muto 1987, cited by Kodaira in Carlsson & Feilitzen 1998, 90).

Sports Programs

Sports can be very violent; Combat sports such as wrestling, especially the more chaotic forms with little rules have influenced children to behave in the same way. As far back as 1954, professional wrestling was banned from Japanese national TV network as some school children were seriously injured and one even killed trying to imitate the wrestlers (Kodaira in Carlsson & Feilitzen 1998, 81). In Israel, children were injured when they tried to copy the antics of some violent sports they saw on television (Lemish in Carlsson & Feilitzen 1998, 136).

Men, and a few women, have always enjoyed watching violent sports — from the days of antiquity in ancient Rome to today. The sports theater of ancient Rome were usually built at a convenient distance from other government buildings for fear of even then of *hooligans*. While we decry today, gladiators, bear fighting, cockfights and the like, they were popular with both men and women until quite recently even in Europe.

Women are also pressured to take up violent sports, especially in the USA. See for instance the passion with which men and other women now view women's boxing![125]   The television sports channels have been the prime moves behind the push for more violent sports involving both women and men because this is a huge moneymaker. Women are also taking an increasing part in combat sports such as karate, because fighting skills that do not depend on pure strength but also dexterity, gives them the self-confidence to defend themselves in case of need. The Amazon of old with her bow and arrows disappeared with the advent of strong heavy arms, but she is coming back today, at least in films. Indeed, one of the most desolating experiences is the number of essentially US made movies and TV films, which show women as aggressive and violent perpetuators of murder. (Will this replace the *calming* effect women traditionally had on male's violence?)

Fantasy and Storytelling

"Conflict and strife are the essence of drama and often result in psychological or physical violence." So said the presidents of TV chains in their first line of 15-point guidelines about violence on television (Guggenheim 1993).

Stories are needed to feed our imagination, as well as to channel our emotions. Story telling is as old as the world. It plays on our fears and need to be comforted, to our identification with good or evil heroes. Stories were orally transmitted, passed down in book form for countless generations, but today they are in images, far more explicit, leaving less room for the imagination to create its own interpretation.

Stories are also important to channel negative feelings and the thirst for revenge. Many people — children included — fantasize about causing serious harm or even killing someone they do not like. The old fairy tales point to a continuing concern with all this. They are important to vent feelings of frustration, fear and misery.

The amount of time spent watching violent scenes and stories is not only at an all time peak, but it has also modified traditional story telling which incorporated culturally determined notions of right and wrong. Folk stories and fairy tales related to a child by a respected peer adult mark the boundaries of acceptable behavior. The presence of the adult also allowed the child to ask questions and to express his or her anxieties and rears regarding a story line to a protecting adult. But watching even fairy tales in an animated cartoon is not the same thing. First the presence of the adult is no longer needed or when present he/she may not want to be interrupted. There is a passive intake of violent scenes. Secondly, unease or insecurity that could arise from the story line has less chance of being expressed and consequently more chance of becoming a repressed phobia that may have later consequences. Finally and most importantly, the sheer volume of violent acts and scenes observed on the screen may overwhelm the child's imagination and thinking about why a certain outcome came about or about the lesson to be learnt.

Violent Sensations & Humor

At the 1997 Cannes Film Festival, the film director, Wim Wenders made the succinct observation, that, "Today's films don't discuss violence. They make use of violence."

A race is on to be the first to come out with some original scene or implement of violence. A story describing the setting on fire of a woman's pubic hair has not only been published but was prominently advertised in a major American newspaper. It will soon be adapted for showing on the screen. A TV mini-series made in Hollywood has shown a mass-murderer cut the spinal chord of his (female) victims so that they could slowly suffocate to death while being conscious all the time.

Children will seek the thrills of screen violence if such programs are available. Just as in storytelling the frisson of fear and suspense may be useful for character development and morality. Yet, too much emphasis on thrill seeking may indicate a disturbed personality. The more aggressive the child, the more he or she will enjoy watching violent films. A study of 5,000 children from 23 countries in 1996-1997 shows that 51 % of children from high aggression neighborhoods preferred "innovative" aggressive media heroes, whereas 37 % from low aggression neighborhoods did so. Globally, 88 % of the children surveyed knew of Arnold Schwarzenegger's *Terminator (*Groebel *reporting about UNESCO's* study in Carlsson & Feilitzen 1998, 181-199). Probably, the more innovative the degree of violence, the more satisfying it is for highly aggressive children. There is also a universal appeal for highly individualistic action heroes that master the most intricate weaponry.

Going to the cinema is still an attractive option for young people all over the world. People between the ages of 14 to 30 represent the major category of moviegoers. It is a socialization process, especially for groups of young men. This is especially so for films where fear, thrill and eroticism intermingle. Producers are well aware of the potential of this market and develop films which they hope will become *cult films* and be seen over and over again, such as *Clockwise Orange* or *Pulp Fiction*.

In many countries of the developing world, cinema is still more popular than TV but, unfortunately, the most violent B-movies seem to have the most popular and the widest distribution in the third world, as any visitor to these countries can attest. What should be shown or not shown in such films? Some critics require a line to be drawn that cannot be drawn, since audiences and cultures all differ. In addition, what may be humorous to one set of people may be considered unsettling violence to another. A few years ago in an open-air movie theatre in Jakarta, my wife and I were shocked by scenes of brutality in a B-movie, which had the mostly male Indonesian audience laughing hysterically... Humorous violence? Movie role models showing violence as fun, and video games where you kill and are rewarded for killing, blur concepts of what is allowed and not allowed when one gets angry or needs *to get even.* The new universal hero could be anyone who mixes violence with humor. Still, even if we allow humorous violence to continue — as it probably should — we should try to ensure that scenes depicting new weaponry, sadism, violent pornography and ethnic stereotyping, and so on, be severely limited. The most dangerous form of screen violence may be the one showing humor as violent acts are committed.

Movie role models showing violence as fun and video games where you *kill* and are rewarded for so doing, blur concepts of what is and is not allowed when one is angry.

Film Heroes as Role Models

Action films need to have an attractive central figure that can inspire young people to imitate him or her. The central figures are powerful men who solve problems though their sheer physical strength rather than their brains. They are the modern Robin Hoods or Zorros, often operating on the borderlines of criminality. Even if the hero is a policeman, he takes liberties with the official code of conduct. There is thus an increasing ambiguity about what is *lawful or unlawful.* Does this increase the confusion in a child's mind about what is right and what is wrong?

The films are characterized by rapid action, the use of powerful weapons and explosives, explicit language with increasingly profanities. Furthermore, the camera works in such a way that the spectator sees the action as if he was in the shoes of the hero. He is made to feel he is facing danger, giving the blows and receiving them without feeling pain.

Film producers look for a hero that can become a cult hero and then, if successful, a series of movies will follow with the same highly desirable hero. Each new film is heavily advertised and creates some kind of fever. In 1999, young Europeans, who could afford it, took the plane to New York to be the first to see the release of the latest Star Treck, others spent a lot of money to buy badly pirated copies of the film or spent hours on the internet to have a copy charged to their computer.

The young increasingly regard violent individuals portrayed on the screen, both hero's and villains, with awe. That is, they would like to be capable of defending themselves, hurting others or being as quick as the screen hero is in response to violence.[126] Children and young people will more likely cite as someone they want to be a film hero than anyone in real life. They will dress like their heroes, copy their speech and attitudes. What is surprising is the identification not just with heroes, but also with the villains and the bad elements in the screenplay.

Desensitization to Violence

Conditioned by repeated exposures to violent scenes, a child gets used to violence and considers it a normal part of life. Desensitization may lead to a greater appetite to see violence or even to commit violence. Producers of action movies will need to escalate the level of violence in order to produce the same impression on the spectator. Another result of desensitization is an increasing callous attitude towards the pain of others. The harm done to others may not be understood because the limits of what is acceptable and not acceptable have been pushed too far.

Before finishing elementary school, the average US child is said to have watched 8,000 murders and 100,000 acts of violence on screen. This will lead that young American to believe that violence is the only mean to resolve conflicts (would we have let him watch 8000 scenes of sexe?)[127] The most popular children's cartoons — *Bugs Bunny and Pals* (TNT Network) and the *Tom & Jerry Kids* (Fox Network) — show as much as 68 and 88 violent acts per hour respectively. In December 1993, a MTV poll conducted by telephone on 800 audience members aged 16-29 found that violence is the most crucial concern facing young people. It also revealed that 44% of the men in the poll owned a gun, that almost half of the teenagers not owning a gun were considering purchasing one in the next year and that two out of three felt they could easily obtain one. Drugs, the economy, unemployment and lack of moral values were the leading causes of violence according to the respondents. In South Bend, Indiana, a survey of 2,508 students from 96 schools revealed that 40% of them knew someone who had been killed or injured by a gun.[128] By the age of 18, the American child will have watched 40,000 murders and 200,000 acts of violence, according to the American Medical Association.[129]

There is also the content, the degree of violence shown. Thirty years ago, very few children had ever seen images of someone being shot, knifed, blown up or raped in front of their bare eyes. Now, the likelihood of a young toddler not seeing such scenes, even very occasionally is remote.

Explicit scenes and tales of murder and mayhem may accentuate the fantasies of those already attracted to sado-masochistic behavior and as with any strong fantasy some, perhaps very few, will then want to act them out. Perhaps there were even more such murders than today. However, now one can state with certainty that the age threshold for violent acts especially those involving shooting is suddenly much lower today than at any time in the past, including a decade ago. Could it be that in terms of content, impact and numbers, many more people are more *desensitized* than hitherto? Have we reached a state of mass culture that provides too much opportunity for desensitization?

Boys and Girls differs

Functional aggression, that is violence related to defense of family, to exploration of distant and hostile lands, to defending one's honor and life has been the stuff of heroes since man began to tell stories. Women have both understood and applauded this kind of necessary violence. But today, we also see much of what Groebel calls *destructive aggression*, that is mass murder, hedonistic torture, humiliation and so on which cannot be explained in terms of survival. It is often these forms of destructive aggression that appeal to boys but rarely to girls (in Carlsson & Feilitzen 1998, 185).

Nevertheless, girls and boys may be influenced by the opposite genders reaction to violence on the screen. Thus, whom you watch a TV movie with is important in terms of how to express your reaction. The type of hero shown also appeals differently to boys and girls. Girls are most sympathetic to violence if it is from an attractive character that is acting benevolently and not out of just cruelty (Zillman, Weaver, Murdorf & Aust 1986).

Dorf Zillman of the University of Alabama divided a sample of viewers in a laboratory setting into those who were exposed to violent movies for a prolonged period of time (daily for a week) and another sample who, over the same period of time, viewed only non-violent movies. He found that women, regardless of personality, are upset but not in awe by prolonged exposure to violence. Men, by contrast, were clearly influenced. Those with "non-emphatic, callous personalities, increased their endorsement of violent resolution of conflict, while men who had previously scored high on empathy tests, rejected violence even more strongly than before viewing the movies, as a way of resolving conflict" (Guggenheim 1993, 32). Thus, according to the author, the effects of exposure on men are not uniform but depend on personality. His research also indicates to me that violent behavior in men who are by nature violent may be reinforced, when viewing such films. Hence, the conclusion that those already of a violent disposition may be made more violent by watching violent movies. The same phenomenon may be true for girls who are inherently violent.

Little boys and girls have always enjoyed violent fairy tales. At some point however, either the physiological changes taking place in young girls or group influence make them turn away from watching or enjoying violent sports and movies. Is this change a physiological one tied up with the secretion of female hormones in larger quantities? It may be interesting to compare enjoyment of violent sports or movies between two groups of girls: one, pre-adolescent and the other, after puberty has occurred.

Sexual aggression

This is once again something that has to be seen both in a historical and cultural context. Soft porn is no longer poor taste in most industrialized countries, but hard pornography is (although the distinctions are increasingly blurred!) What is however both poor taste and dangerous is the increasing linkage between hardcore pornography and "snuff" (real killing and torture videos and adult, usually male acquiescence to owing, sharing and selling such movies).

A vivid example of the effect of a violent movie on subsequent violent behavior was the recent rape of a 5-year-old girl by an eleven year American boy who claimed he was "turned on" by the pornographic cassette his parents had omitted to remove from the TV set.[130] Other examples are the advertisements on the Internet for child pornography, snuff movies and films showing women being forced into sex.

In the USA, 4,524 rapes were committed in 1994 by children aged 18 and below, almost three times the 1985 figure. Some attribute this increase to the increase in sex scenes shown on TV and the easier accessibility for the young of pornographic or sexually explicit films, videos and computer games. In any case, a recent survey in the USA of 2,500 hours of cable TV, less regulated than network TV, reveals that 57 % of the programs shown contain scenes of violence, of which 73 % go unpunished, including many that show males striking females, or females harming males.[131]

In Britain about 40% of sexual abuse was committed by children on other children (cf. Chapter 2). We do not know if this proportion of child abuse by other children always existed or whether it has increased because of greater permissiveness. However, some of the reports from Kodaiva in Japan seem to indicate that much of the increased violence of a sexual nature in Japan may have come about from an increased exposure to sexually violent programs on TV and the Internet. Certainly the Japanese penchant for *Eroduction*, where some magazines, comics, films and videos relishing showing young girls being forced into sex (and enjoying it) is not a healthy development for women.

Control of Violence in Television

Even in the United States, that great producer and marketer of such films, where the First Amendment and private enterprise reign supreme, where freedom to view and carry arms is so valued by so many... — there is an increasingly vocal (some say, effective) lobby, which has convinced politicians, some people in the media, and even some liberal as well as conservative leaning groups that things have got out of hand and that some control is now necessary. A poll commissioned by the Center for Media Education and taken in August 1995 shows that 80 % of American parents believe there are "good reasons to regulate children's television more strictly." As causes for dissatisfaction, 43 % cited violence and 25 % insufficient educational programs. Forty-five percent believed that current programs on commercial TV were having a (undefined) "negative" influence on children, with 10 % saying "very negative"; only 23 % believed current programming is having a positive effect, a meager 6 % saying "very positive." The questions were put to 514 men and 513 women in a random digit dial national sample.

A telling aspect: most respondents blamed movies, television networks and advertisers for the problem — 41 % blaming the networks, 27 % the advertisers — while only 16 % held viewers themselves responsible for the lack of quality. Television and film producers have usually said that it is the viewer that asks for, or is most entertained, by these types of programs and they, like the advertisers "who know their business" are only responding to "demand".

Still, we should note that with the multiplicity of technological inventions involving the use of interactive programs and cable and Internet access, the State, as guardian of morals and discipline, is less and less capable of taking action. Ditto, parents.

Individual responsibility thus increases on the part of the young, to limit their own access and involvement, which calls in turn for better education directed to even very young children about the *pros* and *cons* of mass media. The fact that most American kids now have a TV, a video recorder and a computer in their own rooms is disquieting. Not only will they have spent more time in front of a screen than in a classroom by the time they finish school, but in addition they will have less time to interact with adults or other peers, less likelihood of listening and debating "values" with their parents and more time to brood alone.

While attempts have been made in most industrialized countries to have the most violent programs shown late at night, cinema has no such constraints. The age limits as to who gets to watch what, are mainly for sexually explicit films — nothing stops a 12- or 14-year old in most countries from seeing the most brutal and sadistic movies. If girls and boys are supposedly at risk of influence from watching soft porn, why aren't they for hard-core violence? Since some naively believe they copy what they see in soft core porno films, does it not follow that they will sometimes emulate what they see in violent movies? And incidentally, girls will watch violent films on the cinema screen more than on TV simply because this represents an outing with their boyfriends. Home videos and pay cable are also more attractive to young people than the usual TV fare — precisely where the access of young people seems least regulated. A study recently done at UCLA also revealed that children's TV programs now contain even more violence than adult prime time programs; deaths are not necessarily shown, but a lot of fighting is, on Saturday mornings (TV violence monitoring project, UCLA Center for Communication Policy, Los Angeles, Oct. 1995).

Professor Leon Eron (Guggenheim 1993, 2) of the University of Michigan claims that even after a meeting of the Surgeon General's Scientific Advisory Committee (of which he was a member), with the presidents of ABC, NBC and CBS, all promising to do something about the problem, TV violence was not reduced during either prime time hours or the usual hours when children watched TV. Six months later, in time for Christmas of 1992, they did issue "guidelines", and thankfully some of the violent scenes their chains glorified in were reduced — but these guidelines did not affect the cable TV companies, whose share of the market jumped from 20 % to around 40 % a few months later. Neither cinema nor video or computer games industries were so affected; they continue to portray the most sadistically innovative scenes. The whole question of what to control and how sometimes pales in comparison to the arguments about what type of controls are needed.

Thus, to control content in mass media that is watched even by children raises the problem of freedom of expression. Furthermore, one culture's poison could be another culture's energy drink. Thus, a universal code may be too difficult to create although clearly movies, which show too many details on how to create a weapon of mass destruction or showing the rape of another human being, are universally condemned and not allowed. Yet from that to controlling the production and viewing of movies showing other acts of cruelty and mayhem is a big step. Too high for most commercial studios to take at present.

A Moral Conclusion

Violence on the screen is often portrayed without much attention to about how much harm is done to the victim.

A three-year study "National Television Violence Study" examined the amount and way in which violence is portrayed across 23 channels in the USA. The proportion of violent programs increased overall from 58% in 1994/95 to 61% in 1995/96. Premium cable channels showed the highest number of violent programs at prime-time (85%). Concerning the way in which violence is portrayed, note that 75% of violent scenes contained no remorse, criticism or penalty for the aggression and 55% no form of injuries. Note also that strong anti-violence themes appeared in only 4 % of the shows and the long-term consequences of violence appeared in only 15 %. The conclusion after 6,000 hours of programs from 23 channels between 0600 and 2300 hrs was: "TV violence as portrayed poses a serious risk of harm to children." (Carlsson & Feilitzen 1998, 65). The evidence of serious harm to children still needs to be shown despite all that is been said. For example, the fact that forty percent of the violence was initiated by the *good* characters, to whom children can identify. So did the Greek heroes behave in Iliad and Odysseus!

The Hollywood producer Martin Scorsese has made a film entitled *Casino*. Audiences of over 12 years of age are admitted. In a space of two hours, one can witness some quite original ways of killing — gangsters are shown squashing the victim's head in a vice, burying another victim alive after hitting him with a steel rod, beating to a pulp with baseball bats, knifing others with all sorts of pointed objects, breaking necks, slitting throats, shooting and so on. After watching the 12th such murder, I lost count after about 50 minutes of viewing time, so, as the film went on for another 70 minutes, I can assume that 30-40 beatings, blows and killings may have been seen in 2 hours.

But of more interest is what I would call poor taste influencing others to be in poor taste. Martin Scorsese is said to have shown all this because he wanted audiences "to see how bad violence was, how he abhorred violence!"[132] In a court of law would he be found guilty of inciting psychopathic behavior? And acquitted for reason of normality or insanity? Or that he is merely showing things that are distasteful to someone like me?

Could it be that there are individuals in Hollywood studios, with a syndrome for violence that could be labeled as pathological? Or has the demand for such movies created such a financial windfall that individuals with some inherent artistry in exploiting the most violent scenes become the cherished darling of an indulgent and generous studio?

Do some societies entrust the making of some films, videos and TV programs to individuals who are mentally immature in some way, all in the name of entertainment talent? If we consider that a mark of arrested or slow development may be a penchant for childish fantasies or bouts of violent behavior, then we may be seeing a phenomenon whereby those with a particular talent for transposing violent drama to the screen are in fact those who are still at some childhood development stage. So, some of the filmmakers may be acceptable to these more childish cultures than to cultures who are more mature or *adult*. When they say, in standard response to criticism, that they are providing what their audience wants, they may be right after all...

It is interesting to note that whereas 80% of the French are reported to think that there is too much violence on TV executives and producers are adamant in saying that the public want and enjoy these ratings-evaluated programs. [133] The reason such a discrepancy is interesting lies in the fact that culturally, it may be judged fashionable or desirable to decry TV violence, nonetheless, deep down, people identify with, or enjoy dramatic plays where some violence is portrayed. Is this true for all cultures? I fear it is and where money is to be made from all this, it will become more widespread.

Newspaper Sources and Other Quotations

116 In the USA of course the threat of massive payments as a result of lawsuits limits the question of admitting responsibility for anything.

117 *International Herald Tribune,* 31 Aug. 1998; *The American Psychologist*, Sept. 1998

118 John Markoff. "Logging on causes many to drop out of society." NY Times Services, reproduced in *International Herald Tribune,* 17 Feb. 2000.

119 *The Economist*, 17 Feb. 1996.

120 *Geneva Home Information Bulletin*, 12 Sept. 1996, 3.

121 « Mille Collines, les ondes qui tuent.» *Le Monde*, 21 July 1994.

122 *International Herald Tribune,* 14 Feb. 2000.

123 *International Herald Tribune,* 19-20 Oct. 1996.

124 Juliet Hindell. "Japan grapples with a breakdown in discipline in class.*" International Herald Tribune,* 14 Feb. 2000.

125 There are 5,000 professionals already, *Playboy*, Dec. 1996.

126 School Violence Supplement. *International Herald Tribune,* 14 Feb. 2000.

127 Olivier Peretié. "Faut-il inculper Hollywood d'assassinat?" *Le Nouvel Observateur*, 13-18 October 1994, citing Mark Owen, Congressman of New Jersey.

128 From a non-referenced article I received entitled, "The Role of Media on Youth Violence" by Edenn Sarino..

129 *International Herald Tribune,* 14 Feb. 2000.

130 *Tribune de Genève*, 9 March 1996)

131 ibid

132 *Femina magazine*, Lausanne, 11 March 1996

133 *Tribune de Genève*, 30 October 1996

Epilogue

By focusing on factors that can lead a child to become a young criminal or a violent adult, the preceding account may seem overly pessimistic. The majority of children will emerge as healthy adults from the period of adolescence. They will be more conscious of living if not in a global village, at least in a more cohesive community of nations where certain injustices will not be as tolerated as before.

We have come a long way from the days of public executions and unfettered cruelty to other human beings. More and more elected leaders and even some who are not must now indicate their concerns and positions regarding the treatment of minorities, of women and children. Poorer countries' performances in this realm are used as a condition for international aid. In the 1990s, the world decided to interfere in the internal affairs of countries where human rights were violated by governments. International tribunals can now convict leaders accused of genocides or crimes against humanity. The media is a powerful tool to sensitize people about what is happening both within a specific country, as well as in whole areas of the world. Despite its risks, The Internet is also a powerful tool of communication and denunciation about pedophiles, sadists and fringe groups advocating violence. Women are better aware of their rights and more little girls go to school than ever before learning to think more for themselves. In richer countries at least, children's suffering and feelings of alienation are being listened to more than in preceding generations. Dysfunctional families are receiving more assistance. Great advances in health care, immunization, better family planning, literacy and education have taken place in the past twenty-five years at a pace few of us even in the business of development would have predicted in the 1970s.

But against this background are dangers. In the year 1990 alone, the World Health Organisation (WHO March 1997) calculated that there were 2 million violent deaths around the world, 800,000 recorded suicides, almost 600,000 recorded homicides and a half-million deaths from civil unrest or wars. I do not know how they got these numbers, but I'm glad someone is counting. Better still would be an annual public report listing the most violent countries including those where child suicides and child violence are highest.

Like the physicians of old, we are still hobbled by modesty, superstitions, fears and accusations about the reasons for the different forms violence takes. Yet like an epidemic with multiple foyers of infection we cannot effectively tackle the problem of violence in one country, without looking at its trajectory in others. Looking at violence only in one's culture while not understanding others' is contemptuous – and shortsighted. In still too many countries, children as young as 10 or 11 are used as child soldiers and killers, or as drug dealers and prostitutes. The ages get younger and their access to sophisticated weaponry more common. In South Africa and the United States, we hear of children killers as young as six shooting others.

In Europe the situation of child violence has not reached the level of destruction it has in America in part because of the lesser accessibility to firearms, but it is in the increase. In France, the use of violence in petty crimes, most of which are carried out by teenagers, rose by 40% from 1994 to 1999 and by 141% in the Paris area.[134] In Japan, juvenile crime rose by 14% between 1996 and 1997. Even there, a long time haven of dutiful and peaceful children, there is a growing trend in violent crime by youngsters aged 14-19.[135] Ministry of Education officials and teachers have also just put out another report confirming the fact that attacks on teachers and students have never seemed to be so frequent, a new phenomenon in Japanese society.

To control the rise in child criminality and delinquency, authorities waver between prevention and punishment. Does that justify the mentality of someone like Texas State Representative, Jim Pitts who was introducing a bill in the state legislature to make 11-year olds eligible for the death penalty? Even the Governor of California, Pete Wilson suggested that he might support death eligibility for 14 year olds.[136]

Detention centers and prisons should be more humane. Recidivism for violent youngsters crowding UK jails is said to be as high as 80% two years after release. People should come out of jail not only having paid their due to society but possessing the tools to become useful and more involved citizens. A country's ranking in development terms can surely be partly based on past convicts' rate of rehabilitation.

Minimizing Violence as a Response to Anger and Frustration

The rise in the number of serious crimes and suicides by youths or ever younger children nearly everywhere in the world is a call for attention on the part of children who feel alienated from society and are angry. Aggressive children typically see themselves as victims.

Children have a huge ego and derive satisfaction from knowing they can be successful in love, play and work, but they also think of the future and have aspirations to become like their parents or better than their parents. When they are discriminated against from the start, when they are made to feel they cannot succeed, then they get frustrated and angry. Some of that anger has been the one of the ingredients for some wonderful success stories, but it is also the ingredient for self-destruction and revenge, hence violence. Unhappy and violent children will find solace with other unhappy and violent children or with people all too ready to exploit them. They will gain self-esteem through risk taking, bravado and even acts of barbarity.

I also make the distinction in this book about people who might be born with a certain degree of aggressivity in them, due to certain environmental or biological reasons, and those who become violent in the course of their lives, but my point is that in either case there are ways to minimize the anger and rage. One way is by not adding humiliation to humiliation, that leads to more rage. The interrelationship of rage, power and aggression has been well established (cf. Glick & Roose 1995; Dollard, Doob & Miller 1939; as well as Lewis and Haviland 1993).

Discrimination and Tolerance

Tolerance and full acceptance of the other's differences is a slow and on-going process that needs constant attention. In many countries steps have been taken to ensure full participation of all minority groups despite differences in religion, race, gender or sexual orientation. While much more remains to be done in these countries, they are slowly but surely leading the way to a more tolerant world. Yet hatred about the others is still being instilled in children at early ages.

Many studies have shown that it is impossible to link a violent disposition to a race, rather it is the discrimination suffered by a group at a particular period, whether it was the Irish at turn of the century New York, the Palestinians in today's occupied territories or Tamils in Sri Lanka that leads them to adopt violent tactics. Once a group reaches a certain level of respectability, behaviors change and aggressivity is channeled to other less violent occupations.

The growing child is easily receptive to stories and histories that parents provide him or her. If these are too negative, if they include too much in the form of past injustices and frustrations, of fears and prejudices, they poison a child's brain and can affect his future behavior. Repetitive tales of past frustrations and humiliations lead to anger and bitterness, then open violence.

Here is an example of how hatred can be instilled in an innocent child's mind: Barry Bearak, a New York Times journalist, was interviewing a man in a refugee camp in Macedonia in 1999. The father was trying to convince the journalist how even his five year old son hated the Serbs. The confused boy first said: "Serbs are good" (presumably wanting to please the foreign journalist). "But, who stole our money, burned our house, stole our car?" The father exclaimed. In answer to his father furious cues, the boy answers: "the filthy Serbs." The father then continues: "And what should you do if you meet a Serb like Milosevic?" "I will kill him," the boy dutifully replies to his father beaming with pride.[137]

Another example is South Africa. It is today one of the most violent countries on the globe. The white minority instituted the system of apartheid out of a sense of exclusivity and racial superiority enjoyed by migrant European Huguenots, who had in turn been discriminated against in a largely intolerant and catholic Europe. Apartheid led to the despair, isolation and disintegration of many of South Africa's black population, which found a certain solace in a high consumption of alcohol. Alcoholism leads to high rates of fetal brain damage and anti-social behavior. Many children thus suffer from the alcoholism of their parents. Many then grow up to become rapists and murderers. Some of their principal victims are now the whites who allowed this to happen or did little to change the system. The circle is complete but the suffering goes on.

Exploitation and Greed

Many children become hostages to forms of exploitation and materialism that have been put into place by greed, that says every man is for himself. Yet communism has not fared better in curbing greed once its shackles are removed as we see in present Russia and its former satellites. I am reminded here of what Edgar Morin a reformed French communist, is reported to have once said: "Marxism, my friend has studied economics and the social classes. That's marvelous, my friend. But it forgot to study humanity" (Braudel 1995,340-341). Are we going to be accused one day by our descendants of also forgetting about humanity?

Greed is also fueling some of the drug trade, particularly that of cocaine. Heroin and cocaine use among white youth climbed about 300 percent over the two decades before the 1990's in the USA alone. For black youth, it jumped to a staggering 13 times the rate twenty years before.

And too many countries, notably the Philippines, Thailand, Sri-Lanka, Nepal and Colombia, also allow another type of Western (and Japanese) export to their countries, pedophiles and prostitution merchants. Why do their leaders moan so much about it being a result of poverty instead of really cracking down on many of the known local accomplices that furnish these children to foreigners and local men?

How to control the immense profits from the violence of the drug and sexual exploitation trade? More and more exposure is needed and international trade, commerce and development organizations must be mobilized to provide sanctions to any country allowing such unfettered exploitation.

Women

I have tried in this book to lift some of the taboos involved in admitting that women can also be a source of violence, but I may have not emphasized enough that they are by far, the most common victims of violence. Violence done to women is a violation of their rights and often a disregard of their right to physical integrity. In addition, the sight of a mother being beaten up or abused affects children, especially male children, who can in turn become brutal and violent adolescents. It is a problem especially in societies where there is insufficient discussion about the concept of spouse abuse and the magnitude of the situation.

Take for example, the following data about domestic violence in Eastern Europe: In Romania, 29% of the women admitted to the Forensic Hospital in Bucharest were beaten by an intimate partner. Of the 89 murders committed in Romania in the first few months of 1995, 44 victims or 49% were women killed by their male partners. As for Albania, 20% of women interviewed considered killing themselves to escape from their partners' violence (Stephenson 1996).

The situation may be nearly as bad in some richer countries. Thus, a 1996 Swiss government study on 1500 women aged between 20 and 60 showed that around 40% had suffered abuse at the hands of their lovers or spouses during the previous six months. One in five of these women said they had been raped. An earlier study showed that 32% of 1000 adolescent girls in Geneva had suffered some sort of sexual abuse and that nationally, this figure was close to 25%.[138] Can we only guess at what the magnitude of such abuse is around the rest of the world? The magnitude of abuse of women – and children of course – is only slowly getting into the open. It is an epidemic that we need to learn how to control. Women and children need to be empowered to fight against such abuse and perpetrators of such violence need to be made aware that their behavior is no more acceptable.

The media is a powerful tool to sensitize people to a problem and to change mentalities. In 1997, the Advertising Standards Authority of the UK[139] issued warnings to advertising agencies about the number of advertisements in which men were being demeaned or brutalized by women. An example of "Girl Power" advertisement shows a woman wearing stiletto heels, with her toes shown placed on a nude man's buttocks. Another advertisement for an automobile shows a man clutching painfully his crotch, with a smiling woman and a text saying: "Ask before you borrow it (the car)." There is also an advertisement, which shows a woman flushing a whole series of men down a toilet, courtesy of special effects.[140]

The portrayal of the modern aggressive women as a fighter, mass murderer or sadist may also discredit the traditional role of pacificator usually attributed to women. In play, if a girl gets hurt, the game stops while the other girls comfort the one who has been injured. For boys, the injured one is supposed to leave the playing field and the game continues regardless. Thus, girls need the web of *connectedness* and when they are older and they don't get it, especially if they are in need of comfort, their *trauma* or suffering may become more severe. We should try not only to provide more affection to our children, but also to transmit to both boys and girls the message that it is essential to be aware of the harm they may be doing to themselves and others rather than believing toughness and insensitivity are *cool*.

Despite their increasing political and economic role, women remain the prime caretaker of children and from studies shown the major influence on infant.

Listening to Children from Rich Countries

In 1999, the former American HEW Secretary, Joseph Califano said that in 10 years there has been a 114% increase in the number of abused and neglected children, up from 1.4 million in 1986, to 3 million in 1997.[141] Experts can predict which families will have violent children. Furthermore, aggressive children typically see themselves as victims and almost all have had aggressive or neglectful parents. Children who at age five were rated as aggressive or impulsive were much more likely to be violent adults.

We can also predict other things:

According to a Washington Post-ABC News poll of teenagers after the Littleton, Colorado, school killings, many teenagers believe they know students who might be troubled enough to cause a shooting rampage in their school. About a *third* of the students interviewed, said they have heard a student threaten to kill someone. *Four out of ten* say they know students troubled enough to be potential killers. A *fifth* of the students personally know someone who has brought a gun to school.

About *half* are growing up in homes with guns and *more than half* say it would be easy for them to lay their hands on one. *Two in three* say it would be easy for them to get information on how to make a bomb. Finally, 40% of these students think their school has the potential for an incident similar to the Littleton shootings.[142]

Let's also teach children that when they become parents they must spend time with their children and advise young people about the responsibilities and problems of both parenthood *and marriage*. Violence may have something to do with the stress that unborn children inherit in the womb of many women, who are lonely, neglected, angry or fearful. The reduction of this stress revolves around the better monitoring and support of pregnant women. Perhaps, we should also be more concerned about what we eat or don't eat and where we live, as this also affects our unborn children. Better networks, support groups, educational programs and better care for future mothers' mental and physical needs are needed in order to take the void left by the disappearance of the extended family.

I debunk some theories linking poverty to violence. It is not poverty in itself, but the gap between those who seem to have it all and those who feel they have no chance to get it all, that breeds frustration and anger. Prosperity is not a security against domestic aggression, as some battered wives of rich suburban America can confide, or as children born rich who are ignored or humiliated or pushed too hard to succeed by their parents.

Still poverty should not be equated with lack of opportunities. Better emotional support, better housing, play and shopping areas, better teachers and these unsung heroes, social workers of various types are desirable, especially those who have leadership capabilities and are young. These people deserve a decent salary and national recognition.

Also important is the beautification of housing, play and recreation centers in poor income areas. Low density housing to be preferred over high-density housing. Shopkeepers to be given tax-breaks and subsidies if they open shops in high crime are.

Children, who are brought up in families, who own guns, who have a history of violent behavior, who have an alcoholic or drug addicted mother or father or older sibling, where a care-giver is alone in bringing up children, need close follow up and help. Parents of repeat offenders and their children must attend programs dealing with prevention, information and treatment. The cost of such programs may be extremely small compared to the cost of not reaching out in time. The care and identification of dysfunctional families must however be done with great wisdom and skill in order to avoid further risks of alienation and humiliation.

Developing Countries

Turning to other parts of the world, what of poor countries caught up in cycles of poverty, war, and famines?

I think a lot of the above recommendations can be applied in them as well. I challenge these who say they cannot. I know enough about the dynamics of third-world countries to debunk the self-serving excuses their leaders, intellectuals and apologists will use to say all of this is impossible for them, given their poverty, mentality, cultural traditions. My answer to that is that it does not need money to select wise local leaders and bureaucrats, nor does it need money to monitor the behavior of the more corrupt politicians and oligarchs. If there is a reorientation of certain expenditures from the national budgets, it is surprising how money for social programs can be found. No developing or even rich countries should spend more than 1 or 2% of its budget on defense and security. The figure for some notoriously brutal African, Asian and Middle Eastern countries is around 20 to 30%. The silence of the West is deafening here. Who sold modern jet fighters to Bangladesh and Ethiopia and Eritrea recently? The cost of one such jet fighter is equivalent to six years education budget for the latter two countries, both of which have been engaged in a pitiless desert war for the many years.

Accessibility to Tools of Murder

In 1990, compared to the last two decades, the United States saw the highest juvenile arrest rate for *violent crimes* ever (my italics); teen arrests for forcible rapes had doubled; teen murder rates quadrupled, mostly due to an increase in shootings. During those same two decades, the suicide rate for teenagers tripled, as did the number of children under fourteen who are murder victims (statistics US dept. of Justice, cited in Goleman 1995, 333-334). Eleven thousands armed attacks took place in US *schools* in 1998 (and 4000 rapes!) and 58 people in the US are on death row for crimes committed while they were juveniles.

Parents are taking eight-year olds to shooting ranges, where they practice firing real revolvers using real bullets at moving targets with human features and now we hear of a six-year-old shooting to death another six-year-old in Michigan.

Guns especially in the USA must not be sold to the public. As to the ones in circulation perhaps legislators will one day decide that possession of a gun may be worse than possession of a once of marijuana.

It may be ironic to note that in Colorado, where two high school students recently massacred 15 of their colleagues, (April 1999), the State Assembly was about to loosen restrictions on permits for concealed weapons, was about to ban local lawsuits against weapon manufacturers and preempt local ordinances on possession of firearms. In addition, Denver, the capital was hosting a mammoth three-day annual convention of the National Rifle Association (eventually cut down to one day as a result of the shooting and the mayors brave stand to halt the convention).[143]

However, the Assembly did vote on the day after the massacre, to *limit gun sales to one handgun per person each month* (as if that presented a great step forward!). Furthermore, one legislator has now proposed that the principal and some teachers in every school be allowed to carry handguns in order to prevent such school massacres.[144]

Are these people conscious of what these recommendations will bring?

Media

Television and Internet are wonderful tools to inform, sensitize people to problems and influence them to take positive choices, but they are also powerful tools for some information that can be very negative for some vulnerable children, desensitizing them to the risk of crime both to themselves and to their victims. Some television programs and Internet platforms can even provide children with access to the tools and ideologies that will facilitate them transgressing the limit of what is acceptable behavior. We can do more to limit the diffusion of violent programs to the very young, but what about teenagers? Can we take measure to stop the production of very violent films from the start as a public health measure?

The same prime-time cable TV programs that show an average violence-content of over 80% go to poor countries as well. While their leaders often censor or ban programs dealing with any sort of political opening or opposition, they allow this type of violence-filled programming to fill their airwaves (minus any sexually suggestive scenes of course).

A recent made in Hollywood film I saw on TV showed how a serial killer massacres women by severing part of their nerve cord and letting them die a slow, agonizing death. I saw this dubbed in French on the most popular French TV station (TF1). I understand that being a B-type movie it was dubbed in several other languages and exported to many other countries. How can we allow such films to be made?

Allied to that, let's stop showing that success is linked to making money and that if you appear on TV news as an aggressive hero or in these violent confrontational-type shows, you are somehow an *important personality.*

In the realm of drug and alcohol abuse, delinquency, school absences or unruliness, clear messages should be given to youth. To be effective, such messages for youth should be perfectly tuned to their aspirations, taking into account their admiration for risk-taking, their relative disregard for danger, but also their idealism.

Finally, since my principal aim in writing this book was to look at not only how different cultures operate, but also how we may achieve better understanding of different viewpoints, it is my fervent wish that cross-cultural exchanges, be they through the media, travel or better education in schools be increased: I am convinced that we have much to learn from different cultures and this learning can help us to promote better self-esteem, civility and respect in children.

Newspaper Sources and Other Quotations

134 According to the French National Police Annual Report, Ministry of Interior, Paris, Dec.1999.

135 International Herald Tribune, 13 Jan.1999, 4.

136 "Executing Children." Editorial, *Washington Post*, March 1998.

137 Barry Bearak. "A Hard Life in the Refugee Camps." New York Times Service, *International Herald Tribune*, 29 April 1999.

138 *Tribune de Geneve*, 4 Oct. 1 996, 10.

139 *International Herald Tribune*, 12 Nov. 1997, 15.

140 French TV program, Culture- Pub, M6 channel, 16 Nov. 1997.

141 *International Herald Tribune*, 29 Jan. 1999.

142 "Many US Teenagers Fear Repeat of School Violence." *International Herald Tribune, 28* April 1999, 1.

143 An excellent article on the tricks gun-lobby adherents play as well as the ways they influence politicians to maintain or liberalize gun laws is found in Dennis Warner, "Australia Fights the Gun Control Law." *International Herald Tribune,* 13 August 1996.

144 "Further Fallout: Gun lobby suffers reverses in Colorado." New York Times cited in International *Herald Tribune, 24-26* April 1999, 3.

Bibliography

The full details of all other references such as Newspaper articles, lectures, conversations are given in the footnotes.

Adda, B. *Conflict in Africa: Concepts and Realities.* Princeton University Press, 1976.

Ades, A., & Josipovici, A. *Le Livre de Goha le simple.* Paris: Livre de Poche, 1969.

Allen, G.A., & Futterman, A. "The Biological Basis of Crime: an Historical and Methodological Study-Paper." In *Claims of Genetic Influence on Criminal Behavior Conference,* University of Maryland, College Park, April 1995.

Alston, P. *The Best Interests of the Child.* Oxford: Clarendon Press, 1994.

Assman, J. *Moses the Egyptian.* Cambridge, Mass.: Harvard University Press, 1997.

Azur, J., *Anthropology Today,* 10 June 1994.

Bacon, M.K., Child, I.L. & Barry, H. "A Cross-Cultural Study of Correlates of Crime." *Journal of Abnormal and Social Psychiatry* 66, 1963.

Barrett, D.E. *The Effect of Undernutrition on Chidlren's Behavior.* New York: Gordon and Breach, 1985.

Barry, H., Josephson, L., Lauer, E., & Marshall, C. *Agents and Techniques for Child Training: Cross-Cultural Codes* 6. Pittsburg : University of Pittsburg Press, 1976.

Bassiouni, C., & McCormick, M. "Sexual Violence: An Invisible Weapon of War in the Former Yugoslavia." Chicago: *Occasional Paper No.1,* International Human Rights Law Institute, DePaul University College of Law, 1996.

Basta, S.S. "Health/Nutrition in Low Income Areas of the Third World." *Ecology of Food & Nutrition,* vol. 6, 1977, 113-124.

Basta, S.S. "Amenorrhea-Depression in Famine." *The Lancet,* 1 Oct. 1988.

Basta, S.S. "Iron Deficiency Anaemia and the Productivity of Adult Males in Indonesia." *American Journal of Clinical Nutrition,* 1974.

Berman, J.J., Murphy Berman, V., & Singh, P. "Cross Cultural Similarities & Differences in Perceptions of Fairness." *Journal of Cross-Cultural Psychology.*16, 1985.

Berry, J.W., Dasen, P.R. & Saraswathi *Handbook of Cross Cultural Psychology,* Vol.2. Boston: Allyn & Bacon, 1997.

Bjorklid, P. "Children's Outdoor Environment." *Studies in Education & Psychology.* Stockholm: Institute of Education, 1982.

Bjorkvist, K. & Niemela, P. *Of Mice and Women: Aspects of Female Aggression.* San Diego: Academic Press, 1992.

Bloom, H. *The Lucifer Principle.* New York: The Atlantic Monthly Press, 1995.

Braudel, F. *A History of Civilisation.* New York: Penguin Books, 1995.

Bresciani, E. *Letteratura e Poesia dell'Antico Egitto.* Torino: Einaudi, 1969.

Brett, R., & McCallin, M. *Study on Child Soldiers.* UNICEF, 1996.

Brown, G.W., & Harris, T. *Social origins of Depression: Study of Psychiatric Disorder in Women.* London: Tavistock Press, 1978.

Buchanan, A. "Breaking Intergenerational Patterns of Child Maltreatment." Paper presented at the *10th International Congress on Child Abuse and Neglect,* Kuala Lumpur, 1994.

Burbank, V.K. "Female Aggression in Cross -Cultural Perspective." *Behavior Science Research* 21, 1987.

Capaldi, D.M., &. Patterson G.R "Relation of parental transition to boys adjustment problems: Mothers at risk for transitions and unskilled parenting." *Development Psychology* 27, 1991.

Carey, G., *Understanding and Preventing Violence.* Washington D.C.: National Academy of Science, 1994.

Carlsson, U., & von Feilitzen, C. Children and Media Violence. UNESCO & University of Göteborg: Nordic Information Center for Media and Communication Research (Nordicom), 1998.

Cases O. & Seif, I. "Aggressive Behavior in Mice lacking MAOA." Science 268, June 1995.

Celsing, A. "News on Children and Violence on the Screen." University of Göteborg: Nordicom vol.1, 1997.

Chavez, A., Martinez, C., & Yashine, T. "Nutrition, Behavioral Development & Mother-Child interaction in Young Rural Children." *Federation Proceedings,* 34, 1975, 1574-1582.

Cloninger, C.R. *Nature Genetics,* Jan.1996.

Colborn, T., Dumanoski, D. & Peterson-Myers J. *Our Stolen Future.* New York: Dutton, 1996.

Collard, A. *History of the Indies.* London: Harper Torchbook, 1971.

Coplan, J.D. et al. Proceeding of the National Academy of Sciences 93, Washington D.C., 1919

Covell, K., & Howe, B. "Canadian Youth on Children's Rights." In E. Verhellen & M. Nijhoff. *Monitoring Children's Rights.* The Hague: 1996, 255

Cravisto, J. & Dedicardie, E.R. "Microenvironmental Factors in Severe Protein Caloric Malnutrition." In N. Scrimshaw & M. Behar, *Nutrition and Agricultural Development.* New York: Plenum 1976

Daly, M. & Wilson, M. *Homicide.* New York: Hawthorne, 1988.

Damiaso, A. & Damiaso E. *Nature Neuroscience,* 1999

Dasen, P.R., & Super, C.M. "The usefulness of a cross-cultural approach in studies of malnutrition and psychological development. In P.R. Dasen, J.W. Berry & N., Sartorius (Eds.). *Health and Cross-Cultural Psychology.* Newbury Park, CA: Sage Publications, 1988.

Dasen, P.R., Berry, J.W., & Sartorius, N., *Health and Cross-Cultural Psychology.* Newbury Park, CA: Sage Publications, 1988.

Davenport, C.B., & Laughlin, H. In *Popular Science Monthly* 82, 1913, 33-39.

David, H.R., Dytrych Z., Matejcek, Z., & Schuller, V. *Born Unwanted*, New York: Springer 1988.

De Toqueville. *De la démocratie en Amérique.* Paris: Flammarion, 1981.

De Waal, F.B.M. *Good Natured: The Origins of Right and Wrong in Humans and other Animals.* Cambridge, Mass.: Harvard University Press, 1996.

Devine, J. "Research for Understanding and Reducing Violence." Report by the Guggenheim Foundation, 1993, 21

Dollard, J., Doob, L., & Miller N. *Frustration and Aggression.* New Haven: Yale University Press, 1939.

ECCAN (European Conference on Child Abuse and Neglect), Oslo. *Abstracts*, (eds.) Vanickova et al. Prague: Charles University, 1995

Editorial, *American Journal of Clinical Nutrition* 61, 1995, 1,206-1,212.

Emory, R.E., Kitzman K.M., & Aaron, J. *Mothers Delinquent Behavior Before Marriage and Children's Behavior Problems After Divorce.* University of Virginia, 1996.

Eron, L.D. "Statement to the Harvard School of Public Health, 11 May 1992. reproduced as "The Problem of Media Violence and Children's Behavior." Guggenheim Foundation *Occasional Paper No.7,* 1993, 2.

Eron, L.D., & Heusman, L.R. "The Role of Television in Presocial and Antisocial Behaviour." In *Development of Antisocial and Prosocial Behaviour.* J. Block, D. Olwens & M. Radle-Yarrow (Eds.). New York: Academic Press, 1982.

Farrington, D. In *Children and Violence,* Gulbenkian Foundation, London, 1995, p. 50-62, 127-147, 218 & 262.

Fernstrom, J.D., & Wurtman, R.J. "Brain Serotonin Content: Physiological Regulation by Plasma Neutral Amino Acids." *Science* 178, 1972.

Figley, C.R. *Trauma and its Wake.* New York: Brunner/Mazel, 1985

Finkelhor D. et al. « Child Abuse as an International Issue." *Child Abuse & Neglect,* 12-3-23, 1988.

Fraiberg, S., *The Psychoanalytic Quarterly,* vol. LI, no. 4, 1982.

Frank, R., & Cook, P. *The Winner Take All Society.* New York: The Free Press, 1996.

Furukawa, T. "A study of Temperament and Blood Groups." *Journal of Social Psychology,* 1930, 1,494-1,508.

Fussel, P. *Doing Battle.* New York: Little, Brown & Co., 1996.

Garmezy, N. & Rutter, M. *Stress, Coping and Development in Children.* New York: McGraw-Hill, 1983.

Gelles, R. "Family Violence." *Annual Review of Sociology* 11, 1985.

Gitlin, M.J., & Pasnau, R.O. "Psychiatric Syndrome Linked to Reproductive Function in Women: A Review of Current Knowledge." *American Journal of Psychiatry* 146, 11, Nov. 1989.

Glazer, I.M. "Interfemale Aggression and Resource Scarcity." In *Of Mice and Women: Aspects of Female Aggression.* San Diego: Academic Press, 1992.

Glendenning, V. *Jonathan Swift, A Portrait.* New York: Holt & Co., 1999.

Glick, R.A. &. Roose, S.P. *Rage, Power and Agression.* New Haven: Yale University Press, 1993.

Goleman, D. *Emotional Intelligence.* New York: Bantam, 1995.

Goodall, J. *In the shadow of man.* Boston: Houghton Mittlin, 1971.

Grmek M., Gjidara M., & Simac, N. *Le Nettoyage Ethnique.* Paris: Fayard, 1992.

Guggenheim Foundation *Occasional Paper No.7. New York:* 1993.

Guggenheim Foundation Report: "Research for Understanding and Reducing Violence." New York: 1993.

Gulbenkian Foundation, *Children and Violence.* London, 1995.

Hagerty, R. "Life, Stress and Social Supports." *Journal of Child Neurology* 22, 1980, 391-400.

Heise, L. "Violence against Women, the Hidden Health Burden." *WHO Statistical Quarterly* 46, 1993.

Ho, H.F. In *American Psychiatrist*, 40, 1985, 1212-8.

Hibbeln, J., & Salem, N. *American Journal of Clinical Nutrition* 62, 1995.

Hui, C.H., & Triandis, H.C. "Measurement in Cross-Cultural Psychology." *Journal of American Psychology* 16, 1984(a), 131-152.

Hui, C.H., & Triandis, H.C. "What does Individualism and Collectivism mean?" University of Illinois, Dept. of Psychology: Unpublished, 1984(b).

Ibrahim, S.E. In *Civil Society* 4-44. Cairo: Ibn Khaldoun Center, 1995, 16.

ICCB (International Catholic Child Bureau), *The Family and Child Resilience.* Geneva: 1994.

Johnson, D., & Anderson, D.M. *Revealing Prophets.* London: Currey Press, 1995.

Johnson, D. *New Prophets.* Oxford: Oxford University Press, 1994.

Kagan, A.R., & Levi, L. "Health and Environment-Psychosocial Stimuli." In L. Levi; *Society, Stress and Disease-Childhood and Adolescence.* Oxford: University Press 1975, 241-260.

Kaplan, H.B. *Deviant Behavior in Defense of Self.* New York: Academic Press, 1980.

Kerr, M., Bogues, J. & Kerr, D. "Psychological Functioning of Mothers of Malnourished Children." *Pediatrics* 62, 1978, 778-784.

Khalifa A. In *Civil Society* 4-44. Cairo: Ibn Khaldoun Center, 1995, 4.

Keenan, K. "The Development of Aggression in Toddlers: A Study of

Low Income Families." *Journal of Abnormal Child Psychology* 22, 1994.

Lalette, C. *Textes Sacres et Textes Profanes de L'Ancienne Egypte.* Paris: UNESCO-Gallimard, 1994.

Lamb, M., & Sternberg, K., *Child Care in Context: Cross-Cultural Perspectives.* Englewood, N.J.: Erblum Press, 1992.

Lamb, R. The Bigger Picture : Audio-visual survey and recommendations. UNICEF, 1997.

Leapman, M. *London: The Evolution of a Great City.* London & New York: Wiedenfeld & Nicolson, 1989.

Levi, L. *Society, Stress and Disease-Childhood and Adolescence.* Oxford: University Press 1975.

Levinson, D. *Family Violence in Cross-Cultural Perspective.* Newbury Park, CA.: Sage, 1989.

Lewis, M., & Haviland, J. *Handbook of Emotions.* New York: Guildford Press, 1993.

Lindner, E. G. "How Humiliation Creates Cultural Differences: The Psychology of Intercultural Communication. University of Oslo, Institute of Psychology: Unpublished, 2000.

Lindsay, R.S., & Toft, A.D. "Hypothyroidism." *The Lancet* 349, 1997.

Lore, R.K., & Schultz, L.A. "Control of Human Aggression." *American Psychologist* 48, 1993.

Machel, G. UN Report "Consequences of Armed Conflict on Children." Report to the UN Secretariat, Oct. 1996.

Malone, T.W. *Cognitive Science* 5, 1981, pp. 333-370.

Mark, V.H., & Ervin, F.R. *Violence and the Brain.* New York: Harper and Row, 1970.

Mark, V.H., Sweet, W.H. & Ervin, F.R. "Role of Brain Disease in Riots and Urban Violence." *Journal of the American Medical Association* 201, 1967.

Masters, R., & McGuire, M. *The Neurotransmitter Revolution.* Southern Illinois University Press, 1994.

Maus, M. *Sociology and Psychology: Essays.* London: Routledge, 1979.

McKeigue, P. M., Miller, G.J., & Marmot, M.G. "Coronary Heart Disease in South Asians Overseas: a Review." *Journal of Clinical Epidemiology* 42, 1989, 597-609

McLachlan, J.A. *Estrogens in the Environment.* New York: Elsevier; 1980.

McWhirter, L., Young, V., & Majury, J. "Children's Awareness of Violent Death." *British Journal of Social Psychiatry* 22, 1983.

Minear, L. *Humanitarian Action in the former-Yugoslavia.* Boston University Press, Watson Institute, 1994.

Moffit, T.E. "Life Course Persistent and Adolescent Limited Anti-Social Behaviour." *Psychology Review* 100, 1993, 674-701.

Moffit, T.E. "Measuring Children's Anti-Social Behaviors." *Journal of American Medical Association* 275-5, Feb. 1996.

Montesquieu. *Lettres Persanes.* Paris: Livre de Poche, 1984.

Morris, D., *The Naked Ape.* London: Corgi, 1968

Milunski, A. "Congenital Effects, Folic acid and Homoeobox Genes." *The Lancet* 348, 1996, 419.

Munroe, R.L., & Munroe, R.H. "Co-operation & Competition Among East African & American School Children." *Journal of Social Psychology* 101, 1977.

Murray, C.J.L., & Lopez, A.D. "Mortality by Cause for Eight Regions of The World: Global Burden of Disease." *The Lancet* 349, 9061, 1997, 1,275.

Murray, C.J.L. & Lopez, A.D. *The Global Burden of Disease — a World Health Organisation Collaborative Study.* Cambridge, Mass.: Harvard University Press, 1997.

Needleman, H.L., Riess, J.A., Tobin, M.J., Biesecker, G.E., & Greenhouse, J.B. "Bone Lead Levels and Delinquent Behavior." *Journal of the American Medical Association* 275-5, Feb. 1996.

Niemela, P. "Vicissitudes of Mother's Hate." In K. Bjorkvist, & P. Niemela. *Of Mice and Women: Aspects of Female Aggression.* San Diego: Academic Press, 1992.1992.

Nietzsche, F. W. *The Anti-Christ,* tr. R.J. Hollingdale. Penguin Harmondsworth, 1968.

Olweus, D. "Stability of Aggressive Reaction Patterns in Males: a Review.". *Psych. Bulletin* 86, 1979

The Open University: "Culture and Belief In Europe and the Wider World, 1450-1600." Course A 205. London, 1990.

Ozonoff, D.M. "Fields of Controversy." *The Lancet* 349, January 1997, 74

Patai, D., & Koerige, N. *Professing Feminism: Cautionary Tales from the Strange World of Women's Studies.* New York: New Republic/Basic Books, 1995.

Pike, F.B. *Latin American History.* New York: Harcourt, Brace & World, 1969.

Plotsky, P.M. et al. *Abstract of the Society of Neurosciences,* 321, 1995.

Prescott, J.W. "Body Pleasure and the Origins of Violence." *The Futurist,* April 1968.

Quay H.C. et al., *Handbook of Juvenile Delinquency.* New York: John Wiley & Sons, 1987.

Redlich, C.A., Sparer, J., & Cullen, M.R. "Sick Building Syndrome." *The Lancet* 349, 1997, 1013-1016.

Rhodes, R. "Epidemic of War Deaths." *Science News,* 20 Aug. 1988, 24.

Rivlin, G. *The Plot to Get Bill Gates.* New York: Times Books, 1999.

Robins, L.N. "Sturdy Childhood Predictors of Adult Antisocial Behavior." *Psych. Med.* 8, 1978

Rohner, R.P. "Sex Differences in Aggression - Phylogenetic and Enculturation Perspectives." *Ethos* 4, 1976.

Rose, S., Lowentin, R.C., & Kamin, L. *Not in Our Gene.* London: Penguin 1990.

Rubenstein, J.L., Heeren, T., Houseman, D., Rubin, C., & Stechler, G. "Suicidal Behavior in 'normal' adolescents: Risk and Protective Factors." *The American Orthopsychiatric Association*, University of Boston Medical School, 1989, 59-71.

Rutter, M., & Smith, D. *Disorders in Young People*. New York: John Wiley & Sons, 1995.

Sagan, L.A. *The Health of Nations*. New York: Basic Books 1987.

Scheper-Hughes N. "Child Survival." New York: Reidel, 1987.

Scrimshaw, N., & Behar, M. *Nutrition and Agricultural Development*. New York: Plenum 1976.

Segall, M.H. "More than we need to know about cultures." *Journal of Cross Cultural Psychology* 15, 1984, 153-162.

Segall, M.H. "Psychocultural Antecedents of Male Aggression — Some Implications Involving Gender, Parenting and Adolescence"; in Dasen et al., 1987.

Segall, M.H., Dasen, P.R., Berry, J.W., & Poortinga, Y.H. *Human Behaviour in Global Perspective*. Boston: Allen & Bacon, 1990.

Segall, M.H., Dasen, P.R., Berry, J.W., & Poortinga, Y.H. *Human Behaviour in Global Perspective, Second Edition*. Boston: Allen & Bacon, 1999.

Sereny, G. Cries unheard: Why Children Kill: The Story of Mary Bell. New York, Metropolitan Books, 1999.

Setchell K., Cassidy A., & Bingham, S. "Biological effect of a diet of soy protein rich in isoflavins on the menstrual cycle of premenopausal women." *American Journal of Clinical Nutrition* 60, 1994.

Setchell, K., Zimmer N.L., Cai, J., & Heubi, J.E. "Exposure of Infants to Phyto-Oestroens from Soy-Based Infant Formula." *The Lancet* 350, 1997, 23.

Shilneva L. et al. "Commercial Sexual Exploitation of Children in Latvia." Riga: Higher School of Social Work and Pedagogics (UNICEF), 1996.

Shimmin, R.H. & Shimmin, R.L. "Children's Work in four Cultures — Determinants & Consequences." *American Anthropologist* 86, 1984, 369-379.

Skinner, M.L. "Linking Economic Hardship to Adolescent Aggression." *Journal of Youth and Adolescence* 21, 1992.

Sliwinski, M., *Le Genocide Khmer Rouge*. Geneva & Paris: Harmattan, 1995.

Stein, M. *Child Abuse*. San Diego: Western School Press, 1989.

Stephenson, S. Report on Domestic Violence in Eastern Europe. UNICEF, June 20,1996.

Steptoe, A., & Butler, N. The Lancet 347, 1996, 1789-1792.

Stroun, M. & Harsgor, M. *Israel/Palestine. L'histoire au delà des Mythes*. Geneva: Metropolis, 1996.

Suomi, S.J. Ciba Foundation Symposium, 156, 1991.

Thiesse, A.M., La Création des Identités nationales. Paris: Seuil, 1999.

UN Report of the International Conference for the Protection of War Victims, Geneva, August-September 1993.

UN Report of the UN-sponsored Meeting to Ban Landmines. Geneva, 1996a

UN Secretariat "Small but significant step towards disarmament." *UN Secretariat News*, 10 Dec. 1996b
UN Secretariat Committee on Nutrition News Bulletin 10, 1993
UNDP (United Nations Development Program) *Human Development Report*, 1995.
UNDP *Human Development Report*, 1996
UNFPA *Population Report* of the United Nations Fund for Population Activities, New York, 1995.
UNICEF Innocenti Occasional Papers, No.6, Florence, November 1993.
UNICEF India "Glimpses of Girlhood in India." 1994.
UNICEF *Abstracts of European Conference on Child Abuse*. New York, 1995.
UNICEF Working Paper 127, August 1995.
UNICEF *Progress of Nations Reports*, 1996,1999,2000.
Vaquin, M. *Main basse sur les vivants*. Paris : Fayard, 1999.
Virkkunen, M., & Huttunen, M.O. "Evidence for Abnormal Glucose Tolerance Test among Violent Offenders." *Neuropsychobiology* 8, 1982, 30-40.
Walker, C.D. American Journal of Physiology 268, 1995, 1281-1288
Wartella, E., Olivarez, A., & Jennings, N. "Children and Television Violence in the USA." Nordicom 1998
Wasserman, D. *Science and Social Harm, Genetic Research into Crime and Violence.* University of Maryland, Institute for Philosophy & Public Policy, 1995
Widdowson, E. "Mental Contentment and Physical Growth." *The Lancet* 1, 1951, 1316-1318.
White & Wolraich in a Special Edition devoted to sugars. *American Journal of Clinical Nutrition* 62-1S, 1995.
Whiting, B.B. "Sex identity crisis and physical violence." *American Anthropologist* 67, 1965.
Whiting, B.B., & Whiting, J.W.M. *Children of Six Cultures, a Psycho-cultural Analysis.* Cambridge, Mass.: Harvard University Press, 1975.
Wilson, E.O. *Sociobiology.* Cambridge, Mass.: Harvard University Press, 1975.
Wilson, J.Q. & Hernstein, R. *Crime And Human Nature.* New York: Simon & Schuster, 1986.
World Organisation against Torture Report. Geneva: 1998.
World Health Organisation Report A50-INF.Doc/4, March1997.
World Health Organisation. A Critical Link – Interventions for Physical Growth and Psychological Development – A Review. CHS-CAH 99-3, 1999.
Wu, A., & Pike, M. In *American Journal of Clinical Nutrition* 62, 1995, p.151.
Wurtman, R.J. & Wurtman, J.J. Nutrition and the Brain. New York: Raven, 1977.
Young, T.J. "Poverty and Aggression Management among Native Americans." *Psychology Reports* 69, 1991.
Zillman, D., Weaver, J.B., Murdorf, F.N. & Aust, C.F. Effects of an Opposite Gender Compassion affect to Horror. Journal of Personality and Social Psychology 51, 1986, 586-594

Zohoori, N. et al. *Monitoring Health Conditions in the Russian Federation, 1992-1996.* Chapel Hill: University of North Carolina Press, 1997.

Recommended Reading

The child's mind
Jean Piaget. *The Origins of Intelligence in Children.* New York: International Universities Press, 1952.

The mind and brain
Steven Pinker. *How the Mind Works.* Norton & Co. 1998 (Brain function is admirably expounded in this volume).
G.R. De Long. "Effects of Nutrition on Brain Development in Humans." *American Journal of Clinical Nutrition* vol. 57 supplement, February 1993 (good references for nutrition and brain development).

Biology
A. Mazur, "Effects of Testosterone on Status in Primary Groups." *Folia Primatologica* vol. 26, 1976 (The importance of testosterone in the behavior of primates).
J.H. Walter. "Two new treatable biosynthetic disorders." *The Lancet* vol. 348, August 1996, 558 (Reference to the way that certain genetic-based malfunctions in the metabolism of creatine, serine and transferase lead to seizures, increased aggressivity and poorer child development.

History of violence against women and children
Savitri Goonesekere. "Women's Rights and Children's Rights." *Innocenti Occasional Papers,* UNICEF Florence Center, Sept. 1992 (The legitimisation of violence against children and women in Europe from the Middle Ages, particularly wife-beating and killing).

Stress & Trauma of Hostilities
Dr. Assumpta Naniwe *Phenomenon of Traumatism among Children during the Present Crisis in Burundi, UNICEF Burundi, Jan. 1995* (The effects of war and massacre are scientifically described in a survey by Dr. Assumpta Naniwe of the University of Burundi. To give an idea of the ghastliness of these evils, note that over 90 % of the children in the sample witnessed acts of violence, 15 % the killing of a member of their family, 58 % were themselves attacked — over three in four knowing their attacker, who was in four out of five cases a neighbour — with 15 % wounded, 1.5 % were sexually abused.
Basta, S.S. "L'enfant et la Guerre" Paper for the University of Geneva, *Nord-Sud* XXI, 30 January 1993 (more on child casualties in war and on child

combatants paper for the University of Geneva).

Children : War and Persecution, Proceedings of the Congress of Hamburg (26-29 September 1993), UNICEF Germany & Verlag, Berlin, 1995 (Inheritance of trauma-like characteristics by children from parents who disappeared or were persecuted or were indeed persecutors).

Naniwe. A. "Coping with stress : Palestinian families and Intifada-Related Trauma." *AMIDEAST*, Jerusalem 1994 (The effects of trauma and the punishments inflicted on Palestinians during the Intifada is described in scientific detail by Dr. Assumpta Naniwe of Bethlehem University).

Rupesinghe, K. & Rubia, M.C. *The Culture of Violence*, United Nations University Press, Tokyo 1994 (An account of how military régimes justify total war against political movements, with neither mercy nor capitulation).

Peace Museums Worldwide, UN Library, Geneva 1995 (This is a little-known UN publication, which lists not only some 40 such museums in Japan, Europe and the USA & Canada — note, none in the developing world ! — but also a list of some three dozen UN publications dealing with the process of negotiation for peace).

Index of Authors